BECOMING AN EDUCATIONAL ETHNOGRAPHER

This book provides practical advice on the learning and teaching perspectives of ethnography, including what undertaking research looks like and the experiences it will bring. It considers what it means to be and become an educational ethnographer and builds on an inextricable entanglement between the researchers' field of study and their research trajectories.

With a range of carefully chosen international contributions, this book uses a variety of practical case studies to provide further information about the pros and cons of this research perspective. Chapter authors share the knowledge and experience gained from the research and how it has affected their approach to social phenomena.

This book is an ideal introduction for anyone considering research approach or becoming an educational ethnographer and will be of interest to researchers already working in this field.

Juana M. Sancho-Gil is Emeritus Professor of Educational Technologies in the Faculty of Education, University of Barcelona, Spain.

Fernando Hernández-Hernández is Professor of Contemporary Visualities, Psychology of Art and Arts-based Research in the Unit of Cultural Pedagogies at the Fine Arts Faculty, University of Barcelona, Spain.

BECOMING AN EDUCATIONAL ETHNOGRAPHER

The Challenges and Opportunities of Undertaking Research

Edited by Juana M. Sancho-Gil and Fernando Hernández-Hernández

LONDON AND NEW YORK

First published 2021
by Routledge
2 Park Square, Milton Park, Abingdon, Oxon OX14 4RN

and by Routledge
52 Vanderbilt Avenue, New York, NY 10017

Routledge is an imprint of the Taylor & Francis Group, an informa business

© 2021 selection and editorial matter, Juana M. Sancho-Gil and Fernando Hernández-Hernández; individual chapters, the contributors

The right of Juana M. Sancho-Gil and Fernando Hernández-Hernández to be identified as the authors of the editorial material, and of the authors for their individual chapters, has been asserted in accordance with sections 77 and 78 of the Copyright, Designs and Patents Act 1988.

All rights reserved. No part of this book may be reprinted or reproduced or utilised in any form or by any electronic, mechanical, or other means, now known or hereafter invented, including photocopying and recording, or in any information storage or retrieval system, without permission in writing from the publishers.

Trademark notice: Product or corporate names may be trademarks or registered trademarks, and are used only for identification and explanation without intent to infringe.

British Library Cataloguing in Publication Data
A catalogue record for this book is available from the British Library

Library of Congress Cataloging-in-Publication Data
Names: Sancho Gil, Juana Ma. (Juana María), editor. |
Hernández-Hernández, Fernando, editor.
Title: Becoming an educational ethnographer : the challenges and
opportunities of undertaking research / Edited by Juana M. Sancho-Gil
and Fernando Hernández-Hernández.
Description: Abingdon, Oxon ; New York : Routledge, 2021. | Includes
bibliographical references and index.
Identifiers: LCCN 2020032990 (print) | LCCN 2020032991 (ebook) | ISBN
9780367466480 (hardback) | ISBN 9780367466497 (paperback) | ISBN
9781003030218 (ebook)
Subjects: LCSH: Educational anthropology–Study and teaching. | Educational
anthropology–Research. | Ethnology–Study and teaching. |
Ethnology–Research.
Classification: LCC LB45 .B39 2021 (print) | LCC LB45 (ebook) | DDC
306.43–dc23
LC record available at https://lccn.loc.gov/2020032990
LC ebook record available at https://lccn.loc.gov/2020032991

ISBN: 978-0-367-46648-0 (hbk)
ISBN: 978-0-367-46649-7 (pbk)
ISBN: 978-1-003-03021-8 (ebk)

Typeset in Bembo
by Taylor & Francis Books

Access the Support Material: www.routledge.com/9780367466497

The only constant in life is change. Heraclitus.

Life is a process of becoming, a combination of states we have to go through. Where people fail is that they wish to elect a state and remain in it. This is a kind of death. Anais Nin

CONTENTS

List of tables	*ix*
List of contributors	*x*

1 Researching – and being an ethnographic researcher – as a
process of becoming   1
Juana M. Sancho-Gil and Fernando Hernández-Hernández

PART I
Becoming as moving researcher positionality   15

2 Roots and routes to reading the world as an ethnographer   17
Stephanie Couch

3 Becoming an educational ethnographer by organized
representations of educational realities and 'researching through'   29
Christoph Maeder

4 Becoming educational ethnographer through time and
ontological displacements   40
Juana M. Sancho-Gil

5 Becoming an ethnographer: Living, teaching and learning
ethnographically   52
Audra Skukauskaite

6 The challenges and opportunities of becoming an ethnographer   64
Richard Bacon

viii Contents

PART II
Becoming as an onto-epistemological framework 79

7 What comes after becoming: Virtualities at the end of a doctoral research 81
Aurelio Castro-Varela

8 An ethnographic research based on an ontology of becoming 92
Judit Onsès-Segarra

9 Openness to the unforeseen in a nomadic research process on teachers' learning experiences 104
Fernando Hernández-Hernández

PART III
Becoming as a concept that allows to re-signify the subjectivity 117

10 An accidental institutional ethnographer: Reflections on paradoxes and positionality 119
Garth Stahl

11 Researchers and risk: Exploring vulnerability, subjectivity, and identity in ethnographic research through collage making 130
Cleti Cervoni, Corinne McKamey, and Rhoda Bernard

12 Ethnographic educational research as assemblages of teachers' and researchers' movements and their learning environments 141
Juliane Corrêa

Index 152

TABLES

2.1	Corpus of Records for Producing Data	19
2.2	Six Ways of Learning While Working as a Leader in Education and Becoming as an Ethnographer (1998–2019)	22
5.1	Project Tasks With Underlying Ethnographically-Informed Methodologies	60
6.1	Data and Sources	66
6.2	Event Map of a CEO Becoming an Ethnographer	69
6.3	Phases in the Construction of an AERA Poster	70
6.4	A Spradley Analysis of Semantic Relationships	71
6.5	Event Map of Discursive Events and Actions Supporting an Ethnographic Interview	73
6.6	A Spradley Analysis of Classroom Dialogue (1)	74
6.7	Spradley Analysis of Classroom Dialogue (2)	75

CONTRIBUTORS

Richard Bacon, Ph.D is Chief Executive Officer of Aqua Metrology Systems, a Silicon Valley-based water technology start-up. He is also an advisor to Arrival Education, a UK-based social enterprise that works with leading UK companies to achieve their goals for diversity and inclusion. His research interests focus on ethnographic studies of companies as places of learning to inform initiatives that support the transition of young people, particularly those from underserved groups, into meaningful employment.

Rhoda Bernard is the Managing Director of the Berklee Institute for Arts Education and Special Needs in Boston, Massachusetts, USA. She directs the Graduate Programs in Music Education and teaches graduate seminars in arts education for people with disabilities, and undergraduate service-learning courses in neurodiversity. Her research interests include researcher subjectivity, professional identity, and the intersection of arts education and disability studies.

Aurelio Castro-Varela is adjunct member at the Faculty of Fine Arts of the University of Barcelona and postdoctoral researcher in the HERA project Pleasurescapes, Port Cities' Transnational Forces of Integration. His doctoral research explored the crossroads formed by filmic pedagogies, urban space, and social movements in Barcelona. He is also a member of the research group ESBRINA Subjectivities, Visualities and Contemporary Educational Environments: https://esbrina.eu/en/home/, and of the teaching innovation group Indaga't.

Cleti Cervoni is Professor and former Associate Dean in the School of Education at Salem State University in Salem, Massachusetts, USA. She teaches courses on qualitative research, culturally responsive teaching and directs the Educational Studies program concentration. Her research interests are gender and science education and issues of equity in education.

Juliane Corrêa, Ph.D is Professor of Education at the Federal University of Minas Gerias and her PhD is about Education, Science and Technology. She coordinated the UNESCO Chair in teacher of professional development by distance learning, the GIZ network for the teacher professional development of university and the GRAOS/R&D of educational experiences mediated by ICTs.

Stephanie Couch, Ph.D is the Executive Director of the Lemelson-MIT Program affiliated with the School of Engineering at the Massachusetts Institute of Technology. Her research interests include ethnographic studies of teaching and learning with emerging technologies, educational efforts that address inequities in STEM (science, technology, engineering and mathematics) in both educational and workforce contexts, and studies that can inform understandings of the development of inventors and leading innovators.

Fernando Hernández-Hernández is a full Professor of Contemporary Visualities, Psychology of Art and Arts-based Research in the Unit of Cultural Pedagogies at the Fine Arts Faculty of the University of Barcelona. He is a coordinator of the Doctoral Programme in Arts and Education, and the Master's in Visual Arts and Education: A Constructionist Approach. He belongs to the research group ESBRINA – Contemporary, Subjectivities, Visualities and Educational Environments: https://esbrina.eu/en/home/, coordinates the teaching innovation group Indaga't, and is a member of REUNI+D – University Network for Educational Research and Innovation. Social Change and Challenges for Education in the Digital Age: http://reunid.eu. His research focuses on emerging subjectivities, visual culture and educational innovation and improvement.

Corinne McKamey is the Associate Professor of Culture, Communities, and Education at Rhode Island College in Providence, Rhode Island USA. She co-directs the Youth Development undergraduate program and teaches courses in education and leadership. Her research interests include educational care, youth work, and identity.

Christoph Maeder is Professor of Sociology at the University of Teacher Education, Zurich, Switzerland. He specialises in ethnographic research on 'people-processing organizations' such as schools, welfare bureaucracies, prisons and hospitals. Currently he is engaged in an ethnography of kindergartens in Zürich and doing research on acoustic knowledge using the example bells and other sounding artefacts. Actual publications in English are on educational ethnography and its relation to the sociology of knowledge (The Wiley Handbook of Ethnography of Education 2018), on producing and sharing knowledge with a research field (in: Doing Educational Research, SAGE 2019) and on the problem of the definition of the situation in educational ethnography (in: Rethinking Ethnography in Higher Education, Springer 2020).

xii List of contributors

Judit Onsès-Segarra, Ph.D works as a postdoctoral researcher at the Department of Didactics and Educational Organization at the University of Barcelona. Her research interests include post-qualitative research, new materialisms, cartographies in research, visual documentation of learning processes, and cultural projects in teaching innovation. She is a member of the research group ESBRINA – Subjectivities, Visualities and Contemporary Educational Environments: https://esbrina.eu/en/home/, and of the teaching innovation group Indaga't.

Garth Stahl, Ph.D is an Associate Professor in the School of Education at the University of Queensland and Research Fellow, Australian Research Council (DECRA). His research interests lie on the nexus of neoliberalism and socio-cultural studies of education, identity, equity/inequality, and social change. Currently, his research projects encompass theoretical and empirical studies of learner identities, sociology of schooling in a neoliberal age, educational reform, and gendered subjectivities.

Juana M. Sancho-Gil is Emeritus Professor of Educational Technologies in the Faculty of Education of the University of Barcelona. She was coordinator of the research group ESBRINA – Contemporary, Subjectivities, Visualities and Educational Environments http://esbrina.eu, and of REUNI+D – University Network for Educational Research and Innovation, Social Change and Challenges for Education in the Digital Age: http://reunid.eu. She has extensive experience in promoting research policy, advising research programmes and projects, and assessing and managing research projects at regional, national, and international level. From his passion for education and research, she contributes to building bridges between theory and practice, research, and action, while helping to rethink discourses and visions about the meaning of education in today's world.

Audra Skukauskaite, Ph.D is an Associate Professor in the College of Community Innovation and Education at the University of Central Florida. She is also affiliated with Klaipeda University in Lithuania as a senior research scientist and co-PI on an EU-funded research project. Her research focuses on teaching and learning of qualitative and ethnographic research methodologies and application of discourse-based ethnographic approaches in interdisciplinary projects and fields.

1

RESEARCHING – AND BEING AN ETHNOGRAPHIC RESEARCHER – AS A PROCESS OF BECOMING

Juana M. Sancho-Gil and Fernando Hernández-Hernández

Introduction

This chapter introduces the purpose of this book with a tentative approach to the concept of becoming, its relationship with the praxis of ethnographic research, the movements of researchers and the very notion of what research could be. By following these guidelines, we explore the following questions: How can we face investigation that does not follow a pre-defined path or apply pre-set methods, but opens up to dialogues emerging in the encounter with the experiences of the collaborators and the researcher? What is the effect of research processes when disrupted by the unexpected, and the researcher places themselves in a position of not-knowing? Which is the relevance of researcher's movements through an ethnographic study and how this journey affects inquiry, configuring itself as a relational experience where one is attentive not to the expected, but to what is happening in a non-linear and full of bifurcations process, doubts and places of not-knowing? How do these movements allow exploring other senses of ethnographic research that revise and question some foundations and practices on the supposedly standardized way of doing research and being an ethnographic researcher in education?

The purpose of this book

This book wants to be part of the conversation that began in the 1990s about the onto-epistemological, methodological, and ethical foundations of social and educational research, under the umbrella of the post-qualitative turns. According to St. Pierre (2011, p. 615), these turns 'announce a radical break with the humanist, modernist, imperialist, representationalist, objectivist, rationalist, epistemological, ontological, and methodological assumptions of Western Enlightenment thought and practice'. This movement celebrates the methodological differences and complexity of qualitative research and advocates for greater openness, imagination and risk-taking, especially to carry out research based on 'post-theories' (new materialism, new empiricism, posthumanism). These new ontologies demand methodological displacements, incidents, conceptual leaps, and landslides, as well as theoretical links. In conventional qualitative humanistic research (St. Pierre, 2011) the methodological references and methods that connect them to reality are often considered relatively simple and concrete, compared to more complex or abstract entities that help to generate knowledge, concepts and arguments differently. This framework allows us to think about the meaning of research from another perspective, with other foundations and purposes. But above all, it enables us to argue that research is not just about following a pre-fixed path, in which methods are applied, to give an account of results foreseen in the initial questions (Hernández-Hernández & Revelles Benavente, 2019, p. 27).

As Lather (2007), Koro-Ljungberg et al., (2009), Jackson & Mazzei (2012) and Koro-Ljungberg (2015) have argued, theories (what guides and supports research) and methodologies are interconnected to enable functional relationships. Moreover, we can consider them as political movements against normative science, especially among those academics interested in emerging ontologies and surprising methodologies. When methodologies are considered immanent, changing, and transforming (Deleuze & Guattari, 1980/1987) – and bearers of unknown and unforeseen elements – research practices seem to bring academics closer to openness and imagination. Publications linked to this line of thought try to review, expand, and critically examine the state of normative qualitative research insofar as it has been configured as a space of thought that tends to evade all doubt.

In 2018 we discussed some of these insights in a paper (Sancho-Gil & Hernández-Hernández, 2018) presented in the European Conference of Educational Research at the network of Educational Ethnography, which led to this publication. In this presentation we considered four themes crossed and affected by the notion of becoming, which emerge from the ESBRINA research group[1] ethnographic studies (Domingo et al., 2014; Hernández-Hernández, 2017; Hernández et al., 2012; Hernández-Hernández & Sancho-Gil, 2017; Hernández-Hernández & Sancho-Gil, 2015). These issues are particularly challenging and promising for unveiling the complexities of the multiple layers of institutional cultures. And to question our ontological, epistemological, methodological, and ethical frames in ethnographic research.

1. The first concerned the ever-expanding nature of the ethnographic sites. In the 21st century, the challenge of going beyond the tangible aspects of culture, considering values and what Clifford Geertz (1973) termed as the 'ethos' of the culture, is now greater than ever. It is necessary to overcome the narrow focus on ethnography in one place.
2. The second, to the intra-action between virtual and 'analogical' sites. Something that has given way to notions such as 'digital ethnography' (Murthy,

2008), 'virtual ethnography' (Hine, 2000), 'cyberethnography' (Robinson & Schulz, 2009, 2011), 'internet ethnography' (boyd, 2010; Sade-Beck, 2004), 'ethnography on the internet' (Beaulieu, 2004), 'ethnography of virtual spaces' (Blomberg & Burrel, 2009), 'ethnographic research on the internet' (Garcia et al., 2009), 'internet-related ethnography' (Postill & Pink, 2012) and 'netnography' (Kozinets, 2010).

3. The third one related to the on-growing multimodal nature of information and research evidences. So, the traditional vision of fieldnotes as written (alphabetic) notes (Walford, 2009) is being challenged by the multimodal turn (Dicks et al., 2006; Hernández-Hernández & Sancho-Gil, 2018). A trend strongly driven by the proliferation of digital media that is generating new problems to manage and interpret information. Since, according to boyd (2010, np), 'we've entered an era where data is cheap, but making sense of it is not.'

4. Finally, we referred to the post-qualitative, the new empiricism and the new materialism turns (Lather & St. Pierre, 2013; Barad, 2003), which sustain that theories which guide and support research and methodologies are interconnected to enable conceptual and practical relationships. When methodologies are considered as immanent, changing and transforming (Deleuze & Guattari, 1980/1987) – and carrying unknown and unexpected elements, as we saw in a recent research project on how teachers learn (Hernández et al., 2020) – we are able to review, expand and examine research perspectives.

This framework allows us to think about the meaning of research, and particularly of Ethnography in Education, from other perspectives, with other foundations and purposes. But, above all, it allows us to open our imagination by thinking of research as something other than a pre-determined path, in which methods are applied to account for the results already foreseen in the initial questions. That is why we invite possible readers to be open to things that question and expand our positionalities (Hernández-Hernández & Sancho-Gil, 2015), which are always strategically provisional, and which open up ways for us to continue learning together.

By trying to be part of this conversation, this book examines ethnography in education to disrupt/de-territorialize it. It proposes to experiment with research differently through the concept and experience of 'becoming'. This perspective on ethnography could constitute an expansion of the concept/territory of ethnography.

A 'becoming' approach to ethnography in education could affect observations and interviews that, while guided by the research questions, are not-pre-given from protocols. For instance, in addition to what is documented and what happens in the conversation is the sensation of connecting relations and affect/becoming that come together in the assemblage (e.g. research questions, multimodal fieldnotes, interviews, researcher positionality) (Masny, 2014).

The post-qualitative movement entails the invitation to carry out ethnography in education that does not separate ontology, epistemology, methodology and ethics.

4   J. M. Sancho-Gil & F. Hernández-Hernández

This pays attention to the entanglement between the human, the non-human and the matter. This proposal suggests one assumes ethnography not to be a pre-defined journey, but rather one that opens itself to the possibility of surprise at what happens as the research flow unfolds, concerning the studied phenomenon.

This post-qualitative perspective becomes articulated and agitated around the concept of 'becoming', based on the meaning that Deleuze & Guattari (1980/1987) give it and that Barad (2014, pp. 181–182) develops when she refers to what happens in a research process.

> In an important sense, this story in its ongoing (re)patterning is (re)(con)figuring me. 'I' am neither outside nor inside; 'I' am of the diffraction pattern. Or rather, this 'I' that is not 'me' alone and never was, that is always already multiply dispersed and diffracted throughout spacetime(mattering), including in this paper, in its ongoing being-becoming is of the diffraction pattern.

This orientation towards of 'becoming' generates when, as Lather (2013) points out, researchers, following qualitative research, re-imagine and carry out studies that could produce different knowledge. This research cannot be described in an orderly manner in textbooks or manuals. There are no methodological approaches or instruments that can be learned without a problem. From this movement, one begins to approach research differently, because one adopts an onto-episte-methodology and an ethic that assumes that '[i]ndividuals do not exist as fixed or permanent entities separate from their surroundings but as ongoing relations of becoming in a world that is also always becoming' (Atkinson, 2015, p. 44).

A tentative approach of 'becoming'

The title of this book brings us to the need to discuss the notion of becoming. According to Faber (2011), despite the large differences between Whitehead's 'philosophy of organism' (process thought), Deleuze's 'philosophy of difference' (nomadic thought), and Judith Butler's 'philosophy of gender' (part of feminist philosophy), this notion can be understood

> as being part of—or better, as being at the forefront of—a philosophy for which *Becoming* is eminent. Indeed, in the concept of 'Becoming,' they turn our understanding of the world upside down—with all the philosophical, scientific, aesthetic, and political consequences. 'Becoming,' however, does not play the role of a common denominator enabling us to abstract from their divergent texts, but has the very concerted function of creating an active concept of analysis, struggle, and operation.
>
> *(p. 3)*

For Faber, 'the common field of becoming for Whitehead, Deleuze, and Butler is to understand their revolution in thought as based on (or at least initiated by)

Nietzsche's call for radical becoming' (p. 3), who argued 'there is no "being" behind the doing, acting, becoming. "The doer" is merely invented after the fact—the act is everything' (Nietzsche, 2009, in Faber, 2011, p. 4).

> In this line of thought, the notion of 'subject' is an abstraction post facto of the becoming of forces that happen to manifest themselves 'together'. There is no 'substrate' behind this activity of gathering, only the illusion of an effect disguised as the cause of the activity it originates. Indeed, the revolution, the *metanoia*, that which seems to be the basis, ground, and cause, is, in fact, the effect of its own becoming. *Being is the effect of becoming!*

This statement seems crucial in the context of this book, since it gives rise to the argument that it is impossible to 'be a researcher, an ethnographer' if it is not through a permanent process of becoming. Considering that nothing that becomes changes forever, but rather effects the being, and this 'being' turns into the past, a memory of the becoming. On the other hand, by considering being as the sedimentation of becoming, something can come into being. However, this 'something' is nothing in itself, it is not a substrate; it only functions as a condition of the new becoming.

Deleuze & Guattari (1980/1987) consider that in every event of becoming there are many heterogeneous, always simultaneous components, since each of them is a meanwhile that makes them communicate through zones of indiscernibility, of undecidability; they are variations, modulations, intermezzi, singularities, of a new infinite order (Faber, 2011, p. 6 paraphrased).

For Deleuze & Guattari (1980/1987) the dynamics of *becoming* is a process in which any given multiplicity 'changes in nature as it expands its connections' (p. 8). By deepening the becoming movements Deleuze & Guattari (1994) note 'The actual is not what we are but, rather, what we become, what we are in the process of becoming' (p. 112). This idea of becoming implies, as Lundborg (2009) states, that there is no middle point, or a present, in which the subject can be located. Becoming consists of an unlimited movement that 'produces nothing but itself' (p. 3). It is in this sense that becoming is understood as incorporeal; it is never present as such and has no direct relationship with an already present body. In this way, 'the event does not fall back on an already existing identity of the subject and is not imprisoned within an individual or personal self' (p. 3). Becoming does not have a pre-determined goal.

> It presents only a 'flow of life' that can take on new paths and create new ways of thinking and perceiving. For Deleuze, then, the task is to articulate and make thinkable this process by which there is an event of difference that does not fall back on identity and similarity but affirms the creative and productive elements of the event.
>
> *(Lundborg, 2009, p. 3)*

6 J. M. Sancho-Gil & F. Hernández-Hernández

As suggested above, the concept of becoming has penetrated social and educational research (Atkinson, 2018b; Fendler, 2013, 2018; Semetsky, 2006; St. Pierre, 2013, among others) and ethnography research (Biehl & Locke, 2010; Blair et al., 2011; Kunda, 2013; Masny, 2014; Wallace, 2017) by the influence of authors, such as mentioned Barad, Deleuze, Guattari, who are contributing to revise our ontological, epistemological, methodological and ethics research foundations.

This approach has relevance not only for the formation of educational ethnographers, but to consider that any research process is a process of becoming. Particularly if we assume with Semetsky (2006) that the 'subjects' of the research are subjects-in-process, because

> as *becoming*, (are) always placed between two multiplicities, yet one term does not become the other; the becoming is something *between* the two ... Therefore, *becoming* does not mean becoming the other, but *becoming-other* (p. 6). So, becoming is always relations, is it always in between. Becoming, as Bakko & Merz (2015) point out is 'a force of social indetermination that offers us the opportunity to look at what is, to imagine what could be in its place, and to understand that this "in its place" is always happening'.
>
> *(p. 8)*

This is a key issue for educational ethnographers because in the research process, in our encounters with the others, and with the materiality that embodies all relations, we participated in 'a dynamic series of prehensional relations through which beings try to take account of each other, and such relations are underpinned by a composition of feelings and conceptual processes' (Atkinson, 2018a, p.129).

Becoming ethnographers in a crossroad of trajectories and displacements

In this book, thirteen authors have gathered their reflections, experiences, displacements, drifts and affections in their process of becoming educational ethnographers. They come from various countries, with diverse professional and academic backgrounds, and have different approaches to ethnography. They are in different working positions and have followed diverse professional paths. This implies a broad and diverse vision of the process of becoming ethnographic researchers. Their contributions relate to three broad dimensions of the notion of becoming.

- Becoming as moving positionality in the trajectory of researchers, which allows them to account for their movements and transformations.
- Becoming as an onto–epistemological framework that affects and accounts for the unpredictability of the research process.
- Becoming as a concept that allows to re-signify the subjectivity of researchers and collaborators, as unstable and in permanent reconfiguration.

We have distributed the different chapters in these three areas, not as fixed and closed places, but as indications that allow us to situate the approach of becoming in which the authors of each chapter have located themselves.

Part I.
Becoming as moving researcher positionality

Part I begins with Stephanie Couch's chapter, 'Roots and routes to reading the world as an ethnographer'. She explores the importance of learning how to step back from what we think we know and to set ethnocentrism aside to come to know from the perspective of other individuals or social groups as central to becoming an ethnographer. She examines herself in her having become an ethnographer over twenty-one years. This process has allowed her to read the world in a new way in her efforts to bring about change as a leader in a variety of educational policy and programmatic contexts.

The exploration of how the process of becoming entangles conceptual lenses and relational experiences in the trajectory of the researcher continues in the chapter 'Becoming an educational ethnographer by organized representations of educational realities and 'researching through'', written by Christoph Maeder. In this contribution, he combines theoretical and methodological thoughts which make evident how relevant, innovative, and sophisticated the ethnographic approach could be to the description and analysis of how society and education has become. To illustrate his arguments, he uses selected concepts of organization in ethnography with a reference to educational institution. He proposes to deal with the complex educational realities by means such as participant observation.

In the next chapter, 'Becoming educational ethnographer through time and ontological displacements', Juana M. Sancho-Gil auto-ethnographically reconstructs some significative episodes of her career in the field of education and ethnography, showing how historical, cultural, political contexts and the researcher agency influence becoming processes. The main aim is to share the need to dare going beyond the given answers, pre-established mind frames, prescriptive theories and power relationships, and attentively looking around pondering all possible dimensions, actors, actants and matter, including themselves. The threads that weave this chapter are the relevance of discoveries, crisis, doubts and drifts, leading to new questions, certainties, uncertainties and magnitudes of the unknown, and the constant search for ontological positioning, allowing one to grasp the profound interweaving of social phenomena.

Chapter 5, 'Becoming an ethnographer: Living, teaching and learning ethnographically', by Audra Skukauskaite, focuses on some of the pathways of her life to compose a story of becoming – becoming a researcher, teacher, and scholar – a becoming that spans a lifetime, crosses continents, transcends disciplines, and intersects with the trails of many sojourners along the way. Through this life story, composed and recomposed by the varied elements of personal and professional, social and historical, individual and collective biographies, paints a picture of

8 J. M. Sancho-Gil & F. Hernández-Hernández

becoming as a multi-layered, sociohistorical and collective process. This is a process that keeps on going to capture the divergent elements of life into a cohesive story, which may reverberate with the readers' pathways of becoming.

The last chapter of the first part, 'The challenges and opportunities of becoming an ethnographer' by Rick Bacon, explores the challenges faced by someone from the world of business which sought to enter a community of researchers who practice educational ethnography. The focus of the chapter is the analysis of the process of becoming from 'outsider' to 'insider'. It consists of a reflexive research of a tracer unit, where a CEO-as-ethnographer/researcher-as-CEO studies what is required to read the world through an ethnographic lens and applies that lens to exploring the creation of learning opportunities – internships – in the workplace.

Although all the chapters include the characterization of becoming as a diffraction crossroads, in which biographical and thematic displacements illuminate the positions of the researchers, in this second part, the authors put the focus on the becomings onto-epistemological meaning. They do so by linking it to their completion of doctoral dissertations, and researcher's transformations in the process of an investigation.

Part II.
Becoming as an onto-epistemological framework

Aurelio Castro-Varela, in his chapter, 'What comes after becoming: Virtualities at the end of a doctoral research', elaborates on how the completion of his Ph.D dissertation entailed potentialities that did not entirely come into being. These virtualities arose from the process of becoming a researcher of two case studies in which he was previously involved as a regular member. Becoming an ethnographer of the mode of existence of these two communities, both focused on the display of audio-visual screenings, leading him to trace the more-than-human assemblages during their activities. However, as he should also co-organize them, the fieldwork endured a lack of room stemming from that contorted position. At the end of the writing, he realized that affects had been crucial in the constitution and maintenance of those assemblages, as well as disregarded from his perspective.

In the next chapter, 'An ethnographic research based on an ontology of becoming', Judit Onsès-Segarra starts with a series of questions, linked to her doctoral research, which frame her approach to becoming: Can research be written in an ongoing and processual state? How can a doctoral thesis be approached from an ontology of becoming? From these questions, she shares her experience as an ethnographic researcher while writing her Ph.D thesis, in which she explores the potentialities of visual documentation of learning phenomena in primary schools by adopting Deleuze and Guattari's ontology of becoming. To do so, she explains how it affected her writing processes, and what potentialities and risks it entailed; this is not always well understood or welcomed by other researchers.

To conclude this second part, Fernando Hernández-Hernández focuses his chapter, 'Openness to the unforeseen in a nomadic research process on teachers' learning experiences', on the idea that the researcher positionality as being in becoming makes the inquiry process a relational journey. In this process, one is attentive not to what one expects to find, but to what is happening that is not linear but full of bifurcations, fluxes, doubts and places of not-knowing. This becoming approach emphasizes the importance of making the researcher approach visible and transparent. The chapter explores Fernando's process of becoming from being part of a research project to explore how secondary school teachers experience their learning moves and processes by using ethnographic methods to describe teachers' learning movements in and beyond their/our cartographic encounters.

Part III.
Becoming as a concept that allows to re-signify the subjectivity

Rather than essentializing the 'subject' as singular, fixed, and predictable, Deleuze and Guattari (1980/1987) open-up the possibility of a multiplicitous or patchwork notion of the subject which is in becoming. Which means, as Atkinson points out, that '[i]ndividuals do not exist as fixed or permanent entities separate from their surroundings but as ongoing relations of becoming in a world that is also always becoming' (Atkinson, 2015, p. 44). This idea of the subject in becoming is what is explored, to a large extent, in the three chapters that make up this session.

Garth Stahl initiates the first chapter of this last session, 'An accidental institutional ethnographer: Reflections on paradoxes and positionality', by introducing the debate over the corporatization of schooling; specifically, expanding charter school networks in the United States. The institutional culture is deeply linked to neoliberal practices based on risk and reward to foster a culture of relentless performance. From this starting point, this chapter reflects on his experiences in becoming an accidental institutional ethnographer of a Charter School Management Organization (CMO) where his focus was on his inculcation and the tension between his subjectivity as a participant and identity as a researcher. Considering this tension, he discusses how institutional ethnography (IE) influenced him. To conclude, he reflects on how his role as a researcher represents a negotiation with his positionality and social justice principles.

In the following chapter, 'Researchers and risk: Exploring vulnerability, subjectivity, and identity in ethnographic research through collage making', Corinne McKamey, Cleti Cervoni and Rhoda Bernard use ethnographic methods to work with vulnerable populations and topics and consider ethnographic research as an endeavour that poses considerable risks to the researcher, as well as to the participants. In their work, they have found the arts-based method of collage making to be a particularly useful tool for exposing, reflecting on, understanding and working through the risks that both researchers and participants take. In their experience, this collage work fosters a process of growth, new understandings, and a recognition that the images and beliefs they hold are always changing and unfolding. This process of becoming can help researchers think more deeply about issues of representation and inclusion.

10 J. M. Sancho-Gil & F. Hernández-Hernández

Finally, Juliane Corrêa presents the chapter entitled 'Ethnographic educational research as assemblages of teachers' and researchers' movements and their learning environments', where she deals with her experience as a researcher of school culture and the work context of teachers approaching an unknown reality usually not considered in teacher professional development programs. In this context, she explores three scenes linked to sound space, moving space and shared space as fragments of assemblages that constitute the experience of an event, the materiality of pedagogy. From her readings on post-qualitative turn, cartography and rhizomatic inquiry, she explores how teachers affect and are affected by these learning spaces, how these spaces produce capacities for the bodies to develop the assemblage itself and how teachers and researchers become active participants in a 'pedagogical becoming'.

Crossroads, concepts, positions, drifts

In this book, the different chapters show that research as becoming could be considered as:

- A process that is not linear and does not follow strict limits or normative structures; that diversifies, that can begin and fork at any time.
- Being in becoming assumes that moving without a pre-fixed route can generate a sense of uncertainty and loss of stable, fixed, repetitive and pre-conceptualised historical knowledge.
- Placing oneself in this 'becoming' leads to paying attention to the diverse, the material and the emerging.
- Allowing the possibility of generating ways of thinking and writing practices that offer other views of a reality, which requires consideration from different approaches to inquiry, and to do so as one becomes aware of the transits and detours that one is travelling.
- Challenging, as Snaza & Weaver (2014) point out, the methodocentrism, according to which the methodology and the fidelity to a method are the main concern of the research. This tendency leads to relegating human beings, other living beings, and inanimate objects to a subordinate position from which the intra-actions of these beings are eliminated from the work of the researcher.
- An invitation to 'thinking difference differently, a reappropriation of contradictory available scripts to create alternative practices of research as a site of being and becoming [...] Facing the problems of doing research in this historical time, between the no longer and the not yet, the task is to produce different knowledge and produce knowledge differently' (Lather, 2006, p. 52).
- Not a simple call for a change or expansion of ethnographic methods, but rather a demand for methods not being considered as constraint for research (Koro-Ljungberg, 2015).
- An opportunity to rethink the notions of subject and subjectivity, because understanding 'the subject-in-process, that is, as becoming, is always placed

between two multiplicities, yet one term does not become the other; the becoming is something between the two … Therefore, becoming does not mean becoming the other, but becoming-other (Semetsky, 2006, p. 6, emphasis in original).

All the above does not mean a return to ethnography as a narcissistic approach in the relation with the 'other' or the ethnographer's narrative account (Viveiros de Castro, 2014), but considers the research in intra-action not only with other humans but with other expanded ones.

Note

1 https://esbrina.eu/en/home

References

Atkinson, D. (2015). The Adventure of Pedagogy, Learning and the Not-known. *Subjectivity*, 8 (1), 43–56.

Atkinson, D. (2018a). *Art, Disobedience and Ethics. The Adventure of Pedagogy*. Palgrave.

Atkinson, D. (2018b). Art, Pedagogies and Becoming: The Force of Art and the Individuation of New Worlds. In L. Knight & A. Lasczik Cutcher (eds.), *Arts-Research-Education: Connections and Directions* (pp. 3–16).: Springer. https://doi.org/10.1007/978-3-319-61560-8.

Bakko, M., Merz, S. (2015). Towards an Affective Turn in Social Science Research? Theorising Affect, Rethinking Methods and (Re)Envisioning the Social. *Graduate Journal of Social Science*, 11 (1), 7–14.

Barad, K. (2003). Posthumanist Performativity: Toward an Understanding of how Matter comes to Matter. *Signs*, 28 (3), 801–831.

Barad, K. (2014). Diffracting Diffraction: Cutting Together-Apart. *Parallax*, 20 (3), 168–187, https://doi.org/10.1080/13534645.2014.92762.

Beaulieu, A. (2004). Mediating Ethnography: Objectivity and the Making of Ethnographies of the Internet. *Social epistemology*, 18 (2–3),139–163.

Biehl, J., Locke, P. (2010). Deleuze and the Anthropology of Becoming. *Current Anthropology*, 51 (3), 317–351.

Blair, H., Filipek, J., Lovell, M., McKay, M., Nixon, R., & Sun, M. (2011). Our Journey to Becoming Ethnographers: An Exploration of Rhetorical Structures as Lived Experience. *International Journal of Qualitative Methods*, 10 (2), 140–150.

Blomberg, J., & Burrel, M. (2009). An Ethnographic Approach to Design. In *Human-Computer Interaction* (pp. 87–110). CRC Press.

Bourke, L. (2009). *Reflections on Doing Participatory Research on Health: Participation, Method and Power, International Journal of Social Research Methodology*, 12 (5), 457–474.

boyd, d. (2010). Privacy and Publicity in the Context of Big Data. *WWW*. Raleigh, North Carolina, April 29. http://www.danah.org/papers/talks/2010/WWW2010.html.

Deleuze, G., & Guattari, F. (1980/1987). *Thousand Plateaus* (trans. Brian Massumi). University of Minnesota Press.

Deleuze, G., & Guattari, F. (1991/1994). *What is Philosophy?* (trans. Hugh Tomlinson and Graham Burchell). Verso.

Dicks, B., Soyinka, B., & Coffey, A. (2006). Multimodal Ethnography. *Qualitative Research*, 6, (1), 77–96. https://doi.org/10.1177/1468794106058876.

Domingo, M., Sánchez, J.A., & Sancho, J.M. (2014). Researching on and with Young People: Collaborating and Educating. *Comunicar, Media Education Research Journal*, n. 42, v. XXI, 157–164. http://dx.doi.org/10.3916/C42-2014-15.

Faber (2011). Introduction: Negotiating Becoming. In R. Faber, & A.M. Stephenson, (Eds.), *Secrets of Becoming: Negotiating Whitehead, Deleuze, and Butler.* (pp. 1–52). Fordham Univ Press.

Fendler, R. (2013). Becoming-Learner. Coordinates for Mapping the Space and Subject of Nomadic Pedagogy. *Qualitative Inquiry*, 19 (10), 786–793.

Fendler, R. (2016). *Navigating the eventful space of learning: Mobilities, nomadism and other tactical maneuvers.* Doctoral dissertation. University of Barcelona. Retrieved from: http://diposit.ub.edu/dspace/bitstream/2445/67739/1/FENDLER_RACHEL_PhD_THESIS.pdf

Garcia, A.C., Standlee, A.I., Bechkoff, J., & Cui, Y. (2009). Ethnographic Approaches to the Internet and Computer-Mediated Communication. *Journal of Contemporary Ethnography*, 38 (1), 52–84. http://dx.doi.org/1177/0891241607310839.

Geertz, C. (1973). *The Interpretation of Cultures.* Basic Books.

Hernández, F., Sancho, J., & Fendler, R (2012). When the "(Playing) Field" has no Physical Limits: Ethnographic Research with Young People on their Learning Experiences outside School. In S. Marques da Silva; P. Landri (Eds), *Rethinking Education Ethnography: Researching On-line Communities and Interactions* (pp. 13–25). CIIE.

Hernández-Hernández, F., & Revelles Benavente, B. (2019). La perspectiva post-cualitativa en la investigación educativa: genealogía, movimientos, posibilidades y tensiones. *Educatio Siglo XXI*, 37 (2), 21–48. http://dx.doi.org/10.6018/j/387001.

Hernández-Hernández, F., & Sancho-Gil, J.M. (2015). A Learning Process within an Education Research Group: An Approach to Learning Qualitative Research Methods. *International Journal of Social Research Methodology*, 18 (6), 651–667. http://dx.doi.org/10.1080/13645579.2015.1049468.

Hernández-Hernández, F., & Sancho-Gil, J.M. (2017). Using Meta-ethnographic Analysis to Understand and Represent Youth's Notions and Experiences of Learning in and out of Secondary School. *Ethnography and Education*, 12 (2), 178–193. http://dx.doi.org/10.1080/17457823.2016.1180542.

Hernández-Hernández, F., & Sancho-Gil, J.M. (2018). Writing and Managing Multimodal Field Notes. *Oxford Research Encyclopaedia of Education.* Online Publication Date: Jun 2018. http://dx.doi.org/10.1093/acrefore/9780190264093.013.319.

Hernández-Hernández, F., Aberasturi Apraiz, E., Sancho-Gil, J.M., & Correa Gorospe, J.M. (2020). *¿Cómo aprenden los docentes? Tránsitos entre cartografías, experiencias, corporeidades y afectos.* Octaedro.

Hine, Ch. (2000). *Virtual Ethnography.* SAGE publications.

Jackson, A.Y., & Mazzei, L.A. (2012). *Thinking with Theory in Qualitative Research.* Routledge.

Koro-Ljungberg, M. (2015). *Reconceptualizing Qualitative Research: Methodologies without Methodology.* SAGE publications.

Koro-Ljungberg, M., Yendol-Hoppey, D., Smith, J.J., & Hayes, S.B. (2009). (E)pistemological Awareness, Instantiation of Methods, and Uninformed Methodological Ambiguity in Qualitative Research Projects. *Educational Researcher*, 38 (9), 687–699.

Kozinets, R.V. (2010). *Netnography: Doing Ethnographic Research Online.* SAGE publications.

Kunda, G. (2013). Reflections on Becoming an Ethnographer. *Journal of Organizational Ethnography*, 2 (1), 4–22, http://dx.doi.org/10.1108/JOE-12-2012-0061.

Lather, P. (2007). *Getting Lost: Feminist Efforts Toward a Double(d) Science.* State University of New York Press.

Lather, P. (2013) Methodology-21: What do we do in the Afterward? *International Journal of Qualitative Studies in Education*, 26 (6). 634–645, http://dx.doi.org/10.1080/09518398.2013.78875.

Lather, P., & St. Pierre, E.A. (2013). Post-qualitative Research. *International Journal of Qualitative Studies in Education*, 26 (6), 629–633: http://dx.doi.org/10.1080/09518398.2013.788752.

Lundborg, T. (2009). The *Becoming* of the "Event": A Deleuzian Approach to Understanding the Production of Social and Political "Events". *Theory & Event* 12(1), http://dx.doi.orgdoi:10.1353/tae.0.0042. Retrieved from https://muse.jhu.edu/article/263142.

Masny, D. (2014). Disrupting ethnography through rhizoanalysis. *Qualitative Research in Education*, 3 (3), 345–363.

Murthy, D. (2008). Digital Ethnography: An Examination of the Use of New Technologies for Social Research, *Sociology*, 42 (5), 837–855https://doi.org/10.1177/0038038508094565.

Nietzsche, F. (2009). *On the Genealogy of Morals*. Oxford University Press.

Postill, J., & Pink, S. (2012). Social Media Ethnography: The Digital Researcher in a Messy Web. *Media International Australia*, 145 (1), 123–134.

Robinson, L., & Schulz, J. (2009). New Avenues for Sociological Inquiry: Evolving Forms of Ethnographic Practice. *Sociology*, 43 (4), 685–698. https://doi.org/10.1177/0038038509105415.

Robinson, L., & Schulz, J. (2011). New Fieldsites, New Methods: New Ethnographic Opportunities. In S.N. Hesse-Biber (Ed.), *The Handbook of Emergent Technologies in Social Research*. Oxford University Press.

Sade-Beck, L. (2004). Internet Ethnography: Online and Offline. *International Journal of Qualitative Methods*, 3 (2), 45–51, https://doi.org/10.1177/160940690400300204.

Sancho-Gil, J.M., & Hernández-Hernández, F. (2018). Becoming Educational Ethnographers in the Digital Age. Paper given at the European Conference of Educational Research (ECER). Bolzano, Italy, 3–7 September.

Semetsky, I. (2006). *Deleuze, Education and Becoming*. Sense Publishers.

Snaza, N., Weaver, J. (ed.). (2015). *Posthumanism and Educational Research*. Routledge.

St. Pierre, E. (2011). *Post Qualitative Research: The Critique and the Coming After. In N. K. Denzin & Y. S. Lincoln (eds.) The Sage Handbook of Qualitative Research* (4a edition), (pp. 611–625). SAGE Publications.

St. Pierre, E. (2013). *The posts continue: becoming. International Journal of Qualitative Studies in Education*, 26 (6), 646–657, https://doi.org/10.1080/09518398.2013.78875.

Viveiros de Castro, E. (2014). *Cannibal Metaphysics*. Univocal.

Walford, G. (2009). The Practice of Writing Ethnographic Fieldnotes. *Ethnography and Education*, 4(2), 117–130.

Wallace, M. (2108). *Deterritorializing Dichotomies in Teacher Induction: A (Post)Ethnographic Study of Un/Becoming an Elementary Science Teacher*. Louisiana State University. Doctorate dissertation.

PART I

Becoming as moving researcher positionality

2

ROOTS AND ROUTES TO READING THE WORLD AS AN ETHNOGRAPHER

Stephanie Couch

Initial discovery of ethnography and its usefulness for research in, of, and for education (Bloome et al., 2018) often occurs during graduate studies at a university. This chapter offers a telling case (Mitchell, 1984) of an alternate path of discovery and reports findings from an ongoing study tracing my take-up of the ontological and epistemological perspectives and practices of ethnographers. As the ethnographer conducting this study and given my dual roles of author-as-ethnographer and research subject, I chose to use a pseudonym, 'Dr. C/Ms.C,' for 'self.' The pseudonym supported my attempts to step back from all I thought I knew, avoiding ethnocentrism, to look again as a professional stranger (Agar, 1996b).

The (re)construction of my journey to becoming an ethnographer and findings from the analysis of key events provide an account of ways I am developing ethnographic eyes (Wolcott, 2008) to guide my work in education and in other social contexts. 'Becoming', in this study, is conceptualized as a noun and as an ongoing process of change in which potentialities and capabilities for carrying out studies from an ethnographic perspective develop across time and events. The examination of my progression draws on headnotes of thoughts Dr. C recorded and placed in her archive after the award of a Ph.D in Education by her dissertation committee: The point at which she had successfully negotiated formal access to the social group of 'university scholars.' The following headnote in the archive serves as an anchor or 'rich point' (Agar, 1996a; Agar, 1996b) for beginning the analysis:

> Hours after leaving the committee I reflected on all I had learned through the dissertation process. I thought about the ways of thinking and analyzing social interactions made transparent by my University studies, and the ways I found myself thinking about the conversations I was having with people. In many instances, I noted that I was present in the conversation while also analyzing

18 Stephanie Couch

the dialogue in real time—or dual processing. Noticing and making mental notes of who was doing what, with whom, and so forth happened spontaneously, and I had an uncontrollable urge to find paper to jot down field notes before the mental notes faded away. I hypothesized that these ways of reading the world had become a permanent part of my life... I had developed 'ethnographic eyes' ... the practices had become so ingrained in my thinking processes that [they] would influence ways of coming to understand and to 'know' in differing social contexts in perpetuity.

Research questions guiding the tracing and (re)construction of the journey to becoming an ethnographer

The reflexive stance illustrated in the (re)constructed headnote (or field note) presented above offers evidence of Dr. C's take-up of one of the many practices of ethnographers (Green et al., 2003). Her words suggest that her ways of thinking and working as an ethnographer had become permanently activated by the time her faculty committee approved her dissertation, as opposed to being turned on and off at will. Her description of the ingrained thought processes generated three research questions guiding the study:

Question 1. What actions or events led Dr. C to conduct an ethnographic study on a developing virtual organization and ultimately her receipt of a Ph.D in Education?

Question 2. Who supported Dr. C's development as an ethnographer? How did the individual(s) support her growth and development?

Question 3. How were the roots and routes to Dr. C's becoming an ethnographer related to her work as a leader in education?

Data collection and analysis

Answering the research questions, as I will unfold in the sections that follow, required revisiting records (texts) collected by Dr. C for her dissertation (Couch, 2012). New records were added to the existing ones, and all were re-examined to produce new data (Ellen, 1984) in response to the new research questions. Records from the dissertation research include observation field notes; reconstructed headnotes as a form of field notes; and artifacts such as public documents, email correspondence, documents produced by participants through the activities of the virtual organization and published articles. Additional records include a current curriculum vitae (CV), academic transcripts, artifacts consisting of narratives and related documents from grant proposals written for work purposes during the timeframe addressed by this study, Dr. C's dissertation committee members' CVs, and artifacts from records of university coursework and Dr. C's master's degree project. Table 2.1 summarizes the records.

TABLE 2.1 Corpus of Records for Producing Data

Dates of Records	Range of Records (Re)Examined
2020	Dr. C's curriculum vitae
1981–2012	Ms. C's academic transcripts
2012	Dr. C's published dissertation on the Stepping Project
2010–2019	Publications cited in Dr. C's curriculum vitae (12 total)
2004–2010	Archived narrative text and artifacts from 27 grant proposals
2020	Curricula vitae for Ms. C's three dissertation committee members
2008–2012	Artifacts from Ms. C's coursework at the university
	Artifacts from the Stepping Project:
2007–2009	• 6 grant proposals (one Stepping Project focused on mathematics and one Stepping Project focused on English Language Arts in each of 3 years)
2007–2010	• 6 evaluation reports for the 6 grants

Ethnography in education: Empirical research guided by a philosophy of inquiry, principles and practices

Onto-epistemological theories (Agar, 2006; Green et al., 2012) that have emerged from the fields of anthropology (Bloome et al., 2018; Green et al., 2012; Heath & Street, 2008) and sociology (Hammersley & Atkinson, 2007) guided my process of tracing Dr. C's journey to becoming an ethnographer and my interrogation of the records to answer the research questions. This philosophy or logic of inquiry (Anderson-Levitt, 2006; Birdwhistell, 1977; Couch, 2012; Green et al., 2003; Green et al., 2012) employed by ethnographers in education first emerged in the United States in 1954 (Bloome et al., 2018). Researchers working from this tradition embrace common underlying theories as method and method as theories (Castanheira et al., 2008). An iterative and recursive, abductive reasoning process (Kaplan, 1964) shapes ethnographers' investigations as opposed to pre-determined methods. Principles guiding the process, articulated by Green et al. (2012), include:

Principle 1: Ethnography as a non-linear system.
Principle 2: Leaving aside ethnocentrism.
Principle 3: Identifying boundaries of an event that will be examined to determine what is happening and ways the event may be tied to other events.
Principle 4: Building connections between one bit of life and others.

The primary site of ethnographers' conduct of research is 'in the field,' allowing the researcher to be a participant observer of a particular phenomenon in everyday contexts (Agar, 2006; Ellen, 1984; Hammersley & Atkinson, 2007; Spradley, 1980). Cultural aspects of life within social groups is a central focus. "Culture" is conceptualized from an anthropological perspective as a verb—not a noun (Heath & Street, 2008; Street, 1993; Wolcott, 2008). It is considered to be part of a dynamic process of meaning making realized through ongoing interactions between people, including their talk, behaviour, and interactions with artifacts, objects, or tools (Anderson-Levitt, 2006; Wolcott, 1967).

After negotiating entry to the social group that constitutes the site of study, ethnographers engage with individuals within the group and make records of these interactions over extended periods of time (Anderson-Levitt, 2006; Heath, 1982; Street, 1993). Through this process, ethnographers construct records of events and interactions, and collect artifacts from a wide range of sources. Analysis of the records supports the production of data (Ellen, 1984) used to create warranted accounts of the processes and practices constructed in and through the interactions of members of a social group (Heap, 1985). Thick descriptions (Ellen, 1984; Geertz, 1983; Walford, 2008) of everyday life and meanings of particular words and actions (Bloome et al., 2018; Green & Bridges, 2018) are produced. Attention is paid to collecting, constructing, analyzing, theorizing, and reporting data in a manner that renders and preserves the intrinsic properties of the cultural practices or social actions of the members (Atkinson et al., 2008; Ellen, 1984; Mitchell, 1984).

Participation and observation across time and events, and the collection and systematic analysis of dialogues, artifacts, and field notes, allow researchers to document patterned practices of the ways of thinking, knowing and being within a social group (Gee & Green, 1998). In some instances, however, a full ethnographic study is not possible. When faced with this dilemma—as I was—in this study of the history of an ethnographer's journey, the researcher can conduct research from an ethnographic perspective (Sheridan et al., 2000). Researchers working from an ethnographic perspective continue to draw on theories, a logic of inquiry, and the processes and practices of ethnographers.

This study unfolds the process of tracing Dr. C's journey, making visible how an ethnographic perspective guides the researcher's (re)entry into the archive constructed by Dr. C, thereby enabling the researcher to generate theories from the cultural artifacts in the archive. Analyses of the records reveal ways Dr. C inscribed her lived experiences, making visible who did what to support her journey, with whom, under what conditions, for what purposes, and with what impacts (Green et al., 2003; Sheridan et al., 2000). Warranted accounts (Heath & Street, 2008; Spradley, 1980) presented in the sections that follow were generated by constructing empirical evidence (Spradley, 1980) through documentation of details of time, space, artifacts and human interactions. Theoretical interpretations were then constructed by grounding interpretations of social organization and cultural processes and practices in the ethnographic research literature (Hammersley & Atkinson, 2007; Heath & Street, 2008). By tracing different phases of the study, I make visible how one phase of analysis led to iterative and recursive analyses to gain deeper insights into the process of becoming an ethnographer.

Phases of work involved when a leader in education carried out the historical processes of becoming

The first phase of Dr. C's journey to becoming an ethnographer that I (re)examined from an ethnographic perspective covered a fourteen-year period of time (1998–2012). The decision to employ an ethnographic perspective as a way of knowing is grounded in Hymes' (1996) argument that ethnographers studying social phenomena can adapt anthropological theories for use across many fields of study. Adaptations of the applied theories have been described as: 1) the 'doing' of ethnography, 2) adoption of an ethnographic perspective in which the ethnographer stops short of a comprehensive ethnography as they study aspects of everyday life in a social group, and 3) the use of ethnographic tools (Green & Bloome, 1997; Heath & Street, 2008). The use of archived records to develop an emic understanding of Dr. C's path of becoming builds on those arguments and arguments by Sheridan et al. (2000) that archived records provide opportunities for examining how people inscribe their world or dimensions of that world. In the sections that follow, I will unfold ways in which ethnographic processes, practices, and perspectives guided my reconstruction of Dr. C's ongoing journey to becoming an ethnographer.

Tracing Dr. C's development process from 1998 to 2012 and 2012 to 2019

The (re)construction of Dr. C's journey, (re)presented in Table 2.2, began with mapping key events over a fourteen-year period (1998–2012) to trace the roots and routes leading to the award of a Ph.D in education. This marked the point at which Dr. C realized that she had internalized the practices used by ethnographers to 'read' and theorize social situations and cultures-in-the-making (i.e., culture as a verb). As indicated in Table 2.2, Dr. C embarked on her journey to becoming in 1998, when she left her work as an education policy consultant affiliated with the state legislature to work in higher education by advancing academic programs and partnerships.

After tracing her development during these years, I determined that I needed to map key events over an additional seven-year period (2012–2019) to fully answer the research questions. The phases of research in this abductive, iterative and recursive process (Green et al., 2012) are discussed in the next sections.

Phase 1: Preparing the mind by engaging with educational ethnographers (1998–2012)

In Phase 1 of her journey, as shown in Table 2.2, Dr. C changed leadership roles while engaging in different educational and organizational contexts. Dr. C engaged in ongoing interactions with two university ethnographers, Drs. Judith Green and

22 Stephanie Couch

TABLE 2.2 Six Ways of Learning While Working as a Leader in Education and Becoming as an Ethnographer (1998–2019)

1998–2009 Work Role: Technology in Teaching and Learning	2009–2016 Work Role: STEM Education	2016–2019 Work Role: Invention Education
Forms of Engagement with Ethnographers in Education		
1998–2012 Informal learning by engaging with ethnographers on grant development		2013–2019 Informal learning by continuing to engage with ethnographers as alum
Informal learning during joint program implementation		Learning by engaging ethnographers as consultants/staff
	2008–2012 Learning through formal studies in M.A./Ph.D (Ph.D awarded in 2012)	Learning by working as an ethnographer on research studies

Note. Dr. C's work role prior to 1998 is not reflected due to boundaries established by the researcher

Elizabeth Yeager. Interactions included the writing of grants, research pertaining to the implementation of education programs, and formal university studies. Table 2.2, therefore, makes visible the parallel nature of Dr. C's various roles in leading education initiatives and other actions (ongoing collaborations and dialogues) that contributed to her development in the early stages of her journey. The engagement with ethnographers and opportunities for learning prepared Dr. C's mind for the formal study of ethnography prior to entering a doctoral program with Dr. Green as her advisor.

Phase 2: Learning to think as an ethnographer through graduate studies (2008–2012)

The previous mapping of Dr. C's journey provided a sketch of the interactions and sites of study that generated knowledge and affinity for ethnography as a way of knowing. In the next phase of (re)examining Dr. C's journey, I returned to the archived records to re-examine the years in which she attended graduate school. This process—re-entering the archive to produce data needed to further inform understandings—is consistent with descriptions of ethnographic research as iterative, non-linear and abductive (Agar, 1996b; Agar, 2006; Green et al., 2012). The second phase of the study, therefore, focused on Dr. C's formal studies by (re)examining transcripts and artifacts in course folders she had retained. This phase of analysis revealed opportunities for learning in the period between entry to the master's program in Fall 2008 and the receipt of her Ph.D in spring 2012.

The analyses showed the range of topics studied, including research theories and methods, and topics related to teaching and learning. Resources for learning included members of her dissertation committee, who were also course instructors. Papers produced and her dissertation reflected studies in a wide range of areas including organizational development, innovative teams, the social construction of knowledge, and ethnography.

Analysis of the acknowledgement pages of the dissertation (Couch, 2012) made visible particular sources of influence, including references to her participation in coursework as a distant learner with the help of her fellow students and faculty members who 'integrated the use of new technologies into the courses they taught' so Dr. C could 'gain first-hand knowledge of the many issues involved in the use of technologies in education' (p. v). The acknowledgement page began with a reference to Drs. Green and Yeager in which Dr. C inscribes the encouragement of the two 'digital pioneers' (p. v), who encouraged her to enroll in graduate school, and the 'transformative' nature of the experience. She wrote that her educational experience 'changed nearly every aspect of my life, including the ways in which I now think about personal and professional interactions with others.'

The next phase of my analysis of Dr. C's journey (re)examined her growth and development in the years shown in Table 2.2 that followed her receipt of a doctoral degree. As the 'insider' being studied, I was aware that I had previously entered a headnote in the research records regarding Dr. C's new ways of 'reading' her world at graduation, and her perceived need at that point in time (2012) for further development as an ethnographer beyond graduate school. Additionally, I possessed insider knowledge of the time that passed between the years when Ms. C graduated (becoming Dr. C) and the time when she self-identified as being able to design and carry out ethnographic research studies with confidence as an ethnographer. Given my goal of stepping back from the known, I determined that a third phase of analysis was needed to examine the archived records, sources of influence, and actions taken for the seven years that had passed since Dr. C was awarded a graduate degree. By (re)constructing this period, as depicted in Table 2.2, I was able to render a more complete picture of the roots and routes leading to the time in which Dr. C viewed herself as having reached the point of becoming confident as a practitioner.

Phase 3: Becoming while engaging in ethnographic studies (2012–2019)

To (re)construct Dr. C's history in the third phase of the study, I revisited her CV to determine what it would reveal about the dates, timelines, events, and individuals that may have supported her further development as an ethnographer during the seven years that followed her completion of the Ph.D (2012–2019). The iterative process of analyzing the consequential progression of events (Castanheira et al., 2008) and interconnected bits of life (Green et al., 2012) undertaken by Dr. C made visible six ways of learning—shown in Table 2.2—employed by Dr. C as she developed professional capabilities in and across university leadership contexts.

24 Stephanie Couch

During this period extending beyond graduation, Dr. C led a series of projects in her sites of work and conducted her own research, thereby embedding ethnographic research practices within the programmatic work she led over her seven years of employment and multiple roles at two universities in her post-Ph.D places of work. Ongoing engagement in studies with Drs. Green and Yeager, as well as other ethnographers, was analyzed given Dr. C's account of what was needed to get to a stage of becoming in which she felt confident as a practitioner. The ongoing joint efforts can be conceptualized as a type of collaborative academic apprenticeship (Wellin & Fine, 2001).

Implications of the study of an education leader becoming an ethnographer: The journey continues

The telling case of Dr. C's journey re-presented to this point has demonstrated the over-time nature of becoming an ethnographer in education through engagement with others in both professional collaborations and formal educational contexts. Analysis of the three phases of development made visible that Dr. C had become familiar with ethnography over a ten-year period (1998–2008), before entering a university to pursue a graduate degree. Ongoing engagement with Drs. Green and Yeager constituted a period in which the ethnographers were preparing Dr. C's mind for future graduate-level studies. The second phase of her journey included formal studies during her four years in graduate school (2008–2012), and the third phase involved collaborative learning by engaging with Drs. Green, Yeager and other ethnographers in ethnographic studies over a seven-year period (2012–2019) beyond graduate school.

Findings across all three phases of the study offered evidence that Dr. C's knowledge and capabilities were in an ongoing state of development, or process of becoming-other (Semetsky, 2006), in at least three domains as presented below.

First domain: Becoming knowledgeable of the individuals, social context, and topics studied through actions affiliated with professional roles and graduate studies

As presented in the sections above, Dr. C inscribed her knowledge and representations of reality in relation to the individuals, social context, and topic(s) of study that led her to a growing understanding of how knowledge is socially constructed through ongoing interactions between the graduate student, faculty member, and research subjects (Berger & Luckmann, 1967). In her role of student-as-researcher, analysis of the archived records made visible that she was focused on developing ways of making explicit the ways of thinking, knowing, and being that were taken for granted by social actors familiar with the culture of the particular social groups she was studying (e.g., Hammersley & Atkinson, 2007). Much of the focus in her graduate program courses was on ways of analyzing language in use and meanings inscribed by the actors engaged in particular phenomena. Analyses focused on the language of participants whose interactions were recorded and archived, and on identifying 'frame clashes,' which anthropologist Michael Agar argued is the point at which the researcher realizes 'that you've got a problem with language, and the problem has to do with who you are' (Agar, 1996a, pp. 20–21).

Dr. C reported that the concept of frame clashes continued to allow for the identification of a rich point or place to begin efforts to develop understandings from the perspective of the insider(s) she was studying. She learned that coming to know from the perspective of the insider(s) changes what is known by the researcher. To capture what Dr. C learned through the concept of frame clashes (i.e., differences in frames of reference), I (re)visited Agar's (1996a) publication in which he describes the work of ethnographers. The following captures the challenge that Dr. C identified as central to becoming an ethnographer from a linguistic anthropology perspective:

> You can't use a new language [the participants' language] unless you change the consciousness that is tied to the old one [your own], unless you stretch beyond the circle of grammar and dictionary, out of the old world and into a new one.... Consciousness changes when you think paradigmatically, when you imagine or encounter or learn other things that might have occurred. And once you imagine new things, they have ramifications throughout the system because of the syntagmatic ties between the new things you've learned and the other aspects of your consciousness.
>
> *(Agar, 1996a, p. 48)*

Second domain: Becoming knowledgeable and skilled in the conduct of ethnographic research through ongoing actions affiliated with professional roles

Analysis of Dr. C's assignments and records made visible that as a graduate student engaged in dissertation research, she was engaged in a process of seeking entry into the social group we know as 'university scholars.' Over the course of her program, she developed an understanding that recognition as a scholar is formally bestowed through the award of a graduate degree and is conferred after the student presents evidence (i.e., the final dissertation) demonstrating an understanding of, and ability to employ, the principles and practices valued by the field. As a student aiming to become an ethnographer in education, Dr. C learned that she was expected to demonstrate a logic of inquiry and take-up of the principles described earlier, rather than simply use techniques or methods. For example, in presenting her research in classes and in her dissertation, she learned that avoiding ethnocentrism in claims being made through her research was important—a process that meant setting aside value judgements or a priori expectations of research subjects or outcomes. Part of the process of becoming an ethnographer, she learned, was to step back from what one knows and to look again from the perspective of a professional stranger (Agar, 1996b; Heath & Street, 2008). This process that she came to understand was accomplished, in part, by adherence to a logic of inquiry and through triangulation of multiple forms of data that generate empirical evidence needed for warranted claims (Green & Chian, 2018; Heap, 1985).

26 Stephanie Couch

Third domain: Becoming a reader of the world through ethnographic eyes and ongoing observations and analysis in personal and professional contexts

The third domain related to becoming an ethnographer pertains to the student's ways of thinking, knowing and being in the world, irrespective of his or her deliberate efforts to employ ethnographic principles and practices as part of carrying out a formal study. As a graduate student who engaged in ethnographic studies and the writing of research publications, Dr. C spent many hours engaging with her faculty advisor and with knowledgeable others in exploring ways of thinking, knowing, and being that are made explicit through ongoing dialogues. Over time, efforts to record and then analyze languacultures (Agar, 1996a) in ways that are true to the principles and practices of ethnography became ingrained in Dr. C's consciousness. Through these ongoing interactions, ways of observing, noticing, recording, and then stepping back from the moment and taking reflexive and iterative actions became part of her research repertoire, as documented in her dissertation (Couch, 2012) and subsequent studies and reports (Couch et al., 2018; Couch et al., 2019).

Through the (re)analysis of the records related to this third domain of learning, I have captured processes that Dr. C took up for self as a way of understanding what is happening in daily interactions. The processes, occurring informally, include stepping back, reflecting on and re-examining the emic meanings of words and actions from the perspective of the insider, while avoiding ethnocentrism. The involuntary act of thinking as an ethnographer that I frame constitutes a type of dual processing of lived experiences. Drawing on Berger & Luckmann's (1967) seminal work, *The Social Construction of Reality*, Dr. C's account offers evidence that once an ethnographic lens for reading and analyzing the world has been acquired, the stance shapes the ethnographer's ways of coming to understand differing social contexts and the nature of social reality in perpetuity. This aspect of becoming an ethnographer, skilled in the art of uncovering cultures-in-the-making, was also reflected in Agar's conceptual work on ethnography when he wrote, 'culture changes you into a person who can navigate the modern multicultural world' (Agar, 1996a, p. 21).

The (re)construction of the roots and routes of Dr. C's journey revealed a dual path in which she was developing as an ethnographer while researching and leading the implementation of change initiatives in education as an embedded ethnographer (Couch, 2012). The varied experiences created new ways of thinking, knowing, and being as a researcher, education leader, and in social contexts that are part of her everyday life world. The telling case demonstrates the complementary nature of: 1) developing ethnographic eyes and becoming an ethnographer through formal training in graduate school, 2) work in an occupation or particular job that allows for ethnographic research to be employed as a 'lens' for generating new knowledge to inform practice and change efforts, and 3) ongoing professional collaborations and joint research with other ethnographers.

References

Agar, M. (1996a). *Language Shock: Understanding the Culture of Conversation*. HarperCollins.

Agar, M.H. (1996b). *The professional stranger*. Academic Press.

Agar, M. (2006). An Ethnography by any Other Name… *Forum Qualitative Sozialforschung / Forum: Qualitative Social Research*, 7 (4). http://www.qualitative-research.net/fqs.

Anderson-Levitt, K. (2006). Ethnography. In J. Green, G. Camilli, & P. Elmore (Eds.), *Complementary Methods for Research in Education* (pp. 279–296). American Educational Research Association.

Atkinson, A., Delamont, S., & Housley, W. (2008). *Contours of culture*. AltaMira Press.

Berger, P., & Luckmann, T. (1967). *The Social Construction of Reality*. First Anchor Books.

Birdwhistell, R.L. (1977). Some Discussion of Ethnography, Theory, and Method. In J. Brockman (Ed.), *About Bateson* (pp. 101–141). E.P. Dunon.

Bloome, D., Beauchemin, F., Brady, J., Buescher, E., Kim, M.Y., & Schey, R. (2018). Anthropology of Education, Anthropology in Education, and Anthropology for Education. In H. Callan (Ed.), *The International Encyclopedia of Anthropology* (pp. 1–10). John Wiley & Sons, Ltd.

Castanheira, M., Green, J., & Yeager, B. (2008). Investigating Inclusive Practices: An Interactional Ethnographic Approach. In K. Kumpulainen, C. Hmelo-Silver, & M. Cesar (Eds.), *Investigating Classroom Interaction: Methodologies in Action* (pp. 145–178). Sense Publishers.

Couch, S.R. (2012). An Ethnographic Study of a Developing Virtual Organization in Education. (Doctoral dissertation, University of California, Santa Barbara). Available from ProQuest Dissertations and Theses database. (UMI No. 3507038)

Couch, S., Estabrooks, L.B., & Skukauskaite, A. (2018). Addressing the Gender Gap among Patent Holders through Invention Education Policies. *Technology & Innovation*. 19 (4), 735–749. https://doi.org/10.21300/19.4.2018.735.

Couch, S., Skukauskaite, A., & Estabrooks, L.B. (2019). Invention Education and the Developing Nature of High School Students' Construction of an "Inventor Identity." *Technology & Innovation*, 20 (3), 285–302. https://doi.org/10.21300/20.3.2019.285.

Ellen, R.F. (1984). *Ethnographic Research: A Guide to General Conduct*. Academy Press.

Gee, J., & Green, J. (1998). Discourse Analysis, Literacy and Social Practice. In P.D. Pearson (Ed.), *Review of Research in Education*, 23. (pp. 119–169). American Educational Research Association.

Geertz, C. (1983). *Local Knowledge: Further Essays in Interpretive Anthropology*. Basic Books.

Green, J., & Bloome, D. (1997). Ethnography and Ethnographers of and in Education: A Situated Perspective. In J. Flood, S. B. Heath, & D. Lapp (Eds.), *Handbook of Research on Teaching Literacy through the Communication and Visual Arts* (pp. 181–202). Macmillan.

Green, J.L., & Bridges, S.M. (2018). Interactional Ethnography. In F. Fischer, C.E. Hmelo-Silver, S.R. Goldman, & P. Reimann (Eds), *International Handbook of the Learning Sciences*, (pp. 475–488). Routledge.

Green, J.L., & Chian, M.M. (2018). Triangulation. In B. Frey (Ed), *The SAGE Encyclopedia of Educational Research, Measurement, and Evaluation*. SAGE.

Green, J., Dixon, C.N., & Zaharlick, A. (2003). Ethnography as a Logic of Inquiry. In J. Flood, D. Lapp, N. Squire, & J.M. Jensen (Eds.), *Research in the Teaching of the English Language Arts* (2nd ed., pp. 201–224). Lawrence Erlbaum Associates.

Green, J.L., Skukauskaite, A., & Baker, W.D. (2012). Ethnography as Epistemology: An Introduction to Educational Ethnography. In J. Arthur, M.J. Waring, R. Coe, & L.V. Hedges (Eds.), *Research Methodologies and Methods in Education* (pp. 309–321). SAGE.

28 Stephanie Couch

Hammersley, M. & Atkinson, P. (2007). *Ethnography: Principles in Practice* (3rd ed.). Routledge.

Heap, J. (1985). Discourse in the Production of Classroom Knowledge: Reading Lessons. *Curriculum Inquiry*, 15 (3), 245–279.

Heath, S.B., (1982). Ethnography in Education: Defining the Essentials. In P. Gilmore & A. A. Glatthorn (Eds.), *Children in and out of School: Ethnography and Education* (pp. 33–55). Center for Applied Linguistics.

Heath, S.B., & Street, B.V., with Mills, M. (2008). *On Ethnography: Approaches to Language and Literacy Research*. Teachers College Press.

Hymes, D. (1996). *Ethnography, Linguistics, Narrative Inequality: Toward an Understanding of Voice*. Taylor & Francis.

Kaplan, A. (1964). *The Conduct of Inquiry*. Chandler.

Mitchell, C.J. (1984). Typicality and the Case Study. In R.F. Ellen (Ed.), *Ethnographic Research: A Guide to General Conduct*, (pp. 238–241). Academic Press.

Semetsky, I. (2006). *Deleuze, Education and Becoming*. Sense. https://doi.org/10.1163/9789087900946.

Sheridan, D., Street, B., & Bloome, D. (2000). *Writing Ourselves: Mass-observation and Literacy Practices*. Hampton Press.

Spradley, J.P. (1980). *Participant Observation*. Holt, Rinehart, and Winston.

Street, B.V. (1993). Culture is a Verb: Anthropological Aspects of Language and Cultural Process. In D. Graddol, L. Thompson, and M. Byram (Eds.), *Language and Culture* (pp. 23–43). Multilingual Matters.

Walford, G. (2008). Selecting Sites, and Gaining Ethical and Practical Access. In G. Walford (Ed.), *How to do Educational Ethnography*, (pp. 16–38). Tufnell Press.

Wellin, C., & Fine, G.A. (2001). Ethnography as Work: Career Socialization, Settings and Problems. In P. Atkinson, A. Coffey, S. Delamont, J. Lofland, & L. Lofland (Eds.), *Handbook of ethnography*, (pp. 328–338). SAGE.

Wolcott, H.F. (1967). *A Kwakiutl Village and School*. Holt, Rinehart & Winston.

Wolcott, H.F. (2008). *Ethnography: A Way of Seeing*. AltaMira Press.

3

BECOMING AN EDUCATIONAL ETHNOGRAPHER BY ORGANIZED REPRESENTATIONS OF EDUCATIONAL REALITIES AND 'RESEARCHING THROUGH'

Christoph Maeder

Introduction

To unfold my argument, I am trying first to find answers to the question of why ethnography is important in terms of science before I turn to the realm of the ethnography and organization(s) of education. Education—as opposed to socialization—is undertaken often in institutional contexts like schools, classrooms, in age cohorts of peers and so on. Therefore, a solid concept of the term *organization* is helpful for the ethnographer in order not to get lost. To demonstrate this, I introduce selected *concepts of organization in ethnography*. Finally, I will ask what this means for our work when we are dealing with complex realities and their institutions in education by means of our participant observation. By doing so, I try to develop some substantial dimensions of what 'things' to follow in the fieldwork.

The importance of educational ethnography

As ethnographers we aspire to pin down education as an *organized everyday activity* of people, which is *embedded into a set of institutional 'taken for grantedness assumptions'*, couched by *organizational requirements*, entrenched into *social relations*, surrounded by *material arrangements* and uses, and *guided by shared norms* within the *frameworks of education*. This claim brings me to my first set of questions and theses when it comes to the becoming of educational ethnography. The question I want to raise is: Why does ethnography make sense, even when it is not the only approach or when it comes to volume, even a minor approach to education and its organization? The prominent UK ethnographer Hammersley thought-bogglingly has got us exactly to this point, with such questions in his text as: 'What is ethnography? Can it survive? Should it?' (Hammersley, 2017).

30 Christoph Maeder

Basically, there are three reasons why ethnography is and remains a productive and needed endeavour to describe, analyze and theorize educational processes. *Firstly*, perhaps most of our *knowledge is embodied and kept tacit or implicit in routines of practices* or activities. Such knowledge only becomes accessible for research by direct participant observation when routines linger or fail like the work of Garfinkel (1967) and his incongruity experiments have shown. It cannot be found via interviews and lab-experiments of any kind. It becomes available for research only if an ethnographer turns to these forms of routinized and tacit forms of knowledge, and when she or he tries to describe and analyze this guided by a theory of *interaction, social action* or *social practice*. Silverman has formulated it in a catchy way, saying that as ethnographers we are dealing with 'innumerable inscrutable habits.' And when we look at them, we become aware how 'unremarkably things matter' (Silverman, 2007a, pp. 11–36). A read worthy example of this kind of routinized, embodied and partly tacit knowledge which gives us the competence to act with others can be found in 'Relations in public. Microstudies of the public' (Goffman, 2010, pp. 28–61). There we read a complex analysis of the territorial properties of the interaction order with eight different practical layers analytically coming into play. The actors in their territorial games are under observation by other actors and sometimes act strategically too. Or put simply, sometimes they just lie to outsiders. An example from my own research on so-called 'time-out schools' is the incident where teachers tolerated the deviant behaviour of pupils or even used it knowingly as a power resource in order to keep the class calm: They sent pupils to do errands knowing that the kids would smoke on the way out and back. This made the day easier for all: The teachers got their errands done and the kids got their cigarettes. But it was obviously not something that could be found in an interview.

Related to these arguments of routinized and sometimes hidden aspects of practical realities is my *second argument*. It states that *participant observation* in *real social action* and *situations* is *more meaningful and informative about what is going* on than collecting data in contexts structured by the researcher (see Silverman, 2007b). Despite its known limitations, *participant observation* by an ethnographer is in any case much *less reactive or restrictive* than any form of distant, non-participatory observation, as it is idealized in positivist approaches to social research like interviews, camera perspectives, questionnaires or even experiments. The reason for this is that participant observation does not, of its own accord, prescribe, restrict or exclude any options for social action. But first and foremost, it tries to register and understand them. This is not least because it allows, even forces, the researcher *to learn from the field*. The technical terms here then are the *emic perspective, or the insider's view* and the concept of *serendipity* in ethnographic research. For my own part, I must say that most of my interesting findings in my ethnographic work on prisons, hospitals, welfare offices, unemployment programs, management in a multinational company, schools and a kindergarten and even the uses of animal bells in herding stem from learning to understand what people do, how they do it and how they reflect and talk about this.[1] So, all these fields have become vast learning opportunities for me which finally ignited *serendipity*. This inherent *capacity to find new and unexpected*

Organized representations of educational realities 31

things is a good reason why solid ethnographers want to learn from their fields. They do not categorize fields by reductionist and locally void social science schemes or pedagogical concepts. I think indeed that the possibility of serendipity is one of the key-features of ethnography. It makes it superior to most other forms of social science when it comes to *the production of new knowledge* concerning social groups and their organization.

Thirdly, as a result of the mentioned *socialization* as a kind of *learning of the ethnographers from the people in the field*, data obtained through participant observation can be interpreted and analyzed more substantially along the *relevancies and meanings* of the field. The *phenomenological relevance* and the *adequacy of local structures of meaning* of what is observable enables the understanding of what matters in different social worlds:

> Life-world-analytical ethnography is based on the premise that any world which is not apprehended as a life-world—that is, as the totality of a world that is subjectively experienced—is a fiction. For we do not, in fact, have any knowledge of a world that is not subjectively experienced—of the world per se, as it were.
>
> *(Honer & Hitzler, 2015, p. 1)*

Following these ideas, we will see inevitably the emergence of multiple perspectives in any social setting. *Thick description* (Geertz, 1973) is thus the one suitable technical term here.

The advantages of ethnography can thus be summarized by the terms *implicitness, serendipity* and *contextuality of knowledge*. Together this provides an umbrella argument as to why ethnographies make a lot of sense *in terms of science*. Only by ethnographic means is it possible to register fundamental social processes like education, training and socialization and to understand them and their meaning for the people and for social science. And only ethnography has the capacity to find new and innovative things that are going on in the fields of practice.

What does organization in ethnography mean?

Acknowledging such arguments in favour of ethnography, we still have homework left to do. I must clarify the concept of organization, which I use here when I speak of education as being organized or a being a complex institution: What is meant by the term *organization*, when we say something is organized or has organizational features?

When it comes to *organization*(s), I suggest using interpretive approaches with a tight *affinity to social constructivism*. By this term, I refer to the idea that social reality is inextricably produced in everyday life in its routines of social action as Goffman has put it in his *interaction order* (Goffman, 1983). Organization then becomes *something that is always done locally and emerges out of practical and observable situations* when we see 'people doing things together', according to the dictum by Becker (1970, pp. 3–24). Observing organization this way, we always see something which is accessible for participant observation but at the same time also transcends the situation. It does so when it becomes *hardened* into institutional forms by complex processes of communication and practices of reciprocal typification, joint legitimation, personal and social habitualization and countless repetitions thereof. Finally, something emerges which in everyday life is called routinely and by everyone 'an organization' (see Berger & Luckmann, 1966). All organizations—be it a welfare agency, a school, a university, a hospital, a bank or a police station, etc.—belong to this domain of reified social things we call institutions. They are all made this way, and that is why they all are observable.

Ethnography and the ethnography of education are, as we all know, *no single tales* but rather complex arrays of disciplines, languages, purposes and fields of investigation. Ethnography and the ethnography of education are a blend of traditions along languages, countries, disciplines and uses (Maeder, 2018). So, I only pick one important dimension here, which connects them in a way like that of a thread going through different tissues in a garment. With reference to Morgan (1986), I call it *images of ethnographic organization*.

- The term *social organization* where the organization is treated as a context in order to observe the social production of essential societal aspects of life within a selected type of organization. This concept is usually called 'the social organization of X.' Sudnow's (1967) *Passing On* and *the social organization of dying*, Zerubavel's (1979) *Patterns of Time in Hospital Life* and *the social organization of time*, Gubrium's (1986) *Oldtimers and Alzheimer's* and the descriptive *social organization of senility* are but a few classic examples of this strategy in the realm of medical organizations. These studies—like most others in this tradition—raise and illuminate important issues and their features, which we can almost predictably find embedded in *selected types* of organizations such as *pain* (Heath, 1989) or *shame* (Emerson, 1970) in medical settings, *or boredom in* schools as, for example, Breidenstein (2007) has demonstrated.
- The concept of *organizational culture* is another possibly defining topic for ethnography (Jelinek et al., 1983). This idea seeks to understand organizations through the observation of language use. Linguistic concepts like *metaphors, stories, narratives, gossip* and *other forms of talk* came to be employed by researchers in order to represent and analyze reality construction in organizations. The idea of organizations as *shared meanings* (Smircich, 1983) turned out to be a productive way of doing social research, be it in a bank (Weeks, 2004) or a school (Jeffrey, 2014).
- The *science and laboratory studies* introduced by Latour and Woolgar (1979) which launched what we nowadays call STS-studies (Science, Technology and Society Studies) and the Actor-Network Theory. These ethnographies are concerned with the scrupulous reconstruction of how, under the organizational conditions of a lab, *scientific facts* become made. Taking ethnomethodological concepts like sense-making in interaction, strict sequentiality and organization as a joint production of accomplishments by scientists as a starting

Organized representations of educational realities **33**

point, this approach has led to the more general topic of the *epistemic cultures* and the production of scientific knowledge in general (Knorr-Cetina, 1999).

- The *ethnomethodological workplace studies* (Garfinkel, 1986) conceptualize work and organization as related *accomplishments of actors* interacting in often technologically sophisticated contexts, such as for instance the museum studies by Christian Heath et al. (2002) have shown. There, learning to participate in order to observe the creation of reality is the focus of the ethnographic observation.
- The *grounded theory*, as developed chiefly by Anselm Strauss (1967) and his co-workers, introduces many concepts still used today, such as the ideas of *trajectories* of chains of linked interactions and processes, *going concerns* of the members of an organization or a profession, *awareness contexts* for doing things and others (see Strauss, 1993). Perhaps one of the most influential proposals from this approach with reference to ethnography is the idea of looking at the *negotiating* that goes on nearly permanently in every social setting. While not everything is negotiable in each situation, an astonishing amount of judgement on properties is always at stake. The idea of negotiating as a fundamental property of human communication led to what is known as *the negotiated order approach* (Maines, 1985; Strauss, 1978).
- *Overarching critical schemes and discourse theories*—here we can take in the work of Beach (2018) as an example. He researched the impact of a reorganization of the education system in Sweden by the introduction of markets as a means of coordination, using ethnographic case studies. In his work he carefully looked at the impact of an ideology on local practices contained in and delivered by organizations. A similar analysis of the connection between educational policies and the effects on school organizations, classrooms, etc. is provided by Troman et al. (2006) in the UK line of educational ethnography.

These six different *concepts of organization* have all been used successfully in ethnographic research. They are not exhaustive, but they catch a range of contemporary ethnographic theories with reference to the 'organization-thread' (see Eberle & Maeder, 2016). Furthermore, they illustrate how ethnographic research can be done *with theoretical guidance* in combination with the characteristics mentioned before (*implicitness, serendipity* and *contextuality*).

This way it also becomes clear why *ethnographic research* inevitably *distances the researcher and the researched*, as Fine (2003) has prominently remarked. The way of thinking and reporting of ethnographers about a practice, an organization or a field should not be just a descriptive doubling of the reality. The ethnographer can also perform analysis and contribute to social theory. I think this is an important statement in the context of educational ethnography, which is constantly in *danger to accept normative assumptions of the field* as guiding metaphors. Pedagogical and educational fields arrange themselves steadily along the distinctions of something being correct/incorrect, integrated/excluded, better/worse, fair/unjust, and so on. The neglect of such hard-wired cultural codes of the intervening professions in what

34 Christoph Maeder

van Maanen called 'people processing organizations' (van Maanen, 1978, pp. 19–36) is sociologically naïve. With a theoretical stance as researchers, we better insist on our own agenda of the social in the field of education and better not burden our own tasks with the questions of pedagogy, educational policy, educational administration or other *moral agencies of society*. To strengthen this argument, I reference two famous questions in this regard. One stems from Becker (1967) who asked, 'whose side are we on?', and the other comes from Hammersley (2004) when he inquired, 'should ethnographers be against inequality?'.

The idea of 'researching through'

Given three arguments for ethnography (Atkinson, 2014) and six ways of looking at the organization of the social in educational fields, I finally address how educational ethnographers can create nontrivial insights and understandings linked to theoretical underpinnings. By doing so, they can create new perspectives or in-depth understandings of the organized features of places, spaces, senses, artifacts and practices and their—sometimes even new and hitherto unknown—contributions to the social world of education. My attempt at using the metaphor of on the shoulders of giants by Merton (1965) culminates in the *design of a virtual open space of possibilities* for ethnography. I will call a walk into this idealized space for doing ethnography *'researching through'*. With this rather unwieldly but fitting term, I am borrowing an idea from Sue Wright. She coined the term 'studying through' (Wright & Reinhold, 2011) when doing research on complex institutional orders.

As a *starting point*, I take a challenge which is recurrent and intense in any attempt to teach educational ethnography. As we all know, it is not an easy task to explain to students how ethnographic research is done in the field. We do have some metaphors to describe the task of 'go to where the action is' as Goffman (1967, pp. 149–270) has put it. We are doing *dirty fieldwork* (van Maanen, 1988) and *doing social life* (Lofland, 1976), or we become *professional strangers* following Agar (1996) when we are *fighting familiarity* together with Delamont and Atkinson (1995). But when all the difficult practical questions of field access, permission to record electronic data, lurking around while others work and more have been solved, the big and challenging practical question comes up: What should we look at in the field? There is no simple answer to these topics. But when we do have an idea of what it means to conduct a 'researching through', we might find some handles on which to operate in our complex, organized institutional settings of education.[2]

What to follow in ethnographic research on education?

For the consolidation of the idea of *researching through*, I use a recommendation out of the debate on *multi-sited ethnography* (Falzon, 2009; Marcus, 1995). There the final concept to solve the problem of the distributed and moving features of the social in ethnographic fields was to *follow the actors*. The idea of *researching through*

Organized representations of educational realities   35

then becomes the quest to look for more recommendations of what to follow in the ethnographic literature. Finding the right combination of things puts the theoretical knowledge, the craftsmanship and the literary skills of the ethnographer to the test because *researching through* requires finding the useful combination of *things* to follow for any particular field. And, of course, my compilation here is incomplete: I suggest a principle, not a final lexicon. Every ethnographer is invited to add things to this list too, as long as these things refer to a social scientific theory and are observable by fieldwork.

In the tradition of the *Chicago-School-styled ethnography*, we first *follow the places*. 'Slim's Table' and the learning on race, respectability and masculinity by Duneier (1992) or the ethnography of Fine (1996) on 'Kitchens and the Culture of Restaurant Work', where he describes in great detail how he was trained as a kitchen-hand in four different professional kitchens, are but two placeholders for this approach. And when our interest shifts away from people and their places and we become interested in what is put together and on what levels, we can take Ogbu's (1981) ecological idea as written in 'School ethnography: A multilevel approach' as a model. The motto here is *follow the levels of organization (and outcomes)* and we will realize that on every level we encounter constituent practices. And these situated permutations of routinized social actions as practices, which make education an accomplishment, impose the quest *follow the practices and their events*. This approach has identified the *IRE sequence as a constitutive element for the definition of the pedagogical situation* as Mehan (1974) has shown us. Furthermore, 'Understanding understanding as an instructional matter' became a prominent issue in this perspective as Macbeth (2008) has demonstrated. And a corresponding concept is the idea of Knoblauch's (2005) ways of observation as a 'Focused ethnography.' Here, fingertips, facial gestures, bodily positioning and so on play a pivotal role. This has been translated into educational research as the summary of Trowler (2014) proves when he writes on 'Practice focused ethnographies of higher education: methodological corollaries of a special practice perspective.'

Mobile ethnography, as exemplified by the work of Forsey (2018), has put emphasis on following things like wealth and choice in relation to situated educational institutions – or labour in relation to holydays – like Adler & Adler (2004) did in their book on 'Paradise laborers. Hotel work in the global economy.' Here we learn how one man's paradise becomes another man's work. And last but not least, this kind of look at a local-global dichotomy can be researched by the use of actor-network theory, as Blok (2010) suggested. Taken together, we can deduct the instruction of *follow the phenomenon!* And having spoken of kitchens already, we cannot but ask for following the senses systematically too: Smells, touch, noise, sounds and other senses come into play here and challenge traditional ethnographic approaches, as Pink (2009) suggests. We as ethnographers are like other scientific approaches part of the communities who believe in visual evidence. But there is an alternative perspective on practice as, for example, Vannini et al. (2010) have argued with their idea of sound acts and the bodily performance of sonic alignment. Here the invitation is *follow the senses!* Additionally, we can reach out for the

36 Christoph Maeder

structures and have a look at the Swedish school system by the recent research of Beach (2018). He focuses power and structural injustices in academic selections and educational inequalities from a neo-Marxist class perspective: *Follow the power relations* are the invitations to the educational ethnographer then.

Up to now, I have not mentioned any *artifacts*, although we know from the STS-studies and the corresponding actor-network theory that artifacts matter. They probably even perform some agency of their own depending on the theory of action or theory of social practice that we use. *Follow the artifact* is surely a productive idea for many ethnographic endeavours then. Not only labs are made by artifacts but also classrooms can represent a geography of connections, as Hillman (2012), in his work on networks of humans and materials in classrooms by using handheld technology, has illustrated. Furthermore, in a bureaucratic world like ours, every organization is full of documents, which are an elucidating trace if we follow their uses in everyday life. The concept of *institutional ethnography*, as suggested by Smith (2006), has proven to be of great value if we want to understand what she has called 'text mediated institutional technologies and ruling relations.' *Follow the documents* and their uses is the idea here.

The *ethnography of communication* (Keating 2001) has contributed impressively to our knowledge on education by following speech as discourse. Linguistic anthropology, as exemplified by Alessandro Duranti's work (1997) and that of John Gumperz and Hymes (1972), can teach us how contexts of practices are constructed through speech communication. This research was the root of ethnographies on bilingualism, bidialectism and language in schools (Gumperz & Hernandez-Chavez, 1972): *Follow the language* is the suggestion with reference to Courtney Cazden's (2001) idea about classroom discourse and the language of teaching and learning. And although we cannot reconstruct experience directly because this is an individualistic process, we can do research on what matters in life-worlds. Here the *phenomenological approaches* have to offer a lot, as Honer and Hitzler (2015) argue. The corresponding procedure then is *follow the experience(s)* as you make them or the other tells you! And finally, something like *(N)ethnography*, that is approaches to the internet and computer-mediated communication, must be on our list too. Here the recommendation is to *follow the screens* but also their *users in vivo*, as Garcia et al. (2009) have argued convincingly when it comes to IT-focused ethnography.

Final remark

I stop enumerating important ethnographic ideas and concepts here and I invite the reader to expand the list: be it in what makes ethnography unique, or in terms of organization or things to follow. The remarkable range and possibilities of ethnographic contributions to our scientific knowledge about the societies we live in need such additions and extensions with respect to the people in the fields we observe and as well with regard to the diligent labour of our hard-working colleagues.

Notes

1 Since this is a text in English, I do not quote my ethnographic work here which is written in German.
2 What cannot be elaborated here are the many implications for the data used in ethnography (see: Hernandez-Hernández & Sancho-Gil, 2018).

References

Adler, P.A., & Adler, P. (2004). *Paradise Laborers: Hotel Work in the Global Economy*. ILR Press.

Agar, M.H. (1996). *The Professional Stranger. An Informal Introduction to Ethnography*. Academic Press.

Atkinson, P. (2014). *For Ethnography*. SAGE Publications.

Beach, D. (2018). *Structural Injustices in Swedish Education. Academic Selection and Educational Inequalities*. Cham: Palgrave Macmillan.

Becker, H.S. (1967). Whose side are we on? *Social Problems*, 14 (3), 239–247.

Becker, H. (1970). On Methodology. In H. Becker (Ed.), *Sociological Work. Method and Substance* (pp. 3–24). Aldine Publishing Company.

Berger, P.L., & Luckmann, T. (1966). *The Social Construction of Reality. A Treatise in the Sociology of Knowledge*. Penguin Books.

Blok, A. (2010). Mapping the Super-whale: Towards a Mobile Ethnography of Situated Globalities. *Mobilities*, 5 (4), 507–528.

Breidenstein, G. (2007). The Meaning of Boredom in School Lessons. Participant Observation in the Seventh and Eighth Form. *Ethnography and Education*, 2 (1), 93–108.

Cazden, C.B. (2001). *Classroom Discourse. The Language of Teaching and Learning*. Heinemann.

Delamont, S., & Atkinson, P. (1995). *Fighting Familiarity. Essays on Education and Ethnography*. Hampton Press.

Duneier, M. (1992). *Slim's Table. Race, Respectability, and Masculinity*. University of Chicago Press.

Duranti, A. (1997). *Linguistic Anthropology*. Cambridge University Press.

Eberle, T.S., & Maeder, C. (2016). Organizational Ethnography. In D. Silverman (Ed.), *Qualitative Research. Theory, Method and Practice* (4th and Revised Edition) (pp. 121–136). Sage Publications.

Emerson, J.P. (1970). Behavior in Private Places: Sustaining Definitions of Reality in Gynecological Examinations. *Recent Sociology*, 2, 74–97.

Falzon, M.A. (Ed.). (2009). *Multi-sited Ethnography: Theory, Praxis and Locality in Contemporary Social Research*. Ashgate Publishing.

Fine, G.A. (1996). *Kitchens. The Culture of Restaurant Work*. University of California Press.

Fine, G.A. (2003). Towards a Peopled Ethnography. Developing Theory from Group Life. *Ethnography*, 4 (1), 41–60.

Forsey, M. (2018). Educational Ethnography in and for a Mobile Modernity. In D. Beach, C. Bagley, & S. Marques da Silva (Eds.), *The Wiley Handbook of Ethnography of Education* (pp. 443–454). Wiley Handbooks in Education.

Garcia, A.C., Standlee, A.I., Bechkoff, J., & Cui, Y. (2009). Ethnographic Approaches to the Internet and Computer-mediated Communication. *Journal of Contemporary Ethnography*, 38 (1), 52–84.

Garfinkel, H. (1967). *Studies in Ethnomethodology*. Prentice-Hall.

Garfinkel, H. (Ed.). (1986). *Ethnomethodological Studies of Work*. Routledge & Kegan Paul.

Geertz, C. (1973). Thick Description: Toward an Interpretive Theory of Culture. In *The Interpretation of cultures* (pp. 3–30). Basic Books.

Glaser, B.G., & Strauss, A.L. (1967). *The Discovery of Grounded Theory: Strategies for Qualitative Research*. Aldine Publishing Company.

Goffman, E. (1967). *Interaction Ritual. Essays on the Face-to-Face Behavior*. Pantheon.

Goffman, E. (1983). The Interaction Order. *American Sociological Review*, 48, 1–17.

Goffman, E. (2010). The Territories of the Self. In *Relations in Public. Microstudies of the Public Order* (pp. 28–61). Transaction Publishers.

Gubrium, J.F. (1986). *Oldtimers and Alzheimer's: The Descriptive Organization of Senility*. JAI Press.

Gumperz, J.J., & Hernandez-Chavez, E. (1972). Bilingualism, Bidialectalism, and the Classroom Interaction. In C.B. Cazden, V.P. John, & D. Hymes (Eds.), *Functions of Language in the Classroom* (pp. 84–108). Teachers College Press.

Gumperz, J.J., & Hymes, D.H. (Eds.). (1972). *Directions in Sociolinguistics: The Ethnography of Communication*. Prentice Hall.

Hammersley, M. (2004). Should Ethnographers be against Inequality? On Becker, Value Neutrality and Researcher Partisanship. In B. Jeffrey & G. Walford (Eds.), *Ethnographies of Educational and Cultural Conflicts: Strategies and Resolutions* (pp. 25–43). Elsevier/JAI.

Hammersley, M. (2017). What is ethnography? Can it survive? Should it? *Ethnography and Education*, 1–17.

Heath, C. (1989). Pain Talk: The Expression of Suffering in the Medical Consultation. *Social-Psychology-Quarterly*, 52, 113–125.

Heath, C., Luff, P., vom Lehm, D., Hindmarsh, J., & Cleverly, J. (2002). Crafting Participation: Designing Ecologies, Configuring Experience. *Visual Communication*, 1 (1), 9–33.

Hernandez-Hernandez, F., & Sancho-Gil, J.M. (2018). Writing and Managing Multimodal Field Notes. *Oxford Research Encyclopedia of Education*, 21 (online). https://doi.org/10.1093/acrefore/9780190264093.013.319.

Hillman, T. (2012). A Geography of Connections: Networks of Humans and Materials in Mathematics Classrooms using Handheld Technology. *Forum Qualitative Research*, 13 (1), 50 paragraphs.

Honer, A., & Hitzler, R. (2015). Life-world-analytical Ethnography: A Phenomenology-based Research Approach. *Journal of Contemporary Ethnography, Special Issue Article*, 1–19.

Jeffrey, B. (2014). *The Primary School in Testing Times: A Classic Ethnography of a Creative, Community Engaged, Entrepreneurial and Performative School*. E&E Publishing.

Jelinek, M., Smircich, L., & Hirsch, P. (1983). Introduction: A Code of many Colors. *Administrative Science Quarterly*, 28 (3), 331–338.

Keating, E. (2001). The Ethnography of Communication. In P. Atkinson, A. Coffey, S. Delamont, J. Lofland, et al. (Eds.), *Handbook of Ethnography* (pp. 285–301). SAGE Publications.

Knoblauch, H. (2005). Focused Ethnography. *Forum Qualitative Research*, 6 (3), Art. 44.

Knorr-Cetina, K. (1999). *Epistemic Cultures. How the Sciences make Knowledge*. Harvard University Press.

Latour, B., & Woolgar, S. (1979). *Laboratory Life. The Social Construction of Scientific Facts*. SAGE Publications.

Lofland, J. (1976). *Doing Social Life*. Wiley.

Macbeth, D. (2008). Understanding Understanding as an Instructional Matter. *Journal of Pragmatics*, 43, 438–451.

Maeder, C. (2018). What can be Learnt?: Educational Ethnography, the Sociology of Knowledge, and Ethnomethodology. In D. Beach, C. Bagley, & S. Marques da Silva (Eds.), *The Wiley Handbook of Ethnography of Education* (pp. 135–151). Wiley-Blackwell.

Maines, D.R., & Charlton, J.C. (1985). The Negotiated Order Approach to the Analysis of Social Organization. In A. Faberman & R.S. Perinbanayagam (Eds.), *Foundations of interpretative Sociology: Original Essays in Symbolic Interaction* (pp. 271–308). JAI.

Marcus, G.E. (1995). Ethnography in/of the World System: The Emergence of Multi-sited Ethnography. *Annual Review of Anthropology*, 24, 95–117.

Mehan, H. (1974). Accomplishing Classroom Lessons. In A.V. Cicourel, K.H. Jennings, S. H.M. Jennings, K.C.W. Leiter, R. MacKay, H. Mehan et al. (Eds.), *Language Use and School Performance* (pp. 76–142). Academic Press.

Merton, R.K. (1965). *On the Shoulders of Giants*. The Free Press.

Morgan, G. (1986). *Images of Organization*. SAGE Publications.

Ogbu, J.U. (1981). School Ethnography: A Multilevel Approach. *Anthropology and Education Quarterly*, 14, 3–29.

Pink, S. (2009). *Doing Sensory Ethnography*. SAGE Publications.

Silverman, D. (2007a). Innumerable Inscrutable Habits: Why Unremarkable Things Matter. In *A Very Short, Fairly Interesting and Reasonably Cheap Book about Qualitative Research* (pp. 11–36). SAGE Publications.

Silverman, D. (2007b). On Finding and Manufacturing Qualitative Data. In *A Very Short, Fairly Interesting and Reasonably Cheap Book about Qualitative Research* (pp. 37–60). SAGE Publications.

Smircich, L. (1983). Organizations as Shared Meanings. In L.R. Pondy, P.J. Frost, G. Morgan, & T.C. Dandridge (Eds.), *Organizational Symbolism* (pp. 55–65). JAI Press.

Smith, D.E. (2006). Incorporating Texts into Ethnographic Practice. In D.E. Smith (Ed.), *Institutional Ethnography as Practice* (pp. 65–88). Rowman & Littlefield Publishers.

Strauss, A.L. (1978). *Negotiations. Varieties, Contexts, Processes, and Social Order*. Jossey-Bass.

Strauss, A.L. (1993). *Continual Permutations of Action*. Aldine de Gruyter.

Sudnow, D. (1967). *Passing on: The Social Organisation of Dying*. Prentice Hall.

Troman, G., Jeffrey, B., & Beach, D. (2006). *Researching Education Policy: Ethnographic Experiences*. Tufnell Press.

Trowler, P.R. (2014). Practice Focussed Ethnographies of Higher Education: Methodological Corollaries of a Special Practice Perspective. *European Journal of Higher Education*, 4 (1), 18–29.

van Maanen, J. (1978). People Processing: Strategies of Organizational Socialization. *Organizational Dynamics*, 7 (1), 19–36.

van Maanen, J. (1988). *Tales of the Field. On Writing Ethnography*. University of Chicago Press.

Vannini, P., Waskul, D., Gotschalk, S., & Rambo, C. (2010). Sound Acts: Elocution, Somatic Work, and the Performance of the Sonic Alignment. *Journal of Contemporary Ethnography*, 39 (3), 328–353.

Weeks, J. (2004). *Unpopular Culture. The Ritual of Complaint in a British Bank*. University of Chicago Press.

Wright, S., & Reinhold, S. (2011). "Studying Through": A Strategy for Studying Transformation. or Sex, Lies and British Policy. In C. Shore, S. Wright, & D. Pero (Eds.), *Policy Worlds: Anthropology and the Analysis of Contemporary Power* (pp. 86–104). Bergen Books.

Zerubavel, E. (1979). *Patterns of Time in Hospital Life. A Sociological Perspective*. University of Chicago Press.

4

BECOMING EDUCATIONAL ETHNOGRAPHER THROUGH TIME AND ONTOLOGICAL DISPLACEMENTS

Juana M. Sancho-Gil

Introduction

This chapter relates a long and unfinished journey, a nomadic wandering, which began fifty years ago, when as a young schoolteacher I was sent to a classroom of four- and five-year-olds in a rural town of Spain. This journey is still ongoing. It is a becoming process full of displacements, uncertainties, wonders, dislocations, doubts and discoveries. A nomadic journey that allows me to leave from where I am, to travel to places already known or new and to return to reflect on how the new route has transformed me and my gaze. To reconstruct and share this long and unfinished process of becoming a researcher with an ethnographic outlook, I adopt an auto-ethnographic perspective understood as 'research, writing, story, and method that connect the autobiographical and personal to the cultural, social, and political' (Ellis, 2004, p. xix). In this case, my approach is focused on my experiences situated in the cultural, political, academic and technological contexts in which they have taken and are taking place.

In our research projects[1], we often use auto-ethnographic methods, not only as 'a form or method of research that involves self-observation and reflexive investigation in the context of ethnographic fieldwork and writing' (Maréchal, 2010, p. 43) but because, as educational scholars (as has been recognised by authors such as Kunda (2013) practically all studied phenomena affect us and are part of us (Creus et. al, 2011). Besides, culture, ecology, politics and economics are all embedded. However, the purpose of this chapter is a bit more ambitious, since I am not only referring to a specific problem addressed in a research project, but to an entire career as a teacher and researcher.

Ignorance and grey times as a catapult

> Being is the effect of becoming! (Faber, 2011, p. 4)

In my three years at the Teacher Training College which did not belong to the university[2], they never talked to me about research. There, questions were not welcome. All they had were answers, recipes, and 'must be dones'. But I always had lots of questions, lots of concerns. I was invariably more interested in 'why' than in 'what'. This was a positioning not very convenient or welcome when you live under a dictatorship, and I did so for more than twenty years—many Spaniards did so for many more[3]. But for me, it was highly essential to boost my learning desire.

Since lessons were quite boring—practically everything they explained was in the not very interesting textbooks—I took books, essays[4] and novels to read in the classroom (I was lucky enough to have books at home). And this fostered my passion for reading and learning. At the Teacher Training College, I could learn very little (or nothing) about who the children I was supposed to teach were, what their needs were, and how to teach them something worth coming to school for. The knowledge provided by my own experience as an infant, primary and secondary school pupil and as a student-teacher, the behaviour of my classmates and teachers and their way of teaching, the rules of the school and a short internship gave me a glimpse of the complexity of educational institutions. It also helped my experience as a children's camp monitor. There I could see how different children are and the importance of people's cultural and socio-economic backgrounds. This is something that seems quite common in this profession (Huberman et al., 1993; Sancho & Hernández, 2014).

Entering the (professional) field

I was already aware of my ignorance, so, after passing the national exam to become a public-school teacher, I enrolled at University to study Psychology. Franco's dictatorship was still there. I was lucky that the University had just started evening courses and I was able to combine (with great effort) my work as a teacher from 10 to 5, with three hours of rest at midday, and the University from 7 to 10 at night. This year I was assigned to my first school as a full-time teacher in a village not far away from my city, so that I could travel every day. Although I had never heard of ethnography (a little bit about anthropology, but for me, these were 'exotic' and 'remote' groups), my ethnographic outlook began to grow the first day I arrived at this village.

When I met my twenty-five or so students, aged between four and five, I realised my enormous responsibility. I looked at them and thought that I should look them in the eye, understand their needs, make possible for them what their local environment could not. But I also felt limited. I also realised how different my view of education was from that of the local and national cultures. At a time governed by political and religious control with sanctions and physical and psychological punishment, the old patriarchal-matriarchal motto 'spare the rod and spoil the child' was widely shared. But I did not share it. So, apart from reading anything I could—which was not so much at that time in Spain—I tried to understand people's points of view and discuss with respect my vision about

42 Juana M. Sancho-Gil

education. To my surprise, I found among families and community members much more understanding and acceptance than I expected. They even told me how important it was for them that the teacher showed them things that their context could not offer.

My interest in people's ways of living, and the permanent question that I later posed to university students, especially in research courses: 'Why do you think you think the way you think', began to germinate here. And it was paved along the way with books like *Knowledge and Control*, edited by Michael Young (1971) (especially Nell Keddie's chapter), which I read years later during my master's studies at the London Institute of Education.

A University in grayscale

At the University, under Franco's regime until my last year, I found, again, more questions than answers. I was looking for complexity, for challenges, for studying 'real' people, in 'real' social, cultural, and economic contexts and I found 'objects of study' removed from 'real' life. 'Objects' converted into numbers, classified, standardised, ruled by averages, medians, Ji-squares, Gauss bells, ANOVAs... And professors who presumed to be 'objective' and 'scientific' because they turned their 'object' of study into a number, a mathematical formula. They were convinced that they could 'measure' and 'predict' behaviour. But everything around me (I have always liked to observe social life) was against this discourse, giving me constant evidence that something was not working. And in my Psychology degree, I could not find explanations, in-depth explorations of the complex worlds in which my students and I found ourselves. We were human beings, with bodies, families, communities, countries. How could all this be reduced to a number?

Some subjects briefly contemplated anthropological studies, such as *Coming of Age in Samoa* (Mead, 1973). I found it particularly inspiring but quite far away and 'different' as if our society was 'normal' and 'developed' and theirs 'local, alien, underdeveloped'. Years later, just as I was starting to do ethnographic research, a contra-culture book called *Los papalagi* (Scheurmann, 1977), considered one of the first allegations against globalization and the colonization of others, reinforced in me the importance of the gaze and where we place others and ourselves.

Towards the end of my Psychology degree and going back to school as a full-time teacher (the previous three years I managed to work part-time), I came across another essential hint, from the hand of Roger Barker and the ecological Psychology. We found several of his studies (Barker, 1968; Barker & Gump, 1963; Barker & Wright, 1966) and for us (for me and for Fernando Hernández, with whom we had just started our first research project—Sancho & Hernández, 1981) this was like a revelation, like a 'prize'. So, you could study people in their everyday environments! He did his Ph.D on this topic (Hernández, 1985). My path to ethnography was opening, and my work as a teacher—and, later, my master's studies in England—allowed me to glimpse new horizons.

A school without context

I wanted to work as an educational psychologist, but nothing as such existed at that moment in Spain, so I went back to the public school as a full-time teacher. I was sent to a working-class city near Barcelona, where more than 70% of the inhabitants came from other parts of Spain. As I had a degree in Psychology, I was assigned to a class with almost forty students aged between thirteen and fourteen, who were repeating the course. So, if they wanted the compulsory education diploma, they had to continue in school the following year. In this school and class, I experienced a cultural clash and an enormous push in my becoming a teacher and researcher. And I learnt in the most unusual ways and circumstances.

It was a big school (around one thousand pupils), and the headteacher at this time had still been selected by 'the regime'; Franco died at the beginning of this scholastic year (November 20th). At that time, headteachers were not appointed because of their pedagogical knowledge, but rather for their political loyalty. Until then, I had been working in a rural school where I was the only teacher, and in two small private ones (as a part-timer). So, I had not experienced yet the importance (the weight) of the school culture in the dominant school *dispositif* (as I was later able to name it by reading Foucault, 1980). I could not understand the behaviour of many teachers (especially the principal), nor of some students who seemed uninterested in learning and who often behaved disruptively. I was always trying to get close to them and recognise them, as I was very interested in education. I was surprised at the lack of understanding among the staff—if the school had a science lab and a library, why were the lab supplies and books packaged? Why were they not used? Why did the headteacher not allow me to use all that? And they did not understand me. Most teachers did not understand why I wanted to use this equipment with *repeaters* if *they were already lost*? They did not even think the school had a big deal of responsibility in this situation.

At the beginning, I was no luckier with students. They did not seem to appreciate, as I did, the importance of school learning. The importance of culture, books, access to existing knowledge. I had the impression the school and I came from two different cultures and spoke different languages. At this point, somehow, I began to look at my surroundings as an *exotic culture*. And this made a difference. I told myself it was my responsibility to understand their way of thinking and behaving and the meaning they gave to words. I realised, as later I read in Phillips (2014, p. 10), that 'learning is a phenomenon that involves real people who live in real, complex social contexts from which they cannot be abstracted in any meaningful way'. As an educational ethnographer, without knowing what an ethnographer was, I started to observe my students, to listen and speak to them beyond the class and to explore their cultural environment and values.

This ethnographic look (still unknown to me), allowed me to establish connections that improved my understanding of my students' position and therefore, better communication with them. To finish this section, I will refer to a singular event. I was spending a weekend with friends in a beautiful rural village and went

44 Juana M. Sancho-Gil

to the cinema. They were showing a Bruce Lee film; I do not remember which one. I do not enjoy *fighting* movies so, in Barcelona, I would have never gone to see it. But there was not much to do there, and most of my friends wanted to view it. Throughout the film I was stunned. I was watching my pupils, the boys, who were the most difficult for me! Until then, I had never seen them in the Psychology, Sociology and Pedagogy books I read, and I thought we, teachers, and educational researchers, should know much more about pupils and schools' cultures. Little by little I connected more and more with the students (and many of the teachers) and for my satisfaction, all my class students, despite having reached compulsory school age, remained in school to obtain the certificate. At the end of this school year, I was obligatorily sent to a rural school near the Pyrenees, where I worked for two years and, back in Barcelona, I worked for another year in another working-class school. I underwent three more years full of knowledge and experiences from different students and cultures. Without realising it, I was learning by doing so how to become an educational ethnographer and a better teacher. You do not need to travel far to discover different cultures and values.

The light starts/New horizons

At the end of the 70s, we were in the transition period to democracy, the situation was changing in Spain and a new air was starting to blow, but I needed more. I needed to learn more. So, I decided to apply to become a Spanish assistant teacher in a secondary school in London. My aim: Improving my English, discovering different people, and being able to find more books in bookshops and libraries. And again, this made the difference.

There, I had a very different experience of the school, was able to attend various courses (none of them in ethnography!) and started undertaking research on the school as a social organisation. About people not as 'objects of research', numbers or cognitive entities floating in space, but as social and cultural beings contextualised in families, neighbourhoods and educational institutions. Finally, I began to recognise my students, myself, and the schools I had been working in.

Several seminal works paved this section of the road. In Stephen Ball (1980), *Beachside Comprehensive: A Case study of Secondary Schooling*, I found a great picture of school life, with living people, real school practices, interactions, encounters and misunderstandings, problems, tensions and possibilities. I knew, and know, the map is not the territory, and the deeper I go into ethnography, the more limitations I find, but also the more possibilities (see chapter 3). Balls' book was the inspiration for my first ethnographic research (Sancho, 1987).

Paul Willis (1977)'s book *Learning to Labour: How Working Class Kids get Working Class Jobs*, brought me back to my students of the first working-class school I worked at (see earlier). Willis tried to explain the role of youth culture and socialisation as a means by which schools led working-class students to working-class jobs. My students were there! Many of the conversations I had with the students and teachers at the school I referred to earlier came to mind. I thought that the

Through time and ontological displacements **45**

situations of the social classes were similar regardless of the country, language and national culture. Hence the importance of studying them in detail.

The Man in the Principal's Office: An Ethnography, by Harry Wolcott (1973), was for me another great event. Wolcott spent time as the shadow of an elementary school principal. He revealed that most of his time was spent interacting with teachers, families and students and making decisions as needed and not in his office, carefully deliberating the decisions to be made. How little policymakers and people, in general, knew about the 'real role', in this case of principals. The book also made clear that there was a large discrepancy between principals' professional development and their work practice, something that can also be said of teachers.

My window to educational ethnography had opened a vast and unknown, but somehow sensed, landscape stretched around me.

My enrolment in a master program about *Urban Education: A Comparative Perspective* at the London Institute of Education of London University allowed me to access a new world of possibilities. I 'knew', I felt, education was fundamental, highly complex and full of options—but until I enrolled in this master, I had not been able to explore many of the questions I had been asking myself. Here the cluster grew, but I began to see that they could be studied in multiple ways that did not make them lose their context and complexity. I did not take any specific course on qualitative methodology or ethnography. However, culture, languages, economy, policy, issues were approached from different perspectives. Education was not understood as a prescriptive endeavour, but as a constant field of study in which views, interests, beliefs and scientific paradigms were permanently confronted.

The London Institute of Education was an intellectual festival. Apart from attending classes and seminars in my master's program, whenever time allowed—-I had to keep working—I could attend most of the lectures given at the institution. It is impossible to name all the significant figures I had the opportunity to hear. If I had to select one, I would choose Basil Bernstein. His lectures and the reading of his seminal books, *Class, codes, and control* (Bernstein, 1971, four volumes), allowed me to name and think about many aspects of education I felt were there but did not know how to approach them. The access to the London University libraries and the extended reading list recommended by professors were other fundamental dimensions of this opening horizon.

I spent hours in the library, deepening the ecological perspectives of education (Eggleston, 1977); realising the importance and the complexity of social systems (Hummel & Nagle, 1973); reaffirming the significance of school and class cultures (Galton et al., 1980; Rutter, 1979); reflecting about the fundamental role of teachers (Rosenthal & Jacobson, 1968); beginning to glimpse other ways of doing research (Ball, 1980; Cohen & Manion, 1980; Willis, 1977; Wolcott, 1973), and the enormous responsibility of educational researchers (Bowles & Gintis, 1976; Hamilton & Delamont, 1974). Thirty-eight years after finishing the master's degree, I keep in an archive many of the records I made of each of the works I read. Since the mid-80s, everything is digital!

46 Juana M. Sancho-Gil

Looking back, I see these three years spent in London as a Spanish teacher and master student as a symphony, that still evolves, made of an entanglement of intra-actions (Barad, 2007)[5] between people, devices, symbols, affects, voices, questions, encounters, discoveries. The orchestra did not have and still not have, a conductor. It continues to be driven by curiosity, social commitment, and the desire to learn. Years later, I discovered that I was placing myself in the twists and turns of new materialism and empiricism (St. Pierre et al., 2016) in a new ontology.

(Almost) educational ethnographer

New challenges and opportunities were lying in front of me. As I said, my wish was to work as an educational psychologist and become a researcher, and coming back from England, the opportunity arose. The management team of a newly opened (twelve years) upper secondary school of a working-class city near Barcelona was struggling to secure the services of a psychologist. They did not want a clinical approach, but an educational perspective that offered students professional guidance. For the school staff, this was of high importance as practically all students were the first ones of their family to access secondary education and certainly university. Teachers thought students had problems responding to the academic demands of this educational level and had no experience or information about university or higher vocational training. In this, they agreed with the families. However, at that time, the Catalan Department of Education did not provide schools with this kind of services.

The Parents Association, in agreement with the school management, agreed to hire this service and to take care of the expenses. The Department of Education also accepted the proposal. They contacted me to offer me a ten hours per week job. We negotiated the working terms and decided I would mainly work with students and, to the extent I could, collaborate with teachers and parents. We also agreed I could apply for a small grant to the Institute of Educational Sciences of the University of Barcelona, to carry out a study on *Psycho-pedagogical intervention in the framework of a high school from an ecological perspective*. The main idea was to gather empirical evidence of the need for an educational-psychological guidance service, which would consider the institutional and contextual dimensions of learning and not only 'the problems of the individual student'. Even if as said, I was inspired by Stephen Ball (1980), I founded the proposal as a 'case study', since, at that time in Spain, there seemed to be almost nothing beyond statistical studies (Sancho & Hernández, 2010). The third side of the quadrangle was made up by the part-time job I was offered at the university and the fourth by my enrolment in a Ph.D program on Educational Psychology.

My three years' work as an educational psychologist was challenging and thrilling. However, for the aim of this chapter, I will focus on the 'case study' with an ethnographic gaze I carried out during this time (Ball, 1980 Willis, 1977; Woods, 2005, Wolcott, 1973). Having negotiated at the outset the realisation of the study with the parties involved (at the time I informed the students), I found myself in a privileged and, at the same time, frontier situation. I had both an emic position, as I was looking at the fundamental cultural distinctions that were meaningful for the members of the institution and I was one of them ('insider'), and an etic position, as an 'outsider' looking in (Harris, 1976). Building on my previous background and my continued reading, the data collecting methods were observations, conversations, written accounts, document analyses and above all field notes. I considered them an exceptional approach to account for the complexity of educational phenomena.

All this ethnographic experience provided me with vibrant pictures of the institution life, which served to improve my job with students (also with those of the university), teachers and families and to write the research report. Besides, my role in the school confronted me with an unexpected and enriching circumstance. Teachers were more than convinced that students did not do homework and were not interested in academic knowledge, and insisted on giving them a survey. I argued that in a questionnaire, we only ask what we already know and expect others to agree with us or not. But they insisted and insisted, and I decided to elaborate one with the kind of questions they wanted to be answered, others coming from different studies and considering students' comments. It also gave room for opening students' observations. We also agreed that I would not only analyse results statistically but discuss with teachers, students and parents. And this resulted in unexpected insights into school culture. Here I leant that it is not only data (qualitative or quantitative) that makes research meaningful, but the researchers' onto-epistemological, ethical and methodological positioning.

From the students' answers to the questionnaire I was able to establish a productive dialogue with the school community. I would like to refer to two issues. The first one relates to some students' responses. When asked: How many hours a day, on average, do you spend doing homework and studying outside of school? A total of 34.90% answered around one hour per day, and 43.86% around two. For teachers, this was 'not true'. They thought the same when 54.24% expressed their desire of 'continuing studying until finishing a university degree' and 30.66% wanting 'to keep studying until finishing high school and then go to work'. Students' views were quite different; many of them spent everyday time doing homework—the problem was that the tasks performed were cognitively very little demanding: Passing the class notes to clean, doing exercises. Many of them recognised that they did not 'know how to study'. And yes, most of them insisted on finishing high school, but they did not find the teaching and school knowledge very interesting.

Another critical issue was related to the consumption of cigarettes, alcohol, joints, pills, glue and similar. The consumption percentages apart from cigarettes (23.11% smoked several times per day) were not high. Nevertheless, it seemed crucial to consider those who consumed several times per day wine (1.41%), beer (4.24%), gin-tonic (1.41%), pills (0,47%), glue and similar (0.04%) and joints (0.47% once a day). The person in charge of processing data through SPSS insisted that these figures were not statistically significant. However, for an educator, a single under-age using addictive substances was of great importance, and there

48 Juana M. Sancho-Gil

seemed to be several. Here is where the onto-epistemological, methodological and ethical positioning makes the difference.

Moreover, the ethnographic gaze appeared as a privileged approach to grasp the educational phenomena. Being able to discuss all these issues with all stakeholders allowed a more comprehensive decision-making process for the school. So, evidence-based research helped to foster the improvement of educational processes.

When the research report was ready and submitted to the institution that granted it, I had the opportunity to present it in the national call for educational research awards. I was doubtful, since, as pointed out, at that time, research in Spain was clearly positivist and statistical. Finally, I thought, I would not lose anything either, and the study was so different that either they would throw it in the bin or give me first prize. Surprisingly, they gave me the first prize (Sancho, 1987)! This event gave my academic career a significant push on the path towards a different way of approaching educational research.

New displacements

The following up of this account is my entire academic journey, the penultimate step of which is my position as Professor Emeritus and the new steps of my permanent becoming. On all this long path I have conducted a good number of ethnographic researches and publications. Here are the most representative, in English, of my continuous rithomatic scrollings: Domingo et al. (2014)—focused on young people learning in and out of school with digital technologies; Hernández et al. (2010)—aimed at exploring how Spanish primary and secondary school teachers deal with changes over time; Sancho et al. (2017)—based on how primary school teachers construct their professional subjectivity at Teachers College and the first working years. I have participated in lively discussions in Network 19 Ethnography in the European Conferences on Educational Research (ECER), from which emerged the need to rethink ethnography in the digital age (Hernández et al., 2013). In this forum I have problematised the fact that ethnography mostly focuses on 'weak' populations and cultures (Sancho-Gil, 2017). I spent a lot of time forming younger scholars in an increasingly complex world and contributing to developing alternative approaches to what a method could be, as a place of encounters among people, experiences and knowledges (Hernández-Hernández & Sancho-Gil, 2017), as becoming an ethnographer is a permanent move.

The orchestra continues to compose itself, diversifying, with new instruments, voices, movements, worlds, contexts, forces, literacies and people. It resonates in my body, awakens my curiosity and moves my affections.

Notes

1 Developed by the research group ESBRINA: https://esbrina.eu/en/home/
2 In Spain, teacher training only became a university degree in 1970. I finished in 1967 as high secondary school diploma was not required, only lower secondary education.

Through time and ontological displacements **49**

3 After 3 years of Civil War (1936–1939), Spain lived under a dictatorship until 1978.
4 One particular event was especially important for my process of becoming. In the class of 'Formation of the National Spirit' (political indoctrination for me), on November 20, 1967, as always, I got bored and began to read 'Emile, or On Education' by Rousseau. The teacher began to read the following text from a Spaniard, sentenced to death that day in 1936, accused of conspiracy and military rebellion against the government of the Second Republic: 'When in March 1762 an evil man, whose name was John James Rousseau, published "The Social Contract"'. This frightened me, and I quietly put the book in my desk drawer—but I realised that I was reading 'the right text'.
5 According to Barad (2007), the universe includes phenomena characterised by the ontological inseparability of intra-active agencies. Intra-action refers to non-arbitrary and non-deterministic causal events through which matter-in-the-process-of-becoming envelops iteratively in its continuous differential materialisation. Phenomena or objects do not precede their interaction but emerge through intra-actions.

References

Ball, S. (1980). *Beachside Comprehensive: A Case Study of Secondary Schooling*. Cambridge University Press.

Barad, K. (2007). *Meeting the Universe Halfway: Quantum Physics and the Entanglement of Matter and Meaning*. Duke University Press.

Barker, R., & Gump, P. (1963) *Big School, Small School*. Stanford University Press.

Barker, R., & Wright, H. (1966). *One Boy's Day; a Specimen Record of Behavior*. Archon Books.

Barker, R. (1968) *Ecological Psychology: Concepts and Methods for Studying the Environment of Human Behavior*. Stanford University Press.

Bernstein, B. (1971). *Class, Codes, and Control* (4 volumes). Routledge and Kegan Paul.

Bowles, S., & Gintis, H. (1976). *Schooling in Capitalist America: Educational Reform and the Contradictions of Economic Life*. New York: Basic Books.

Cohen, L., & Manion, L. (1980). *Research Methods in Education*. Croom Helm.

Creus, A., Montané, A., & Sancho, J.M. (2011). Reconstrucción del Proceso de una Investigación Autobiográfica en Educación Superior. In F. Hernández & M. Rifà (Coord.), *Investigación Autobiográfica y Cambio Social* (pp. 49–72). Octaedro.

de Tiavea, T., Scheurmann, E. & Swarte, J. (1977). *Los Papalagi: los Célebres Discursos de un Jefe Samoano*. Integra.

Domingo, M., Sánchez, J.A., & Sancho, J.M. (2014). Researching on and with Young People: Collaborating and Educating. *Comunicar*, 42 (XXI), 157–164. http://dx.doi.org/10.3916/C42-2014-15.

Eggleston, J. (1977). *The Ecology of the School*. Methuen.

Ellis, C. (2004). *The Ethnographic I: A Methodological Novel about Autoethnography*. AltaMira Press.

Faber (2011). Introduction: Negotiating Becoming. In R. Faber, & A.M. Stephenson (Eds.), *Secrets of Becoming: Negotiating Whitehead, Deleuze, and Butler*. (pp. 1–52). Fordham University Press.

Foucault, M. (1980). *Power/Knowledge: Selected Interviews and Other Writings 1972–1977*. Vintage.

Galton, M.J., Simon, B., & Croll, P. (1980). *Inside the Primary Classroom*. Routledge and Kegan Paul.

Hamilton, D., & Delamont, S. (1974). Classroom Research: A Cautionary Tale. *Research in Education*, 11 (1), 1–16.

Harris, M. (1976). *History and Significance of the Emic/Etic Distinction – Annual Review of Anthropology*, 5, 329–350.

Hernández, F. (1985). *La Psicología Ecológica de R. G. Barker como Metodología de Análisis de la Cotidianidad.* Unpublished Ph.D. Universitat de Barcelona.

Hernández, F., Fendler, R., & Sancho, J.M. (Eds.). (2013). *Rethinking Educational Ethnography: Researching On-line Communities and Interactions.* Universitat de Barcelona. http://hdl.handle.net/2445/44009.

Hernández, F., Sancho, J.M., Creus, A., & Montané, A. (2010). Becoming University Scholars: Inside Professional Autoethnographies. *Journal of Research Practice*, 6 (1), Article M7. Retrieved [May 13, 2011], from http://jrp.icaap.org/index.php/jrp/article/view/204/188.

Hernández-Hernández, F., & Sancho-Gil, J.M. (2017). Using Meta-ethnographic Analysis to Understand and Represent Youth's Notions and Experiences of Learning in and out of Secondary School. *Ethnography and Education*, 12 (2), 178–193. http://dx.doi.org/10.1080/17457823.2016.1180542.

Hernández-Hernández, F., & Sancho-Gil, J. (2018-06-25). Writing and Managing Multimodal Field Notes. *Oxford Research Encyclopedia of Education.* http://dx.doi.org/10.1093/acrefore/9780190264093.013.319.

Huberman, A., Grounauer, M., & Marti, J. (1993). *The Lives of Teachers (Teacher development).* Teachers College Press.

Hummel, R.C., & Nagle, J.M. (1973). *Urban Education in America: Problems and Prospects.* Oxford University Press.

Keddie, N. (1970) Classroom Knowledge. In M.F.D. Young (Ed.), *Knowledge and Control: New Directions for Sociology of Education* (pp. 47–69). Collier-Macmillan.

Kunda, G. (2013). Reflections on Becoming an Ethnographer. *Journal of Organizational Ethnography*, 2 (1), 4–44.

Maréchal, G. (2010). Autoethnography. In A.J. Mills, G. Durepos & E. Wiebe (Eds.), *Encyclopedia of Case Study Research* (Vol. 2, pp. 43–45). Sage Publications.

Mead, M. (1973). *Coming of Age in Samoa: A Psychological Study of Primitive Youth for Western Civilisation.* Morrow.

Phillips, D.C. (2014). Research in the Hard Sciences, and in very hard 'softer' domains. *Educational Researcher*, 43 (1), 9–11. https://doi.org/10.3102/0013189X13520293.

Rosenthal, R., & Jacobson, L. (1968). *Pygmalion in the classroom; teacher expectation and pupils' intellectual development.* Holt, Rinehart and Winston.

Rutter, M. (1979). *Fifteen Thousand Hours. Secondary Schools and Their Effects on Children.* Open Books.

Sancho, J.M. (1987). *Entre Pasillos y Clases.* Sendai y Ministerio de Educación y Ciencia. https://cutt.ly/cf3wv7H

Sancho, J.M. & Hernández (1981). *Interacción Ambiental en el Parvulario.* Publicaciones del ICE de la Universidad de Barcelona.

Sancho, J.M., & Hernández, F. (2010). Education Studies in Spain: Insights, Issues, and Failures. In D.K. Sharpes (Ed.), *Handbook on International Studies in Education* (pp. 201–217). Information Age Publishing.

Sancho, J.M. & Hernández-Hernández, F. (Coord.) (2014). *Maestros al Vaivén. Aprender a ser Docente en el Mundo Actual.* Ediciones Octaedro SL.

Sancho, J.M., Hernández, F., Creus, A., Domingo, L., & Montané, A. (2017). Primary School Teachers' Professional Identity: An Ethnographic Study. In Borgnakke, K., Dovemark, M., & Marques da Silva, S. (Ed.), *The Postmodern Professional: Contemporary Learning Practices, Dilemmas, and Perspectives* (pp. 92–109). Turfnell Press.

Sancho-Gil, J.M. (2017, August 22–25). *Ethnography of the Unknown, Unspoken, (In)visible.* ECER2017Convention. Copenhagen, Denmark.

Scheurmann, E. (1989). *Los Papalagi: Los Célebres Discursos de un Jefe Samoano*. Integral.

St. Pierre, E., Jackson, A., & Mazzei, L. (2016). New Empiricisms and New Materialisms: Conditions for New Inquiry. *Cultural Studies ⊠ Critical Methodologies*, 16 (2), 99–110.

Willis, P. (1977). *Learning to Labour: How Working Class Kids get Working Class Jobs*. Saxon House.

Wolcott, H.F. (1973). *The Man in the Principal's Office: An Ethnography*. Holt, Rinehart & Winston.

Woods, P. (2005). *Inside Schools: Ethnography in Schools*. Routledge.

5

BECOMING AN ETHNOGRAPHER

Living, teaching and learning ethnographically

Audra Skukauskaite

Writing about the many ways of 'composing a life', anthropologist Mary Catherine Bateson (2004) talks about stories as 'lenses for interpreting experience' (p. 67) and as ways through which we work with continuities and discontinuities of our lives to construct versions of the past, present and foundations for the future. She argues that the ability to create many versions of our life stories engenders both freedom and 'creative responsibility' (p. 68) to compose stories that speak and respond to particular contexts, times and audiences. Building on Bateson's idea of composing a life, here I share stories of becoming an ethnographer through living and listening, teaching and learning with sojourners around the world. To me, teaching and researching are part of the continuous process of becoming. As many of the teachers I interviewed at the beginning of my career said, 'I teach and I learn' (Skukauskaite, 2009, p. 204) and, as I learn with and from others, as I expand the ways of knowing, seeing, and being, I continuously become and live-into-being new stories and their interpretive potentials.

A prequel: When histories and human lives intersect to lay foundations for new becomings

I had many versions of the beginnings of this chapter and they all started at different moments in time, in different countries and encounters. But the more beginnings I wrote, the more I recalled a recent conversation with a professional colleague and friend who said that my story needed to be heard. As we sat on her balcony gazing at the majestic pelicans and their reflections flying over the calm waters of the Gulf of Mexico in Florida, we talked about ethnography as a way of seeing and being in the world, a way of learning with and from others, and a way of continuously creating connections and new ways of working with continuities, discontinuities and liminal spaces of our complex lives. When my friend asked how and why I became an ethnographer, I answered 'it made sense'. When I encountered ethnography, it made sense because I had already lived it; I connected with it viscerally—its concepts, principles, actions and goals reflected the ways I had lived in rapidly changing worlds and in the many liminal spaces of diverse national, academic and epistemological languacultures (Agar, 1994, 2019).

I came of age at a time and in a country that was transforming before my eyes. After Lithuania declared its independence from the soviet Union in 1990, all of a sudden the history, literature and even English language textbooks became unusable, and new ways of learning, knowing and acting as independent Lithuanians were being created. The national movements of the 1980s, the Baltic Way of 1989 and the Lithuanian people's resilience to maintain our newly regained freedom despite the soviet tanks, armies and economic blockades rolling in and over people, revealed the conflicting views of reality and social, economic and political ideologies that constructed those 'realities'. These conflicts also sparked re-envisioning of new possibilities and foregrounding the previously forbidden histories, literature, discourses and social networks that have made the independence possible. The lives, conversations and stories that were lived behind closed doors for decades were now celebrated and (re)composed into new coherences (Linde, 1993). The almost-millennium-long history of Lithuania and its ancient language that struggled for survival under the oppressors became the backbones of freedom and democracy. The pasts of independent Lithuania over the centuries were now creating new futures.

I lived those transformations. I saw the multiple ideologies and worlds clashing and collapsing. I participated in the Baltic Way in 1989—the human chain of people across Lithuania, Latvia and Estonia joining hands in protest against occupation and singing one freedom song in three languages. When the soviet tanks started rolling into the Lithuanian cities in an attempt to crush the new independence, I joined the multitudes around the country protecting key organizations (TV towers, phone and telegraph stations, government buildings) with our bodies, songs and campfires. When the soviet economic blockade cut off gas and hot water, we went for runs in the middle of winter to heat our bodies to take cold showers. Many stories could be composed from those days, yet one of the enduring threads I have woven into my evolving life story is the possibility of multiple perspectives. I saw the multiple lives lived and (re)composed; I heard the power of language, poetry and song to spark and sustain resistance and create new possibilities; I lived the different histories and their juxtapositions. History, contexts, language, social networks and individual actions within the collective story mattered. They were fluid and created possible worlds. Ethnography is about understanding and co-creating those possible ever-changing, hybrid worlds (Agar, 2019) and cultures-in-the making (Collins & Green, 1992; Heath & Street, 2008).

Becoming a researcher: Coming to ethnography through responsive listening to research participants

I didn't know what ethnography was or what it could offer until my Ph.D studies at the University of California, Santa Barbara. Encountering ethnography in my qualitative research classes, I was curious about it, but it still seemed more appropriate for my colleagues and professors who conducted studies in classrooms or other more clearly bounded settings. I was interested in learning about teaching and the impacts of educational reforms on the lives of teachers in Lithuania—I wasn't going to study a specific cultural group, so ethnography did not fit my research questions. Little did I know that it wasn't so much the research question or the boundaries of a group studied, but the epistemology of ethnography (Green et al., 2012) that would draw me in and become a foundation for my career in research methodology.

I did not set out to do ethnography or adopt an ethnographic perspective (Green & Bloome, 1997; Skukauskaitė et al., 2017). I planned an interview-based qualitative-interpretive (aka basic qualitative) study (Merriam, 2002) with representatives of three generations of English teachers in Lithuania. I wanted to know about their work as teachers thirteen to fourteen years after the independence, how the educational reforms guided or impacted their teaching, and how they continued to learn through formal and informal professional development opportunities. In open-ended interview conversations (Skukauskaite, 2017) the teachers not only shared many insights about their teaching lives but also inscribed criteria for understanding their lives. Throughout the conversations (two to three over two years with each of the nine participants) all teachers referenced history, policies and various people, thus demonstrating that their stories could be understood only in the sociohistorical contexts of their personal, professional and national histories. The teachers led me to ethnography.

The teachers I interviewed showed me the importance of ethnographic principles for understanding and constructing representations of their lives. When asked about their work *now*, they shared their *histories* of becoming teachers or talked about teaching *then in contrast to now*. They did not answer my open-ended questions in linear ways but wove multiple threads of their lifeworlds throughout the interview conversations (Skukauskaite, 2017). The teachers talked about students, parents, administration, books, trips, economics, society and many other aspects of their teaching lives. The richness of their stories and the complexity of the worlds we were co-constructing in the interview conversations made my initial research questions about teacher learning and impact of reforms too narrow and almost irrelevant. We still covered those topics, but there was so much more in those conversations that I did not expect (Skukauskaite, 2006). So I listened. Listening and trying to understand the many layers of the teachers' lives led me to the ethnographic principles I had first encountered in my doctoral classes.

Ethnographic principles proposed by Green, Dixon and Zaharlick (2003) reverberated throughout the discourse of the teachers I interviewed. When teachers talked about their teaching practices and the changing conditions of their work, they made visible the ethnographic principle of *studying cultural practices* by exploring people's actions across times and events. When they referenced various texts, events and their personal, professional and societal histories to paint a picture of their complex teaching lives, they inscribed the *contrastive perspective* that required me to look beyond the interviews to construct a deeper understanding of their stories. They also signalled the *holistic perspective* and the need to explore part-whole-relationships between moments in the conversation and overall stories; between one and all participants; between teacher discourse and policies referenced; and between teaching and sociohistorical contexts.

As I analyzed the interviews, I (re)turned to ethnography as a way of seeing people-in-inter/action in the multifaceted contexts of their lives, from their points of view, within groups and histories they were composing. Listening to my participants, following their leads, and responding to their ways of constructing knowledge in the interview conversations led me to Interactional Ethnography and discourse-based ethnographic approaches (Bloome et al., 2005; Kelly & Green, 2019). I came to adopt interactional ethnography as a way of thinking, being, learning and becoming. I am continuously becoming an Interactional Ethnographer as I continue learning *with* and *alongside* my research colleagues, partners, participants and readers. I also bring ethnographic ways of thinking, being and becoming into my teaching of research.

Becoming a professor of research methodologies: Teaching ethnographically

Coming to ethnography through responsive listening and analysis of my research participants' discursive constructions of their lifeworlds helped me realize that research methodology was a way to continuously engage in life-long-learning and to study any topic or question systematically. Consequently, in my Ph.D program I took more than ten research courses; assisted and collaborated in multiple research projects and served as assistant editor for the *Handbook of Complementary Methods in Education Research* (Green et al., 2006), which exposed me to multiple methodologies and ways of reading across traditions. Given my interest in understanding multifaceted social worlds, I specialized in qualitative and ethnographic methodologies, joined qualitative research networks and became a research methodologist and professor of qualitative research and research design. I teach research methodologies and their underlying epistemologies as ways of studying varied dimensions of the complex human and material worlds which we construct, inhabit and continuously change. Learning how to research opens the worlds of possibilities to explore the 'lively science' of social research (Agar, 2013).

Among the variety of research methodology courses I taught over my career, I often had the privilege to teach the introductory qualitative research course required in most doctoral programs. The course is challenging for the students and for me, but I love teaching it because it opens doors to exploring new ways of thinking, learning, interacting, connecting and becoming.

Every qualitative research professor has their own particular ways of teaching, influenced by their own studies, professors, disciplines, values, onto-epistemological stances and goals for themselves, students and the field. My way of teaching qualitative research methodologies is grounded in my ontological, epistemological and axiological perspectives of constructing socially just and culturally responsive contributions to the worlds we create. Ethnographic principles guide my teaching and my emphasis on learning to see through 'ethnographic eyes' (Frank, 1999) while developing reflexivity about the ways our pasts, values and experiences influence our ways of seeing and becoming.

I emphasize reflexivity, transparency, and the need to understand foundations and histories of varied research approaches so we can work creatively and build on, transform or create new knowledge (Golde, 2006). I often use arts-based strategies to nudge students to look in different ways (Skukauskaite et al., 2019). One year I asked students to paint or draw as a way of reflecting on their learning of qualitative research. Many students commented on the discomfort but also the opportunity of that experience. As one student summarized, teaching to learn, see and engage differently creates 'apprehension' but also 'opportunities to learn about ourselves', to see the 'artist within' (RC, 2015) and to develop new ways of looking that enhance the learning of qualitative research and deepen student personal and professional journeys (Skukauskaite et al., 2018). This kind of learning is ethnographic, for it teaches us to step outside our comfort zones, fight familiarity (Delamont, 2013; Skukauskaite, 2019) and try on new perspectives and new actions.

I purposefully design my courses for discomfort (Skukauskaite et al., 2018) since the discomfort students encounter and co-create helps us all explore the roots and many pathways that become possible when we step outside our comfort zones. Agar (1994) calls such discomforts rich points, or moments when our prior knowledge, language and expectations (our 'languacultures') clash with what we observe in our interactions with others. As we resolve those rich points, we learn about ourselves and the languacultures of others. Rich points are everywhere (Agar, 1994) and are the foundation of an ethnographic principle that emphasizes the *nonlinearity of ethnography* (Green et al., 2012). This principle points to ethnography's *abductive logic* in creating new understandings by challenging the old and enfolding developing new learnings into both forward and backward mapping of the languacultural encounters.

Facing discomforts and engaging in reflexivity in teaching and learning qualitative research (Skukauskaite et al., 2019) is also built on the ethnographic principles of *cultural relevance* (Green et al., 2003; Heath, 1982) and *leaving aside ethnocentrism* (Green et al., 2012). These principles encourage ethnographers to step back from personal views and seek to understand the emic (insider) perspectives of those with whom we research and interact. I remind students that emic and etic (outsider) are not polar opposites but a dynamic continuum that we constantly co-negotiate in the field. If, as ethnographers and researchers, we seek to understand the possible worlds of others, we first need to understand our subjectivities and suspend them, so we can deeply listen and *be* with others in their lifeworlds.

Teaching and learning ethnographically is often a harrowing journey that requires vulnerability as well as critique and support, but the majority of my students rise to the challenge and finish the course with deeper understandings of themselves and qualitative research (Skukauskaite et al., 2018; Skukauskaite et al., 2019). At the end of the semester I ask students to write learning essays and do self-assessments, which provide them with an opportunity to reflect on the journey. Many comment not only on the challenges and discomforts, but also the depth of learning they experience in the class. Echoing the statements of many, a student (VQ, 2016) shared that her experiences of learning qualitative research required her to challenge her own assumptions, become 'open minded' and allow the 'new ideas and thoughts' to 'challenge her beliefs', thus opening doors for new ways of understanding. She summarized her experience in the course by writing:

> I soon realized that I was in for a challenge that I had not experienced before. This was the moment when I realized that I was no longer in an ordinary world of completing a PhD course. I was now entering into a journey, a new way of learning. Not just learning about qualitative research, but learning about myself as a PhD scholar.

The journey of learning about ourselves, qualitative research and ways of seeing, becoming and acting in the world differently continues both for students and for me as a teacher. It is often uncomfortable and exhausting, but I continue teaching ethnographically because I see the epiphanies and changes that lead to new possibilities of co-creating more open, tolerant and socially just worlds.

I continue learning every time I teach. I also look for the opportunities to fight my own familiarities and extend learning opportunities in new ways and new spaces, including consulting and co-researching in a developing field of invention education (Couch et al., 2019), writing an analytic commentary on science education studies (Skukauskaite, 2019) and collaborating with colleagues in Lithuania to bring educational ethnography to Lithuania and the study of complex social problems.

Extending ethnographic ways of becoming to new situations

Throughout my career in academia in the U.S., I have maintained ties with Lithuania and insider-supported efforts of enhancing Lithuanian education. Teaching action research to Lithuanian teachers and school administrators through the American Partnership for Lithuanian Education program, conducting qualitative research and, more recently, teaching a variety of qualitative research seminars to faculty and graduate students across Lithuania, over the past two decades I have sought to understand the *insider* needs of the educators and join them in addressing those needs through whatever expertise I can offer. In 2014, I met Dr. Liudmila Rupšienė, a professor of research methodologies at Klaipėda University. She was interested in expanding research methodology potentials in Lithuania and we brainstormed what *we* could do to support Lithuanian scholars in learning and doing qualitative research.

58   Audra Skukauskaite

Like the teacher participants in the beginning of my research journey, Dr. Rupšienė inscribed an ethnographic perspective when she *holistically* explained the ways the fifty-year soviet occupation had stifled the development of qualitative research in the country. Without knowing she was using ethnographic principles, she constructed a *contrastive framework* that showed how differences between then vs now, soviet vs post-soviet, Lithuanian vs western, English vs Lithuanian created particular challenges and opportunities for Lithuanian scholars wanting to learn and do qualitative research (Skukauskaitė & Rupšienė, 2017). From her *emic perspective* as a scholar and research professor, Dr. Rupšienė argued that Lithuania needed more exposure to and experience with qualitative research methodologies beyond phenomenology, interpretive phenomenological analysis and grounded theory that had already become popular among Lithuanian doctoral students. Dr. Rupšienė's insider perspectives matched my own outsider observations and we set out to collaborate; this collaboration continues to this day and enfolds new scholars.

One of our first efforts was to bring educational ethnography to Lithuania. We invited the international *Rethinking Educational Ethnography* network to hold their conference in Lithuania in 2016, which led to a special issue on ethnography in the *Acta Paedagocia Vilnensia* journal (Skukauskaitė et al., 2017). Seminars on ethnography, interactional ethnography, narrative, discourse analysis and other qualitative approaches were also conducted at Klaipėda University and were attended by professors and doctoral students from around the country. More scholars started publishing qualitative research articles and dissertations, but many lamented that most of their learning was still from books or one-shot seminars and they lacked understanding needed to develop high quality research that could be published in international journals.

Seeking to address this local need, in collaboration with Dr. Rupšienė and other insiders, we set out to design a research project that could engage people in learning ethnographic epistemologies while participating in interconnected research seminars and conducting a large-scale research project. The project received European Union funding administered through the Lithuanian Research Council. The project was grounded in the four ethnographic principles proposed by Green, Skukauskaite and Baker (2012) in a chapter that expanded on the 2003 principles (Green et al., 2003) and presented ethnography as an epistemology, not a set of research methods.

The principles include:

1.   Ethnography as epistemology is *nonlinear* and is grounded in an abductive logic which enables backward and forward mapping to identify and examine rich points and construct telling cases that make visible the languacultures being studied.
2.   Ethnography calls for researchers to *set aside ethnocentrism* and engage in reflexivity in order to develop understandings of the emic/insider points of view within local situations.

3. Ethnography involves *identifying boundaries* of what counts as relevant to insiders by utilizing a contrastive analysis and following participant discourse, actions, and referential trails within and across individuals, groups, times, events and kinds of information.
4. Ethnography requires *making connections* among multiple insider perspectives and their individual and collective histories as well as intertextual connections among multiple sources of data and theoretical lenses brought to (orienting theories) and developed within the study (explanatory theories).

The four principles were embedded in all aspects of the multi-year project, whose goal was to 'research specialist training to provide holistic help to people with disabilities in the health care system while improving researcher competencies.' We designed five tasks and ethnographically-informed methodologies to achieve them (represented in Table 5.1). Ethnographic principles underlying each methodology are marked P1-P4.

Table 5.1 demonstrates that ethnographic epistemology guided the conceptualization and design of the project throughout. However, implementation of the project created a multitude of challenges that we did not foresee. They ranged from misalignment of intended scope and personnel needs for the project and the funded budget, to lack of expected expertise on the team in specific health care fields, to interpersonal conflicts and changes in research based on what was and was not possible in situ. The challenges made visible the influence of soviet history that garnered Lithuanian people's fears about being observed or interviewed on record, despite all affirmations that ethnography does not evaluate. The challenges also brought forth the gaps in knowledge, interest and/or understanding of research and underlying epistemologies guiding the project. The long-distance collaboration of PIs from different countries, linguistic differences and professional and personal preferences of international and local PIs also made visible the differences in languacultural work patterns, needs and commitments.

Though these challenges led to tensions among members of the project, they also created rich points and opportunities for learning and rethinking ethnography in new ways. I have had to re-examine my own understandings of ethnography as I mediated among team members, tried to explain the languacultural realities of U. S. and Lithuanian research contexts or attempted to translate deep conceptual foundations of ethnography into the Lithuanian academic language that did not have a long history nor vocabulary for ethnography.

The project, its possibilities and its challenges have opened doors to new ways of becoming and being an ethnographic researcher and teacher in the midst of change and languacultural contrasts. I now understand in deeper ways the human nature of ethnographic work, its possibilities and impossibilities when enacting ethnography in contexts where ethnography is new and work expectations are driven by a multitude of factors within and beyond the researcher's control. In facing the challenges and my own discomforts in teaching, doing

60 Audra Skukauskaite

TABLE 5.1 Project Tasks With Underlying Ethnographically-Informed Methodologies

Task	Methodologies and underlying principles (P1–4)
Examine the help people with disabilities receive in the health care system in order to create a foundation (baseline) for improving specialist training for holistic care	• Life history interviews (2–3 per participant) of people with disabilities, family members, and healthcare specialists (P2, P4) • Walk-along interviews (P1, P3) • Surveys of the 3 groups. Survey questions developed based on the data from the interviews (P2, P3, P4)
Analyse specialist training to provide holistic help for people with disabilities in the healthcare system	• Document and policy analyses (P1, P3, P4) • Ethnographic interviews with students, faculty, administrators, others (P2) • Observations of specialist preparation (P2, P3)
Through an ethnographic action research approach, improve the preparation of healthcare specialists to work with people with disabilities	• Action research to improve specialist training (P1–4) • Pre- and post-survey of students and faculty engaged in action research (P4)
Developing researcher competencies in the course of implementing the project	• Conduct interconnected seminar series led by international researchers who are part of an epistemologically aligned network (P1, P4) • Participate in international internships/visiting scholar programs led by international researchers (P2, P4) • International scholars (PI and co-PI) collaborate with Lithuanian scholars to design the project (P1–4) • Outsiders advise and guide based on knowledge generated by insiders on the ground (P2, P3)
Utilizing knowledge, understanding and developed research competencies for furthering science and practice (publications, dissemination and future grant applications)	• Publish in high quality international journals and other venues that meet the requirements of the funder (P2–4) • Publish monographs, research studies and textbooks as aligned in the project tasks (P4) • Divide publication tasks among project researchers (P1, P3)

and learning ethnography, I am seeing more clearly ethnography as a space of possibilities where 'more than one ethnography is possible, but not all ethnographies are acceptable' (Agar, 2006, par. 26). After all, ethnography is an epistemology, a philosophy of research (Anderson-Levitt, 2006), a way of thinking (Atkinson, 2017) and being (Madden, 2010) driven by ethnographic principles and logic but adaptable to varied contexts in culturally sensitive and responsive ways (Agar, 2006; Green et al., 2012; Heath & Street, 2008). Doing, teaching and learning ethnography across multiple institutions, contexts, disciplines and moments in history, with varied configurations of actors, I am continuously becoming an ethnographer—an observer, listener, reader, research partner and a human, with my own vulnerabilities, preferences, expertise and interests. My overarching commitment to lifelong learning will continue carrying me into and through new ways of becoming.

Composing a future life

Ethnography as a way of thinking, learning, seeing, being and becoming is a foundation for creating new versions of the life stories we use to interpret our experiences. Ethnographic epistemology is a way of continuous, collective and embodied learning. Bateson (2004) argued that learning is what 'defines our humanness' (p. 8) and connects us with the world. I have adapted her motto 'we are not what we know but what we are willing to learn' (p. 8) as my own, for it reflects the ethnographic commitment to continuous becoming that I value and try to live-into-being. As the stories I composed in this chapter demonstrate, this becoming is contextual and interpersonal. Becoming does not happen in a vacuum; it does not stop; it does not act alone. It creates, reflects and refracts my/our ways of thinking, acting, knowing and interacting as part of an ongoing historical, human, material and social world. As we act, we learn and we change. We are becoming.

In her memoir entitled *Becoming*, Michelle Obama (2018) summarized becoming as a 'forward motion, a means of evolving, a way to reach continuously toward a better self' (p. 148 Kindle). It is a process that requires 'patience and rigor' while also calling us to exploration, creativity, reflexivity and connections to all living human, nature, material and imagined dimensions of our storied and storying lives. Becoming is composing our future lives.

Acknowledgement: A part of this work was funded by the European Social Fund according to the activity 'Improvement of researchers' qualification by implementing world-class R&D projects' of Measure No.09.3.3-LMT-K-712

References

Agar, M. (1994). *Language Shock: Understanding the Culture of Conversation*. Quill.

Agar, M. (2006). An Ethnography by any Other Name… *Forum Qualitative Sozialforschung/Forum: Qualitative Social Research*, 7 (4). Retrieved 6/18/2008, from http://www.qualitative-research.net/fqs.

Agar, M. (2013). *The Lively Science: Remodeling Human Social Research*. Mill City Press.

Agar, M. (2019). *Culture: How to Make it Work in a World of Hybrids* (Kindle ed.). Rowman & Littlefield.

Anderson-Levitt, K. (2006). Ethnography. In J.L. Green, G. Camilli, & P.B. Elmore (Eds.), *Handbook of Complementary Methods in Education Research* (pp. 279–296). Lawrence Erlbaum for AERA.

Atkinson, P. (2017). *Thinking Ethnographically*. Sage.

Bateson, M.C. (2004). *Willing to Learn: Passages of Personal Discovery*. Steerforth Press.

Bloome, D., Carter, S.P., Christian, B.M., Otto, S., & Shuart-Faris, N. (2005). *Discourse Analysis and the Study of Classroom Language and Literacy Events: A Microethnographic Perspective*. Lawrence Erlbaum.

Collins, E.C., & Green, J.L. (1992). Learning in Classroom Settings: Making or Breaking a Culture. In H. Marshall (Ed.), *Redefining Student Learning: Roots of Educational Restructuring* (pp. 59–85). Ablex.

Couch, S., Skukauskaite, A., & Green, J.L. (2019). Invention Education: Preparing the Next Generation of Innovators. *Technology & Innovation*, 20 (3), 161–163. https://doi.org/10.21300/20.3.2019.161.

Delamont, S. (2013). *Key Themes in the Ethnography of Education: Achievements and Agendas.* Sage.

Frank, C.R. (1999). *Ethnographic Eyes: A Teacher's Guide to Classroom Observation.* Heinemann.

Golde, C.M. (2006). Preparing Stewards of the Discipline. In C.M. Golde & G.E. Walker (Eds.), *Envisioning the Future of Doctoral Education: Preparing Stewards of the Discipline. Carnegie Essays on the Doctorate* (pp. 3–20). Jossey-Bass.

Green, J.L., & Bloome, D. (1997). Ethnography and Ethnographers of and in Education: A Situated Perspective. In J. Flood, S.B. Heath, & D. Lapp (Eds.), *Handbook of Research on Teaching Literacy through the Communicative and Visual Arts* (pp. 181–202). International Reading Association & MacMillan.

Green, J.L., Camilli, G., Elmore, P.B., Skukauskaite, A., & Grace, E. (Eds.). (2006). *Handbook of Complementary Methods in Education Research.* Lawrence Erlbaum for AERA.

Green, J.L., Dixon, C.N., & Zaharlick, A. (2003). Ethnography as a Logic of Inquiry. In J. Flood, D. Lapp, J.R. Squire, & J. Jensen (Eds.), *Handbook of Research on Teaching the English Language Arts* (2nd ed., pp. 201–224). Lawrence Erlbaum.

Green, J.L., Skukauskaite, A., & Baker, W.D. (2012). Ethnography as Epistemology: An Introduction to Educational Ethnography. In J. Arthur, M.J. Waring, R. Coe, & L.V. Hedges (Eds.), *Research Methodologies and Methods in Education* (pp. 309–321). Sage.

Heath, S.B. (1982). Ethnography in Education: Defining the Essentials. In P. Gillmore & A. A. Glatthorn (Eds.), *Children in and out of School: Ethnography and Education* (pp. 33–55). Center for Applied Linguistics.

Heath, S.B., & Street, B.V. (2008). *On Ethnography: Approaches to Language and Literacy Research.* Teachers College Press.

Kelly, G.J., & Green, J.L. (2019). Framing Issues of Theory and Methods for the Study of Science and Engineering Education. In G.J. Kelly & J.L. Green (Eds.), *Theory and Methods for Sociocultural Research in Science and Engineering Education* (pp. 1–28). Routledge.

Linde, C. (1993). *Life Stories: The Creation of Coherence.* Oxford University Press.

Madden, R. (2010). *Being Ethnographic: A Guide to the Theory and Practice of Ethnography.* Sage.

Merriam, S.B. (2002). *Qualitative Research in Practice. Examples for Discussion and Analysis.* Jossey-Bass.

Obama, M. (2018). *Becoming.* Crown Publishing.

RC reflection, 2015.

Skukauskaite, A. (2006). *Developing an Analytic System for Grounded Interpretations: Studying the Impact of Educational Changes on Teachers in Lithuania* [Ph.D., University of California, Santa Barbara]. ProQuest Dissertations & Theses Full Text.

Skukauskaite, A. (2009). "I Teach and I Learn": Teacher Learning Across Generations in the Context of the European Lifelong Learning Programme. *Lifelong Learning in Europe, 4,* 204–215.

Skukauskaite, A. (2017). Systematic Analyses of Layered Meanings Inscribed in Interview Conversations: An Interactional Ethnographic Perspective and its Conceptual Foundations. *Acta Paedagogica Vilnensia, 39* (2), 45–60. https://doi.org/10.15388/ActPaed.2017.39.11466.

Skukauskaite, A. (2019). Constructing Transparency in Designing and Conducting Multilayered Research in Science and Engineering Education — Potentials and Challenges of Ethnographically Informed Discourse-based Methodologies. In G.J. Kelly & J.L. Green (Eds.), *Theory and Methods for Sociocultural Research in Science and Engineering Education* (pp. 234–255). Routledge.

Skukauskaite, A., Noske, P., & Gonzales, M. (2018). Designing for Discomfort: Preparing Scholars for Journeys Through Qualitative Research. *International Review of Qualitative Research*, 11 (3), 334–349. https://doi.org/10.1525/irqr.2018.11.3.334.

Skukauskaitė, A., & Rupšienė, L. (2017). Teaching and Learning Qualitative Methodologies in the Context of Developing Doctoral Education in Lithuania. *Acta Paedagogica Vilnensia*, 39 (2), 61–82. https://doi.org/10.15388/ActPaed.2017.39.11470.

Skukauskaitė, A., Rupšienė, L., Player Koro, C., & Beach, D. (2017). Rethinking Educational Ethnography: Methodological Quandaries and Possibilities. Editorial Introduction. *Acta Paedagogica Vilnensia*, 39 (2), 9–14. https://doi.org/10.15388/ActPaed.2017.39.11451.

Skukauskaite, A., Yilmazli Trout, I., & Robinson, K. (2019, January 17). *Deepening Reflexivity Through Art in Learning Qualitative Research*. The Qualitative Report Conference, Fort Lauderdale, FL.

VQ reflection, 2016.

6

THE CHALLENGES AND OPPORTUNITIES OF BECOMING AN ETHNOGRAPHER

Richard Bacon

On a CEO becoming an ethnographer

This is a study based on warranted claims (Heap, 1995) of the period that began when I embarked on my journey to enter the community of scholars called international ethnographers to the moment, four years later, when I first was publicly identified as a member of that community. This account is, in itself, an ethnographic study of my developing deep reasoning and thinking as an ethnographer that took place in multiple contexts, through multiple dialogic events with multiple actors over time as I came to understand what I needed to know and do in order to make sense of workplace-based learning initiatives.

In 2006, the company of which I was CEO partnered with Arrival Education (AE), a London-based social enterprise, to offer a workplace-based program that brought together the company's junior managers with diverse K12 students from undeserved backgrounds in a mentoring program designed to develop employees' management skills and improve students' access to academic and career opportunities. The positive impact of the program gave me the idea that this program could be extended to the USA where I was CEO of a technology start-up in California. I shared this idea with Dr. SC, who questioned my belief in the transferability of the program to different countries and different social contexts. This frame clash between my beliefs and Dr. SC's lived experience prompted her to recommend that I contact Professor JLG, at the University of California Santa Barbara (UCSB), to explore the opportunity to study with her interactional ethnography that has as its roots anthropology, sociology and linguistics and that has been widely used as a way of understanding the developing complex, dynamic and multifaceted worlds of classroom-based learning (Green et al., 2012)

Subsequently, I was accepted into a doctoral program at UCSB that lead to my doctoral thesis (Bacon, 2018) that was written from my perspective of a

CEO-as-ethnographer/ethnographer-as-CEO. The invitation by the Editors to contribute to this publication provides me with the opportunity to offer a reflexive account of 'becoming an ethnographer' and led me to frame the following questions:

What does a business leader need to know and be able to do as an ethnographer to understand what is being proposed and accomplished in a given social context?

What supports the business leader's development as an ethnographer?

How is the business leader's role as an ethnographer acknowledged by self and others?

To answer these questions, I adopt an interactional ethnographic approach (Green & Bridges, 2018) to (re)present my journey of 'becoming' an ethnographer within a community of researchers called interactional ethnographers. By tracing that journey, I (re)present the processes and practices that over time led to me 'becoming' an interactional ethnographer. My approach is designed to make visible the reflexive, non-linear, iterative, abductive nature of this journey and how each step to 'becoming' raised new questions, actions, and insights.

Framing this study: Key theoretical perspectives

Guiding my ethnographic approach in this study are three core constructs that are central to my analysis of my journey to becoming an interactional ethnographer. The first of these is that the (re)presentation of my lived experience goes beyond story-telling and constitutes a *telling case study* as defined by Mitchell (1984):

the detailed presentation of ethnographic data relating to some *sequence of events* from which the analyst seeks to make some theoretical inference. The events themselves may relate to any level of social organization, a whole society, some section of a community, a family or an individual. What distinguishes [telling] case studies from more general ethnographic reportage is the detail and particularity of the account. Each case study is a description of a specific configuration of events in which some distinctive set of actors have been involved in some defined situation at some particular point of time.

(p. 222)

In this telling case study, the distinctive actors on my journey are those with whom I interacted over time when, as a CEO, I engaged in discursive activities that had as their intended purpose my being accepted into a community of scholars called interactional ethnographers.

The second construct is framed by the work of Hill-Bonnet et al., (2012) who define social and academic identities as being '(re)formulated in, and through, ongoing discursive work of members in particular events as well as for the

66 Richard Bacon

collective'. (p. 320). The third construct captures the dynamic and reflexive processes in such ongoing discursive events as made visible by Bakhtin (1986).

> Sooner or later what is heard and actively understood will find its response in the subsequent speech or behavior of the listener. In most cases, genres of complex cultural communication are intended precisely for this kind of actively responsive understanding with delayed action. Everything that we have said here also pertains to written and read speech, with the appropriate adjustments and additions.
>
> *(pp. 68–69)*

These three constructs provide the foundation for this telling case study in which I will present evidence of how what I heard and understood was subsequently reflected in my actions and utterances. In this process of analysis, I demonstrate the argument of Ellen (1984) that ethnographers produce data, from which texts about cultural processes and practices are constructed.

Data collection and analysis

The inscription of this telling case study begins with a description of how I constructed an archive of records and artefacts for the time period during which, as indicated previously, I sought to become a member of a community of scholars called interactional ethnographers. These records are presented in Table 6.1.

TABLE 6.1 Data and Sources

Data	Source
Emails	Gmail and Yahoo accounts. Professor JLG's email archive
Recommended readings and references	Emails Class reading lists Online accounts purchase history
Word, PowerPoint, pdf documents, class and AERA poster presentations	Email attachments, electronic folders in Google Drive and DropBox
Calendar	Gmail and Yahoo accounts
UCSB Transcript	UCSB website
Headnotes	Transcribed records of CEO's recall of discursive events
Class handouts with contemporaneous notes	CEO's records
Class assignments submitted	CEO's records
Handwritten notes from meals with Professor JLG	CEO's records

In order to uncover these records, I first used headnotes grounded in my lived experiences to identify the names of those with whom I had engaged in discourse during the period covered by this study. Using these names and terms such as 'ethnography', I deployed a keyword search engine to my emails from the period to uncover email-based discourse in which these names and terms appeared. I transcribed these emails with their date stamps, sender and recipient identifiers and placed them in the archive in chronological order. While examining the transcribed emails, I uncovered emails that contained recommendation(s) for readings (literature) which I recorded along with the name of those who had provided them to me and when, and then placed these citations into a bibliography (e.g. Agar, 1994).

In order to determine which citations I had subsequently taken up to guide my understanding of ethnographic perspectives and practices, I searched my electronic records (Google Drive and DropBox) for evidence of downloaded versions of them and the date when I had downloaded each of them. Some of the recommended readings were books; therefore, in order to determine if I had taken up the reading recommendation, I analysed and recorded the history of my online book purchases.

The transcribed emails in the archive also contained links to academic articles and attachments in the forms of Word, PowerPoint and PDF documents. I downloaded these academic articles and attachments and placed them in the archive with the details of who had sent them to me and when. I also downloaded my UCSB transcript and placed this in the archive along with copies of my professional and personal calendars. I interrogated these artefacts to identify my travel, UCSB class attendance and meetings with my UCSB advisor, Professor JLG, and others.

In order to analyse these discursive events, I stepped back from the known (Heath & Street, 2008) and sought to make visible the roots and routes to my 'becoming' an interactional ethnographer by uncovering how what I heard and understood was subsequently reflected in my actions and utterances. In conducting my analysis, I followed Giddens (1984) and examined the records of these events for patterns of discourse, behaviours and flows of conduct. My analysis was guided by two questions (Green et al., 2012):

1. Who said what to whom, when, where, under what conditions, for what purpose and in what context?
2. What were the outcomes for the participants in these discursive events as made evident by subsequent discourse and actions?

In Table 6.2, I present the results of my analysis in the form of a detailed event map that makes visible my pathway to developing as an interactional ethnographer during the period that began with the frame clash that occurred in my initial meeting with Dr. SC until I presented my research in a poster session alongside other interactional ethnographers at the 2017 American Education Research

68 Richard Bacon

Association (AERA) Conference. I identified this presentation as a second 'rich point' (Agar, 1994) because it was the moment when my hitherto recognized role as a CEO clashed publicly with my emerging role as an interactional ethnographer that was being acknowledged by the education research profession outside UCSB for the first time.

My analysis of this period uncovered five phases:

1. Preparing my mind for becoming a student of ethnography.
2. Negotiating entry to a place of study.
3. Engaging with peers and mentors in gaining an understanding of ethnography.
4. Acting for myself and others as an ethnographer.
5. Gaining external recognition as a member of a community of ethnographers.

An analysis of each of these phases of my journey to becoming an ethnographer now follows and is presented in reverse chronological order, so as to uncover the roots and routes to each phase that culminated in the participation of the CEO-ethnographer in a conference of an international community of scholars in education.

Gaining external recognition as a member of a community of ethnographers

My examination of the records in the archive indicates that I presented a poster entitled, 'The Challenges Faced by a Company in Constructing a Work-Place Based Learning and Development Opportunity Called an Internship' at the 2017 (AERA) Conference in San Antonio, Texas. An inscription of the poster is presented in Appendix 6.1. My analysis in Table 6.3 makes visible that the roots and routes by which I, CEO-ethnographer, came to be present in this social context were found in an invitation from Professor JLG to me and five of my UCSB peers to submit a proposal for a structured poster session at the AERA Conference. This culminated with my presentation of a poster at the Conference. As will be made visible later, my participation as CEO-ethnographer and that of my peers in this discursive event had been anticipated by Professor JLG several months before she had issued the invitation.

As evidenced in Table 6.3, the construction of my AERA poster was the outcome of multiple actions and dialogue with Professor JLG, who acted for me as a cultural guide to the AERA site. Using Spradley (1979) as a resource, my analysis of the semantic relationships presented in Table 6.4 makes visible the provision of particular resources by Professor JLG to me.

The extracts of the transcribed emails in Table 6.4 reveal my collaborative dialogic exchanges with both Professor JLG and her citations (Guba, Agar, Graduate Student H – pseudonym). These served to inform my (co)construction of my AERA poster. These utterances make visible the guiding principles and practices of

TABLE 6.2 Event Map of a CEO Becoming an Ethnographer

Time	2013			2014			2015	2016	2017
	April – June	July – December	January	Winter Term	Fall Term	Winter Term			
Phases of action taken	Preparing mind for becoming a student of ethnography	Negotiating entry into UCSB		Engaging with mentors and peers in gaining an understanding of ethnography		Acting for self and others as an ethnographer			Gaining external recognition as a member of community of ethnographers
Discursive Processes	Engaging with Dr. SC on education projects	Contacting, entering into discourse with and meeting Professor J LG.	Being included as a recipient of Professor JLG's email to others	Formally applying to UCSB	Attending and participating in Professor JLG's Classes: Classroom Cultures and Classroom Ethnography		UCSB Class: Research Methods. Entering the field (ethnographic interviewing)	Invited to join a community of ethnographers' application to AERA 2017 Conference.	Presenting poster to AERA 2017 Conference

TABLE 6.3 Phases in the Construction of an AERA Poster

Event Date	Nov 28th 2016	July 17th - 23rd 2016	23rd July 2016	January 7th – April 24trh 2017	30th April 2017
Action	Professor JLG invites me and five other graduate students to submit to Division D Graduate Student In-Progress Research Gala at AERA 2017	Drafting and submitting a poster abstract for a session organized by Professor JLG for Language and Social Progress, Special Interest Group at AERA	Submission of five doctoral student abstracts to AERA	Preparing an AERA poster	Presenting a poster at the AERA
Actors	Professor JLG in discourse with CEO-as-ethnographer and five UCSB doctoral students	Professor JLG in discourse CEO-as-ethnographer,	Professor. JLG in discourse with CEO-as-ethnographer and five UCSB graduate students	Professor. JLG in discourse with CEO-as-ethnographer	Professor. JLG in discourse with CEO-ethnographer
Discursive event	I encourage you to submit if you are ready. Division D Graduate Student In-Progress Research Gala. The Division D Graduate Student Council is again sponsoring the 'Division D Graduate Student In-Progress Research Gala' at the annual AERA meeting. This session is an opportunity for Division D graduate students to present their research in an interactive poster session.	Perhaps add a couple of words to tie it to national calls—they not only speak to the need but frame the need to create principles for developing internships, not just proposing the need for or something of the sort. Need for further research before establishing programs or policies and how ethnographic perspective can inform designers of initiatives.	Greetings Good Colleagues, I wanted to let you know that our submission for the Structured Poster Session was accepted by the AERA system	You might look at the Guba Research Methods and Methodologies in Education and the Baker Green. That will help you think about what you did and how you did it. This is not about the finding so much as the logic in use. Laying out the logic in use and the perspectives guiding your analyses as well as data collection	Hi Rick, your work contributed a rich part for today. Thank you for being a risk taker. Professor JLG

On becoming an ethnographer 71

TABLE 6.4 A Spradley Analysis of Semantic Relationships

Spradley Semantic Relationship	Professor JLG's Resources and Recommendation
X is a way of providing resources	You might look at Guba in *Research Methods and Methodologies in Education* and the *Baker Green* (2012). That will help you think about what you did and how you did it
X is a way of making visible what needs to be known by a researcher	This is not about the finding so much as the logic in use. Laying out the logic in use and the perspectives guiding your analyses as well as data collection
X is a way of identifying a rich point	Please add something about what frames the stepping back and the rich point. Agar (1994) has a description if you want or you can frame it through what constitutes an IE logic of inquiry
X is a way of making visible expectations of a scholar presenting at a conference	I am attaching Graduate Student H (pseudonym)'s poster. She has detailed the framework and you might want to adapt some of her arguments to yours
X is a way of making visible findings from a research study	Perhaps you want to identify what was learned that supported earlier work and what is new. Help the reader and visitor see the importance of what you located
X is a way of extending knowledge of research outcomes	Some words about the failures are important also. Those are 'findings' or rather theoretically identified factors previously unstudied by others. What was learned from the failures would be important in the final section or in that section and how do the failures contrast with the success? What elements led to the success?

ethnographic research that, as with this study, required me to step back and reflect on what I need to know and understand as I approached it and how to make visible my findings to others.

Acting for self and others as an ethnographer

Ethnographic conversations (Spradley, 1979) are used by researchers to understand social phenomena through discourse with participants in those particular social situations. Analysis of the classes I attended at UCSB indicates that a course led by Professor JB provided instruction in ethnographic interviewing. The course included an exercise that required members of the class, working in pairs, to identify an issue, conduct ethnographic interviews to explore the issue, and present their findings to the class. An analysis of my headnotes and the transcribed presentation indicates that Doctoral Student G (pseudonym), a first-generation Latina, and I chose to study 'The Challenges facing Latino High School Students in Gaining

72   Richard Bacon

Access to College'. I initially analysed the data of the discursive events that took place during this study and produced a timeline for these before proceeding to analyse that data for patterns of who said what, to whom, for what purpose, and with what outcomes.

In Table 6.5, I make visible the progression that my fellow doctoral student and I made as we developed an ethnographic project and the opportunities for learning the practices of ethnographic interviewing that this presented. This provides evidence of how multiple resources (faculty, readings and partners), a practice-orientated experience and multifaceted discursive events with multiple actors/cultural guides all featured in my journey to 'becoming' an interactional ethnographer.

Engaging with mentors and peers in gaining an understanding of ethnography

In this section I explore how Professor JLG served as a cultural guide for me and others. I have taken for analysis the period during which I attended Professor JLG's Winter 2014 and Fall 2014 classes that were entitled 'Classroom Cultures' and 'Classroom Ethnography'. In analysing the records (e.g. class notes, my calendar and notes of meetings outside the class with Professor JLG) I uncovered a pattern of discursive events that took place over time between:

- A. Professor JLG and all class attendees.
- Professor JLG and myself.

As previously framed, I conducted a Spradley analysis of each of these groups' discursive events:

- An analysis of Discourse between Professor JLG and Class attendees.

In Table 6.6, I make visible the role of Professor JLG and the emphasis placed by her on ethnography being a philosophy of inquiry.

Professor JLG is observed to have anticipated potential outcomes for her students both in terms of going public ('build a base for publishing articles and presenting at conferences') and working with others to (co)construct ethnographic studies ('work with a partner to learn interactively since many ethnographic projects involve teams'). This dialogue served to foreground future discursive events on my journey to 'becoming' that were to include an ethnographic interview exercise and presentation at the AERA Conference in 2017.

- An analysis of the discourse between the CEO and Professor JLG.

My analysis of the archived records shows that I often dined with Professor JLG on the evening before or after her class. My headnotes indicate that these discursive events focused on my studies. Further analysis presented in Table 6.7 reveals that in

TABLE 6.5 Event Map of Discursive Events and Actions Supporting an Ethnographic Interview

2015

	January 6th–14th	January 20th	January 20th–27th	January 28th	January 31s	February 2nd –16th	February 17th
Discursive event	Classes in Research Methods in Education	Identifying a study partner	Preparing to conduct an ethnographic interview. Negotiating a problem to study	Identifying an informant and negotiating an interview	Ethnographic interview	Sharing of interview transcripts, analysis of records, negotiation Inscription of presentation of research (PowerPoint)	Presentation to class of findings of research
X is a way of	Preparing the mind		Entering the field		Conducting ethnographic research	Going public with research findings	
Discursive actions	Reading Spradley (1979)	Dear Dr. F*(pseudonym for a Latina Professor at a California State University) Dr. SC suggested I contact you. As part of one of my assignments this term in the Qualitative Interviewing Class, I would like to interview someone with a perspective on the challenges facing Latino students who wish to gain entry to College.			(To Dr. F from me) 'could you give me your perspective on the issues that are going on outside the school which influence how the students decide to go to college'.	Dear Dr. JB, (pseudonym for class instructor) I am emailing you our PowerPoint presentation in case my laptop has technical difficulties.	

74 Richard Bacon

TABLE 6.6 A Spradley Analysis of Classroom Dialogue (1)

Spradley Semantic Relationship	Professor JLG to Class
X is a way of greeting students into the field of ethnography	Greetings Classroom Ethnography colleagues I am looking forward to supporting you in exploring how this philosophy of inquiry can guide your research

X is a way of explaining the role of the Professor	the initiator of this social circle
	    to help you prepare your mind for this class to support you in developing background knowledge needed to actually engage in ethnographic work I have developed a series of background readings that will help you prepare to engage in ethnographic work
	    partner in ethnography

X is a way of using wiki as a dialogic space	[for] developing common knowledge (Edwards and Mercer, 1987) and learning how (ways of) to develop (developing) (Vygotsky, 1978) a social circle (not a class, a group, a community—Bakhtin, 1986)
X is a way to set the goals of the class	construct the culture of our developing course construct the cultural processes and practices in this developing community explore not only what is happening in class but also the things you need to know, understand and do to contribute to the developing culture of learning with, through and from each other. develop dialogic cultural processes and practices read the articles, think about how you read the text as a dialogue with the author deep discussions about analysis of ethnographic records build a base for publishing articles and presenting at conferences work with a partner to learn interactively since many ethnographic projects involve teams

emails between Professor JLG and myself that followed class or dinner, Professor JLG provided me with additional resources. This provides another layer of insight into the steps by which I was 'becoming' an ethnographer through on-going discourse with a cultural guide that was not confined to the classroom.

My analysis of the dialogic exchanges via email between me and Professor JLG made visible an utterance of Professor JLG in which she declares the importance of analysing discursive events from multiple angles of vision and from a non-judgemental basis:

> Your analysis and reflections provide a basis to make visible what is invisible from different angles on a common problem. As someone entering, your notes become a critical basis, a rich point, for conceptually exploring issues you raise without judging.

On becoming an ethnographer **75**

TABLE 6.7 Spradley Analysis of Classroom Dialogue (2)

Spradley Sematic Analysis	Professor JLG's reading recommendations
X is a way of providing resources	This is a chapter from RF Ellen's book on *Ethnographic Research* (1984) I am also including a chapter on multi-cultural education by James Banks (2008) that explores positionality of researcher and research Now read Arthur, Coe, Waring and Hedges (2012)' first three chapters and then let's talk. Please read *On Ethnography* by Heath and Street (2008) and then we can talk

In the continuation of this dialogue, Professor JLG, citing Frederiksen and Donin (2015) states that 'You have made visible the "shifting sands of you own thinking, if this is the right metaphor"'. This analysis provides evidence that my taking up of ethnography as a philosophy of inquiry took place over time and was made visible to Professor JLG through my subsequent utterances and actions.

The semantic relationship analyses in this section make visible how across different times, places and social contexts, I entered into formal and informal discursive events with Professor JLG about what it means to 'become' an ethnographer and describes how Professor JLG engaged me and others in developing an understanding of the processes and practices of ethnography as a philosophy of inquiry, not a method. Through this analysis of the transcribed dialogues between Professor JLG and class members and with me makes visible that becoming was not a pre-ordained, linear progression but a complex interwoven series of dynamic, discursive interactions that took place over time in a range of social contexts (classrooms, remote locations, restaurants and cafés).

Negotiating entry to a community of ethnographic scholars

In analysing the archive, I traced my initial approach and subsequent discourse with Professor JLG while I was engaged in seeking entry to UCSB and the opportunity to study with Professor JLG. The records of my actions and discursive events revealed many overlapping layers of interactions that began on July 24th 2013 and included an email from Dr. AS (pseudonym) to Professor JLG, who forwarded it to eleven people, including me and Dr. SC (an ethnographer known to me), with the inscription:

...we located this piece that I thought you might find intriguing. Let me know what you think. Seems relevant to me on a lot of levels. What do you think?

76 Richard Bacon

The attachment to the email was a paper written by Dr. AS (pseudonym) entitled 'An ethnographic approach to reading, analysing, and engaging in dialogues with texts'. This was the first time I had been included in such a group email that referenced a subject which Professor JLG considered would be 'intriguing' and 'relevant' for a group, which included me, and from which she invited its members' thoughts. This suggests that at the time of sending this email, Professor JLG considered that I was part of a group with whom she shared intriguing artefacts. (An analysis of Professor JLG's emails to members of classes which I subsequently attended in 2014 and 2015 indicate that five of the recipients were doctoral students of Professor JLG at that time of this email and another was Dr. SC, a prior student of Professor JLG).

My analysis of the archive reveals the steps I took to negotiate access to UCSB and makes visible that Professor JLG played the role of 'cultural guide' by 'preparing my mind' through the provision of introductory readings of widely cited authorities in the field of ethnography and by asking me to write extended essays 'to make certain you understood the time commitment and the concepts as well... So, I was concerned that you understood what we were about and what you would be doing'.

Preparing my mind for becoming a student of ethnography

My analysis of the archive indicates that from April to July 2013, I advised on a program being led by Dr. SC from California State University (CSU) that supported students from local colleges with employment opportunities in leading local companies as part of a Corporate Education Engagement program. My headnotes indicate that in the course of this, Dr. SC suggested that I might benefit from gaining a better understanding of workplace-based education programs and that she, in becoming an ethnographer, had gained ways of seeing and understanding what takes place in learning spaces that had informed her work as an educationist and education policy activist. In the course of this conversation, Dr. SC recommended that I read Spradley (1979) and Agar (1986) and offered to introduce me to Professor JLG at UCSB, who had been her Ph.D advisor for her ethnographic dissertation and was a leading, internationally recognised interactional ethnographer. The records show that I purchased the two books on July 9th 2013 and contacted Professor JLG on July 27th 2013 to introduce myself, then subsequently applied to UCSB to study with her.

Findings

This reflexive study has made visible that the CEO 'becoming' an ethnographer was an intentional series of actions and discursive events that comprised complex ongoing processes from the moment he entered the field. It also makes visible how that journey was not a solitary exercise but took place over time through unplanned, ongoing discourses with cultural guides, including Professors, peers and those whose theories and observations are inscribed in books and other media with whom (co)construction of knowledge and ideas took place. This study has offered evidence of how, over time, I evolved from a novice when I entered the field to becoming learner-as-teacher/teacher-as-learner (Freire, 1998) when I presented my research findings at the 2017 AERA Conference. That becoming has continued; this text has been (co)constructed with interactional ethnographers with whom I have shared earlier drafts upon which they have commented.

Bibliography

Agar, M. (1986). *Speaking of Ethnography*. Sage Publications.

Agar, M. (1994). *Language Shock: Understanding the culture of conversation*. William Morrow.

Bacon, R.J. (2018) *An Ethnographic Study of the Complexities of Designing and Gaining Access to an Internship* (Doctoral dissertation, University of California, Santa Barbara). Available from ProQuest Dissertations and Theses database. (UMI No. 10845368)

Bakhtin, M.M. (1986). *Speech and Other Late Essays*. University of Texas Press.

Banks, J.A. (2008). *An Introduction to Multicultural Education*. Pearson/Allyn and Bacon.

Edwards, D., Mercer, N. (1987). *Common Knowledge: The Development of Understanding in the classroom*. Methuen.

Ellen, R.A. (Ed) (1984). *Ethnographic Research. A Guide to General Conduct*. Academic Press.

Frederiksen, C.H., & Donin, J. (2015). Discourse and Learning in Contexts of Educational Interaction. In N. Markee (Ed.), *The Handbook of Classroom Discourse and Interaction*, First Edition (pp. 96–114). John Wiley & Sons, Inc.

Freire, P. (1998) *Pedagogy of Freedom: Ethics, Democracy, And Civic Courage*. Rowman & Littlefield.

Giddens, A. (1984). *The Constitution of Society: Outline of the Theory of Structuration*. Polity Press.

Green, J.L., & Bridges, S.M. (2018). Interactional Ethnography. In F. Fischer, C.E. Hmelo-Silver, S.R. Goldman, & P. Reimann (Eds), *International handbook of the learning sciences*, (pp. 475–488). Routledge.

Green, J.L., Skukauskaite, A., & Baker, W.D. (2012). Ethnography as Epistemology: An Introduction to Educational Ethnography. In J. Arthur, M.J. Waring, R. Coe, & L.V. Hedges (Eds), *Research Methods and Methodologies in Education* (pp. 3019–3321). Sage.

Heap, J. (1995). The Status of Claims in "Qualitative" Educational Research. *Curriculum Inquiry*, 25 (3), 271–292.

Heath, S.B., & Street, B.V. (2008). *On Ethnography: Approaches to Language and Literacy Research*. Teachers College: NCRLL/National Conference on Research in Language and Literacy.

Hill-Bonnet, L., Green, J., Yeager, B, Reid, J. (2013). Exploring Dialogic Opportunities for Learning and (Re)negotiating Selves: An Ethnographic Telling Case of Learning to be Social Scientists. In M.B. Ligorio & M. César. (Eds.), *The Interplays Between Dialogical Learning and Dialogical Self*. Charlotte, NC: Information Age Publishing.

Mitchell, J. (1984). Typicality and the case study. In R. Ellen (Ed.), *Ethnographic Research: A Guide to General Conduct*. (pp. 237–241). Academic Press.

Spradley, J.P. (1979). *The Ethnographic Interview*. Wadsworth Cengage.

Vygotsky, L.S. (1978). *Mind in Society: The Development of Higher Psychological Processes*. Harvard University Press.

Walford, G. (2001). *Doing Qualitative Educational Research: A Personal Guide to the Research Process*. Continuum.

PART II

Becoming as an onto-epistemological framework

7

WHAT COMES AFTER BECOMING

Virtualities at the end of a doctoral research

Aurelio Castro-Varela

Introduction

Very often, the writing of a doctoral dissertation does not fit well the academic duty of having to come to an end. In my own experience, a line of virtualities crossed the path towards that end and broadened it with new requirements. In particular, while I was starting an ending part which in reality was not a conclusion—one of the case studies still went on and I was also fully involved in its activities—a quotation of Gilles Deleuze and Félix Guattari (1987) came to highlight a region of the research that had remained in the shadows until then. The quotation belonged to *A Thousand Plateaus.* I had read it before but had not made complete sense of its implications:

> Assemblages are passional, they are compositions of desire. Desire has nothing to do with a natural or spontaneous determination; there is no desire but assembling, assembled, desire. The rationality, the efficiency, of an assemblage does not exist without the passions the assemblage brings into play, without the desires that constitute it as much as it constitutes them.
>
> *(p. 399)*

The title of my Ph.D dissertation is *Aesthetics of the audio-visual screening. Assembly, fiction and right to the city in Poble Sec, Barcelona.*[1] I defended it in January of 2018. It explores the aesthetic, political and pedagogical practice of two collectives arisen from the 15M Movement[2] and located in the same area: The Occupy Poble Sec Cinema Forum (OPSC) and the Fiction Workshop (FW). Both turned the screening of images into the primary method for their events, using a fluid filmic apparatus to get and move through several spots in the neighbourhood (see Castro-Varela, 2018b). Besides being a member of the two collectives and co-founder of the latter, I also carried out an ethnography from 2012 to 2014 about their mode of doing and existing. Such anthropological study was focused on the assemblage of human and nonhuman entities needed for supporting them. The fragile but also careful socio-material shape that they took, as well as the paradoxes and tensions they had collectively to deal with, led me to refer to that form of existence as 'in-common'.

The film sessions organized by the OPSC from January to July of 2012, and by the FW from the spring of 2012 to the fall of 2014, sought to produce collective knowledge within several social centres and public institutions of Poble Sec. The projection of a fiction or documentary film, in the case of the OPSC; and of short movies addressed to urbanistic issues, in the case of the FW, usually gave rise to a public debate in a circle. During these meetings, the just-seen sequences were discussed and *translated* to the current political situation. In the OPSC sessions, for instance, Twenty Years is Nothing (*Veinte años no es nada*, Joaquim Jordà, 2005) led to consider how political struggles had been damped down during the Spanish transition to democracy and subsequently ignored in later official accounts; and Videograms of a Revolution (Ujica & Farocki, 1992) was chosen to look at the production of symbolic violence in the 2012 general strike, the largest in Spain during the recent economic crisis.

Both collectives led the 15M political sphere—settled in Poble Sec from July of 2011 through a popular assembly—to connect better with the everyday life of the neighbourhood. The public also gathered heterogeneous people and groups, some of them ideologically dissimilar to the very movement. On the one hand, issues such as the Spanish Transition to democracy, the political meaning of a strike in that crisis context, or the notions of public space and coexistence concerning a remodelled square of Poble Sec, were brought up for discussion through the viewing of a film. On the other hand, the dark room where that film was screened—and which could be an auditorium, a meeting room, or a kitchen—gave way to the transformation of the audience into participants of a kind of open classroom. This practice was in tune with the tradition of filmic pedagogies, according to which the cinema becomes a school that brings the real closer and allows to think it better (Daney, 2004). Besides, it heavily relied on the meeting and alliance of manifold spatial, technical, and bodily pieces.

On this point, *assemblage* is a concept which I had learnt from Actor-Network Theory (ANT) (Callon, 1987; Latour, 2005). In contrast with a 'science of the social' that always draws on external 'social factors' to explain specific matters of fact (Latour, 2005, pp. 1–17), my research looked to trace the associations taking place in and around audio-visual screenings, as well as the ambivalences and controversies distinguishing a particular form of existence on their own. In broad terms, this was the agenda of issues that I resolved to tackle during the fieldwork:

> My ethnographic approach to both case studies aimed to explore in depth the entanglement that the film screenings gave rise to. This meant firstly recognizing which actors—human and non-human—took part in them, and what agency—understood as the power to create or modify a given situation—each

actor had in running them. Other questions arose on the heels of this general one: how ideas and discourses were related to the construction and existence of the OPSC and FW, and to what extent what they did can also be understood as ideas and modes of being in themselves; how the screenings provoked disagreements or discussions about the relationships constituting the daily life of the neighbourhood, and what relational politics the screenings in turn involved; what kind of space-temporalities enabled the production of and were produced by the OPSC and FW activities; what divergences, approaches or openings took place between the case studies, the context of the Poble Sec people's assembly and the whole area; and lastly, what traces were left by the novelty of this aesthetic-cum-political assemblage.

(Castro-Varela, 2018a, pp. 32–33).

A matter of affects

At the end of the writing I started to grasp some limitations related to the ANT onto-epistemic and methodological perspective. One of them had precisely to do with the existential features of the screenings, of which I had just given a thorough account for three chapters. In the OPSC and FW sessions, the way of tying the projection of the movie and the following debate, the filmic contents and the urban or political problematics translated from them, the devices and the screening venues, the bodies and the furniture, and all of this with each other, not only stemmed from a matter of connectivity. It also entailed a common sensibility while and for achieving it. The importance of care practices in order to manage the precarity of the technical apparatus, the length of the sessions or the places for meeting and screening—whose conditions were far from being as comfortable and immersive as those of a conventional cinema—required shared, collective forces always going on. It was not just to play a film, but to prepare food and drinks, set up the room, energize the debate, and create a proper atmosphere for staying at ease for two or three hours.

Thus, that mode of existence fed on a *sympoeitic*—i.e. 'partnered all the way down' (Haraway, 2016, p. 33)—display of energy. And to some extent, this feature was at odds with the ANT tendency to usually approach the formation and functioning of stable forms of association. The affective and reproductive forces needed for supporting those forms—specially assemblages which, as in the case of OPSC and FW, had to undergo a persistent fragility—were not taken sufficiently into consideration in Bruno Latour's or Michel Callon's view. Precisely in both case studies a shared existence taking place in and around the screenings of images went through a regular tension between fluidity and vulnerability, spatial appropriation and maintenance, collective dispositions and arrangements that should start almost every time from scratch. If care practices—understood in a broad sense—were crucial for holding that socio-material entanglement with *feet of clay*, which affects held in turn the determination for restarting the whole process once and again? Or should we talk better about a form of reciprocity?

84 Aurelio Castro-Varela

In any case, the ANT's kind of *actualism*, which I noticed when revising the experiences of OPSC and FW, was criticized too, by other theoretical approaches to the concept of assemblage:

> Via the labour of tracing associations actor-network theory seeks to relate humans and non-humans in their co-production of the world, and in this work of relating the properties of parts – objects, artefacts, technical practices, humans, and so on – form *logically necessary* relations in the constitution of an actor-network. In DeLanda's vocabulary the actor-network becomes a 'seamless whole' that fully assimilates its component parts; nothing stands outside the descriptions that actor-network theory performs (Hetherington and Law, 2000: 128; Lee and Brown, 1994). The problem is that seeing entities as fully determined by their present relations makes it difficult to understand the efficacy of 'parts' by making the relational configuration into a homogeneous whole.
>
> *(Anderson & al., 2012, p. 179).*

The association of entities happening during the OPSC and FW sessions also challenged the idea of a 'seamless whole': The fragility of that order led us to be constantly keeping it on track through varying tasks of care. We could compare it to an 'ontological choreography' (Thompson, 2005) which utilizes a dynamic coordination for performing a kind of filmic relational dance. Was the desire of being together, within and despite of that precarity, the fuel for setting that dance in motion? Or was this dance a consequence of that desire? Perhaps both things at the same time?

Throughout the dissertation, I did offer several descriptions of the affective reactions of the audience during the screenings. These descriptions drew on the understanding of Raymond Bellour (2013) of filmic spectatorship as a kind of hypnotic circuit between the viewers and the movie. In particular, he refers to the 'affective attunement' which takes place at the cinema and goes beyond discrete emotions such as anger, happiness, disappointment, fear, surprise, etc. Following the psychologist Daniel Stern (1985), Bellour considers these 'vitality affects'— instead of categorical ones—those which mobilize the encounter between the body of the spectators and the visual corporeality of a film. While with the category affects, 'for some time and especially since Darwin, we have wished to give human emotions a recognizable meaning', on the other hand vitality affects involve 'the expressive translation of an interior feeling' and are aroused by 'changes in state, appetites and motivational tensions' (Bellour, 2013, pp. 171–172). Stern himself (1985, p. 80), cited by Bellour (2013), defines them as follows: 'There are a thousand smiles, a thousand getting-out-of-chairs, a thousand variations of performance of any and all movements, and each one presents a different vitality affect'.

In line with Bellour's framework, the final thesis report sought to expose *dynamically* the play of actions and reactions between the screen and the audience: Sighs and laughs, murmurs and silences, modulations of breathing in a sign of attention, etc. However, such attempts did not expand on the moments surrounding the projections, for instance the spatial production of each event or the dialogical activities to which the screenings gave rise. This transfilmic flow of affects remained *off-camera*. In this chapter, I do not seek to fill that gap but to rethink it as a virtuality at the end of the research—i.e., as a potentiality that still is coming into being. In this respect, feminist affect theories help me glimpse the passions that constituted, inasmuch as they were constituted by *in-common* assemblages. I look back as a way of looking forward with another lens. But this work cannot be untangled from the main becoming which I experienced during the fieldwork: going researcher.

Going researcher

No virtuality would be properly thought without reference to the *contorted position* I had to adopt while approaching both case studies. As I explain in this section, this contortion was in fact the becoming after which any possibility could come.

I got involved with the Poble Sec neighbourhood assembly as a resident rather than as an ethnographer, subsequently joining the coordinating group of the OPSC in January 2012 and helping to organize the film sessions until they ended in July of that year. By then I was also writing a Ph.D thesis project on the aesthetics of audiovisual screenings, and so I started to consider—and finally decided on—the inclusion of the cinema forum as a case study. Something similar occurred with the second case study, the Fiction Workshop—a film activist collective formed in 2012 thanks to a grant from the Sala d'Art Jove[3]—although on this occasion I already knew, along with my colleagues, that my Ph.D research would study our practice. The fact is that I was a member of the two groups before approaching them ethnographically.

That ethnographic contortion also emerged after having re-imagined the classic scene of the field encounter, based on a clear distinction between natives and researcher. But this re-imagining did not happen in terms of the 'epistemic partnership' suggested by Douglas R. Holmes and George E. Marcus (2008; cf. Marcus, 2013) and followed by Adolfo Estalella and Tomás Sánchez Criado (2016) and others (see Corsín Jiménez & Estalella, 2016; Corsín Jiménez, 2014; Lafuente et al., 2013) writing on 15M Movement contexts and groups. Though my recursive engagement with both case studies did imply a kind of experimental fieldwork, it did not consist of a 'theoretical innovation' (Rappaport, 2008) nor a coproduction of ethnographic knowledge. The OPSC and FW sessions already attempted to produce situated knowledge based on anyone's participation, and it was this shared condition, rather than expertise, which had constructed my relationship with the projects from the outset. In return, ethnography could offer an account of their trajectory and mode of existence and, first and foremost, a piece of memory taken from its practice at work; for if politics is about people who have no time to do it (see Rancière, 2004, pp. 42–45), then the description of how it is practised seems to be doubly asynchronous.

On the one hand, I was already a native, and therefore access to, and participation in, the actors' dynamics and relationships were easily achieved. On the other hand, this put my research into a state of perpetual precariousness. 'If […] we attempt often to "walk the margins" that separate ourselves as researchers from those whom we research', Valli Kanuha (2000, p. 441) argues, 'the native researcher is the margin'. It was for this reason that, rather than going native, the epistemological design of the study was conceptualised as *going researcher*, that is, shuttling back and forth continuously between the two positions: Sometimes sharing in the coordinating group's tasks and concerns for each session, and sometimes viewing the OPSC and FW activities as an otherness whose functioning transcended my participation. The usual ethnographic tension between the roles of observer and participant (Adler & Adler, 1994) turned into a slalom requiring, on my part, a situated understanding rather than a distanced gaze.

The advantage of having unfettered access to the groups' practice as a participant entailed some trouble in setting a research schedule exterior to that process. Firstly, my fieldwork often had to overcome a constant lack of time[4]. I could only be present as a co-organizer of the events and then, for the movie, as a regular spectator. The adoption of a low profile during the film projections responded to the decision of not disturbing the audience. I always tried to place myself at a point— usually in the background or near to the entrance—from which I could perceive what was happening in the rest of the room. But that was all. Starting with the screenings and continuing with the preparations for the sessions or debates that followed, I was empirically positioned in the same place as both native and researcher. Or rather, the latter remained embedded in the former.

Despite that overlap, the issues involved by the two roles were different. If the native was worried—together with his fellows—about which movie to show, who to invite to the debate, the availability of a specific public site or the technical arrangements needed for a public square, the researcher approached the means and connections through which these actions were carried out and, in this regard, the mode of existence sustaining the whole practice. If the OCPS and FW experienced controversies, I had to take a stand in them since I was a member of both groups; but as an ethnographer I sought to trace the terms in which they arose and developed.

After the sessions, I had to inhabit a room of my own to arrive at an understanding of how the screenings had been assembled. Reviewing the dozens of emails sent in organizing each event helped me to grasp more clearly what concerns had guided the preparation of the encounters and to which joints attention should be paid. It was not about seeing everything, but rather about seeing better, especially the connections. In this way, going back to the OCPS and FW meeting minutes and virtual exchanges made me entirely go researcher of their (our) assemblages. But in doing so I also put aside the passions driving and brought into life by the very process of assembling. I could focus on them during the screenings because, as a simple spectator, I was free to immerse myself in the situation and perceive how the film scenes were affecting the audience. Apart from this, the native participant condition, added to the effort of going researcher by tracing associations, did not give me room for expanding on affective issues. So this is what comes—as virtuality—after that becoming.

Approaching transfilmic affects

Anna Hickey-Moody (2016) has re-read 'through a feminist lens' (p. 258) the concept of *affectus* which Deleuze (1990, 1998, 2003) takes from Spinoza. In so doing, she looks to understand better the posthuman material exchanges raised through artistic practices. In her perspective, art is always pedagogical since it affects us and provides us with new ways of seeing, feeling and engaging with reality. Hickey-Moody also considers that 'practices of art production, ways of seeing, spaces and places of viewing are plugged into one another and aug-mented' (Ibid., p. 259). This understanding fits the experience of OPSC and FW but cannot be limited to the agency of the screen. Even if the projection of films played a central role during the sessions, preparative meetings, the dis-semination of the event, the organization of the spaces, the arrangement of the filmic apparatus, the distribution of furniture, the bodily and dialogical activities following the movie, or final cleanings, were also part of the artistic process. I call *transfilmic affects* to the driving forces of that in-common mode of doing, in the sense that they simultaneously included and exceeded the space-time of screenings.

These transfilmic affects were also related to a kind of *affective climate* spread out by the 15M Movement in several areas of Barcelona, including Poble Sec. I described that ambience at the beginning of the dissertation in the following way: 'As if fellowship—the affect that puts us close and in sight within the neighbour-hood from and after the 15M Movement—had as reverse angle the persistence of a kind of anonymity' (Castro-Varela, 2018a, p. 49). An OPSC participant also recalls it as based on an increasing capacity of acting, that is, as *affectus*: 'All of a sudden the neighbourhood was happiness and tenderness. It was about meeting up at the public space and think about how we were capable of doing everything. Now we want a vegetable garden, an athenaeum, a square, a festivity. I remember the feeling of everything becoming possible' (Ibid., p. 218).

How could this located affective climate, in general, and particularly the flow of affects co-constituting the OPSC and FW assemblages, be approached by ethno-graphy? If events are by definition *that* escaping pre-existing representational frames and bringing, according to Dennis Atkinson (2012), 'a disturbance, a rupture, a puncturing of ways of understanding or acting' (p. 6), was not that climate *eventful* by stirring up a collective desire of learning and assembling? How to refer then to that *eventfulness*? At the same time, how was that desire sustained and intensified through new assemblages and learning processes (such as the OPSC's and FW's)? And concerning the transfilmic affects, how should they be brought forth, descri-bed, and accounted for? I try to outline a brief, virtual way of responding to these methodological questions keeping in mind that categorial terms, as in the case of spectatorship, are not suitable to affections. That outline draws (for now) on general orientations from Kathleen Stewart's (2007) and Elizabeth de Freitas' (2018) approaches.

On the one hand, Stewart defines ordinary affects as 'something' that 'throws itself together in a moment as an event and a sensation' (2007, p. 1). Also, this 'something' does not work through meanings. It lies instead on the intensities that it builds, and on the thoughts and feelings that it makes possible:

> The question they beg is not what they might mean in an order of representations, or whether they are good or bad in an overarching scheme of things, but where they might go and what potential modes of knowing, relating, and attending to things are already somehow present in them in a state of potentiality and resonance.
>
> *(p. 3)*

Thus, Stewart's ethnographic account of affects consists in performing in writing some of their intensity and texture. She focuses on the pressure points and forms of attention and attachment which organize the ordinary. From that perspective, everyday things become 'tentative though forceful compositions of disparate and moving elements' (p. 6). For instance, 'the watching and waiting for an event to unfold, the details of scenes, the strange or predictable progression in which one thing leads to another, the still life that gives pause, the resonance that lingers, the lines along which signs rush and form relays, the layering of immanent experience' (Ibid.). Many literary and philosophical models—such as Laurent Berlant's books, Ian McEwan's *Atonement* (2001) or Roland Barthes' *A Lover's Discourse* (1978)—aided Stewart in weaving that textual contact zone.

Elizabeth de Freitas (2018), on the other hand, proposes the notion of 'transindividual sympathy' for thinking of the flow of affects crossing a posthuman learning ecology. That flow precedes and goes beyond the mere individual existence of people inhabiting any ecosystem. 'Transindividual sympathy' means a 'making with' giving rise to a 'process of becoming other that does not erase the other' (p. 5). According to de Freitas, 'one can identify three pivotal processes at work in sympathy—a *contagion* of feeling, a *common sense* or shared sensibility, and a *compassion* for the other entailing "response-ability"' (p. 6). It is important to remark that such agreement does not mean 'erasure of distinctive manner' (p. 7). Mapping strategies as a form of experimenting with the real and a way of following affects 'in their twisting, braiding and knotting emergence' (p. 2) are called to make us grasp that sympathetic dimension. However, they fail in case of not recognizing, or just equalizing, degrees of power.

De Freitas' understanding puts affects as capable of circulating across bodily reactions. It means that transindividual sympathy relies on minor movements contributing to 'passionate attachments': 'In other words, the micro-ethnographic scale plugs into the transdividual scale of the collective endeavour' (p. 8). How can visual maps approach this complex affective milieu? She considers the potential of sensor technologies in mapping such ecology—especially if it has to do with learning—subverting thereby the use that normative science and control society have made of them. Biosensors entail a 'wordily sensibility' which registers atmospheric affects, sensations and intensities going on below the bandwidth of human consciousness. Also, the maps arising from this data can show a multiplicity of heterogeneous flows beyond the 'directional, irreversible arrow of time' (p. 15). The affective activity remains therefore outside the timescale of the human and needs to be relinked to 'the power of thought and *intensive matter*' (Ibid.).

Both Stewart and de Freitas provide methodological orientations to research transfilmic or other kinds of affects. They are sensitive events rather than meanings. They have to be followed in their leaps and intensities, rather than represented. They circulate across bodies and connect, in doing so, minor matter movements, passionate attachments and atmospheric milieus. A performative writing and/or a biosensitive mapping are also proposed as tentative tools for experimenting with and enacting that affective territory.

When the end comes

When a doctoral dissertation comes to an end, it is supposed to be grounded on, give an account of, and/or guarantee the author becoming a Ph.D In this chapter I explore what comes after that becoming as a virtuality—that is, as a potentiality that has not been actualised yet. In my case, the ethnographic tracing of OPSC and FW screening assemblages left quite aside an understanding of them as desiring compositions. This blind corner also stems from the process of going researcher, which I carried out from 2012 to 2014. Being a member of both case studies implied that I had to deal with a constant lack of time for developing an ethnography about them. Any research needs to adjust the means on which it counts and the aims it addresses. This fitting implies that some onto-epistemic and methodological potentialities do not find room to come into being. My point is that even though they are not actual, they are real (Deleuze, 1995, pp. 208–214) and need to be taken as part of the whole project.

Finally, I have outlined a possible approach to transfilmic affects, so-called because they crossed the assemblages of the two case studies during, around and beyond the film projections. I had paid exclusive attention to the reactions of spectators and disregarded that passionate envelope, as well as the *climate* that brought to Poble Sec a collective desire for learning and assembling. Affects have no 'respect for or knowledge of [...] the boundary between the self and the world' (Kluchin, 2012, p. 1). Neither respect for representational knowledge, I would add. Kathleen Stewart and Elizabeth de Freitas offer in this sense methodological orientations to deal with that opacity without turning it into categorial transparency. When the end comes, it is time to get in new old troubles.

Notes

1 Close to Barcelona's historic centre and flanked by the mountain of Montjuïc and Parallel Avenue, Poble Sec is a seventy-acres neighbourhood of the district of Sants-Montjuïc.
2 The *Indignados* or 15M Movement was a grassroots protest movement demanding a radical change in the Spanish democracy after the 2008 crisis. It began in May of 2011 with thousands of mainly young people occupying the central squares of several cities. In June the occupation of Plaça Catalunya in Barcelona came to a close and dispersed to the neighbourhoods, creating local area assemblies. One of these was formed in Poble Sec.
3 'Sala d'Art Jove is a Government of Catalonia facility which runs a series of experimental processes intended to interrelate artistic practice, work with young people, arts education and cultural production'. Retrieved from http://oriolfontdevila.net/sala-dart-jove/
4 In the case of OPSC, I had to write many fieldnotes sometime after helping to run the film sessions. With the first screenings this was several weeks later, approximately in June 2012. After autumn I began to revise and complete my field diary by interviewing six different people: Three of them also members of the organising group, and three spectators. By then I also informed the committee of my intention to turn the OPSC activities into a case study for the thesis, to which they kindly agreed.

References

Adler, P., & Adler, P.A. (1994). Observational Techniques. In N.K. Denzin & Y. Lincoln (Eds.), *Handbook of Qualitative Research* (pp. 377–392). Sage.

Anderson, B., Kearnes, M., McFarlane, C. & Swanton, D. (2012). On Assemblages and Geography. *Dialogues in Human Geography*, 2 (2), 171–189. doi:10.1177/2043820612449261.

Atkinson, D. (2012). Contemporary Art and Art in Education: The New, Emancipation and Truth. *International Journal of Art & Design Education*, 31 (1), 5–18. doi:10.1111/j.1476-8070.2012.01724.

Bellour, R. (2013). *El Cuerpo del Cine: Hipnosis, Emociones, Animalidades*. Shangrila Textos Aparte.

Callon, M. (1987). Society in the Making: The Study of Technology as a Tool for Sociological Analysis. In W.E. Bijker, T.P. Hughes & T. Pinch (Eds.), *The Social Construction of Technological Systems: New Directions in the Sociology and History of Technology* (pp. 83–103). MIT Press.

Castro-Varela, A. (2018a). *Estética de la Proyección Audiovisual. Asamblea, Ficción y Derecho a la Ciudad en Poble Sec, Barcelona* (Doctoral dissertation, University of Barcelona, Barcelona, Spain). Retrieved from http://hdl.handle.net/10803/461980.

Castro-Varela, A. (2018b). 'Going Researcher' in the Occupy Poble Sec Cinema Forum: Listening to the Screenings and Tracing a Fluid Assemblage of Learning and Care. *Ethnography and Education Journal*, 13 (3), 396–412. doi:10.1080/17457823.2018.1448999.

Corsín Jiménez, A. (2014). The Right to Infrastructure: A Prototype for Open Source Urbanism. *Environment and Planning D: Society and Space*, 32 (2), 342–362. doi:10.1068/d13077p.

Corsín Jiménez, A., & Estalella, A. (2013). Asambleas al Aire: La Arquitectura Ambulatoria de una Política en Suspensión. *Revista de Antropología Experimental*, 13, 73–88. Retrieved from http://hdl.handle.net/10261/85038.

Corsín Jiménez, A., & Estalella, A. (2016). Ecologies in Beta: The City as Infrastructure of Apprenticeships. In P. Harvey, C.B. Jensen & A. Morita (Eds.), *Infrastructure and Social Complexity: A Routledge Companion* (pp. 141–156). Routledge.

Daney, S. (2004). *Cine, Arte del Presente*. Santiago Arcos Editor.

De Freitas, E. (2018, October). *The Multidimensional Mapping of Transindividual Sympathy*. Paper presented at the Cartographic Approaches to Teachers' Corporeal, Ecological and Nomadic Learning Conference, Fundació Tàpies, Barcelona, Spain.

Deleuze, G. (1990). *The Logic of Sense*. Colombia University Press.

Deleuze, G. (1995). *Difference and Repetition*. Colombia University Press.

Deleuze, G. (1998). *Spinoza: Practical Philosophy*. City Light Books.

Deleuze, G. (2003). *Francis Bacon: The Logic of Sensation*. University of Minnesota Press.

Deleuze, G. & Guattari, F. (1987). *A Thousand Plateaus*. University of Minnesota Press.

Estalella, A. & Sánchez Criado, T. (2016). Experimentación Etnográfica: Infraestructuras de Campo y Re-aprendizajes de la Antropología. *Revista de Dialectología y Tradiciones Populares*, lxxi (1), 9–30. doi:10.3989/rdtp.2016.01.001.01.

Haraway, D. (2016). *Staying with the Trouble. Making Kin in the Chthulucene*. Duke University Press.

Hetherington, K., & Law, J. (2000). After Networks. *Environment and Planning D: Society and Space*, 18, 127–132. doi:doi:10.1068/d216t

Hickey-Moody, A. (2016). A Femifesta for Posthuman Art Education: Visions and Becomings. In C.A. Taylor & C. Hughes (Eds.), *Posthuman Research Practices in Education* (pp. 258–266). Springer.

Holmes, D.R. & Marcus, G.E. (2008). Collaboration Today and the Re-imagination of the Classic Scene of Fieldwork Encounter. *Collaborative Anthropologies*, 1 (1), 81–101. doi:10.1353/cla.0.0003.

Jordà, J. (Director). (2005). *Veinte Años no es Nada* [Twenty Years is Nothing] [Film]. Ovideo.

Kanuha, V.K. (2000). 'Being' Native Versus 'Going Native': Conducting Social Work Research as an Insider. *Social Work*, 45 (5), 439–447. doi:10.1093/sw/45.5.439.

Kluchin, A.S. (2012). *The Allure of Affect: Rigor, Style, and Unintelligibility in Kristeva and Irigaray*. (Doctoral Dissertation, Columbia University, New York, USA). doi:10.7916/D86D5R1G.

Lafuente, A., Alonso, A., & Rodríguez, J. (2013). *¡Todos Sabios! Ciencia Ciudadana y Conocimiento Expandido*. Cátedra.

Latour, B. (2005). *Reassembling the Social: An Introduction to Actor-Network-Theory*. Oxford University Press.

Lee, N., & Brown, S. (1994). Otherness and the Actor Network: The Undiscovered Continent. *American Behavioural Scientist*, 37 (6): 772–790. doi:doi:10.1177/0002764294037006005

Marcus, G.E. (2013). Experimental Forms for the Expression of Norms in the Ethnography of the Contemporary. *Hau: Journal of Ethnographic Theory*, 3 (2), 197–217. doi:10.14318/hau3.2.011.

Massumi, B. (1987). Translator's Foreword: Pleasures of Philosophy. In G. Deleuze and F. Guattari, *A Thousand Plateaus* (pp. ix–xv). University of Minnesota Press.

Rancière, J. (2004). *The Politics of Aesthetics. The Distribution of the Sensible*. Continuum.

Rappaport, J. (2008). Beyond Participant Observation: Collaborative Ethnography as Theoretical Innovation. *Collaborative Anthropologies*, 1 (1), 1–31. doi:10.1353/cla.0.0014.

Stern, D. (1985). *The Interpersonal World of the Infant: A View from Psychoanalysis and Developmental Psychology*. Basic Books.

Stewart, K. (2007). *Ordinary Affects*. Duke University Press.

Thompson, C. (2005). *Making Parents: The Ontological Choreography of Reproductive Technologies*. MIT Press.

Ujica, A. & Farocki, H. (Directors). (1992). *Videogramme einer Revolution* [Videograms of a Revolution] [Film]. Bremer Institut Film & Fernsehen; Harun Farocki Filmproduktion.

8

AN ETHNOGRAPHIC RESEARCH BASED ON AN ONTOLOGY OF BECOMING

Judit Onsès-Segarra

Introduction

Can a Ph.D thesis be built like a rhizome, like a living map? It made more sense to me first of all, because the thesis that this chapter talks about was developed when I still did not know that I wanted to carry out a doctoral dissertation, so it began as an extension and growth of an already existing rhizome. And secondly because it shows the developed processes of research in a state of becoming.

Drawing on Deleuze and Guattari's concept of becoming, I carried out research and defended a doctoral thesis (Onsès, 2018) developed rhizomatically, within which I explored the potentialities of visual documentation of learning phenomena in primary school, as well as alternatives in research and educational fields. The research was linked to European project *Do It Yourself in Education: Expanding Digital Competence to Foster Student Agency and Collaborative Learning* (DIYLab).[1] It connected with the aim of the project to expand students' digital competence, agency, and creativity, and involved two groups of pupils between ten and eleven years old from Barcelona (Spain). The fieldwork consisted of several different sessions in which different groups of children visually documented their learning processes while I visually recorded how they were recording and learning.

The objective was to escape from dichotomous thinking and representational logic, proposing the research and educational phenomena instead as an entanglement in which subjects, objects, spaces, concepts, times and thoughts affected continuously and were affected by each other, (re)configuring the phenomenon itself. According to Onsès & Hernández-Hernández (2017), during the research, 'the subjects were inseparable from visual documentation because they became subjects in an involving process of documentation' (p. 63), in which children and ethnographer embroiled in an ontology of becoming. Thus, the research and the

Ontology of becoming and ethnographic research **93**

evolution of the dissertation were understood as an open system, as a tentative work, in which future lines of research were pointed out; a Ph.D research for learning and daring, understanding inquiry as an adventure.

The concept of rhizome has been taken from Deleuze & Guattari (1987) who, in turn, took it from botany and reterritorialized it in philosophy. They are interested in the concept of rhizome (and I am) because 'itself assumes very diverse forms, from ramified surface extension in all directions to concretion into bulbs and tubers' (p. 7); since

> any point of a rhizome can be connected to anything other, and must be … A rhizome ceaselessly establishes connections between semiotic chains, organizations of power, and circumstances relative to the arts, sciences, and social struggles.
>
> *(Ibid., p. 7)*

If I understand thought as a rhizome, if thinking behaves like a rhizome, if ideas and experiences make rhizome, I could only think about the research and Ph.D thesis from there. So the report showed how during my four-year Ph.D, my life, the ethnographic fieldwork I carried out in a primary school and the writing became entangled. Namely, what I lived, what I learned, what was thought and thinkable, what I knew and what is about to be known was narrated and assembled in a continuum way. That involved risk and experimentation. It required a do-on-the-go attitude, a state of becoming, to be in the rhizome. It meant being open to new connections that could occur in doing fieldwork and mapping in the writing in the same rhizome making. In a research like this, ethnographers have to be predisposed to the fact that the investigation and also themselves can be broken, altered, 'connectable … adapted to any kind of mounting [of texts, of images, with] multiple entryways, [with their] lines of flight' (Deleuze and Guattari, 1987, p. 7, my claudators). That thesis intended to be like Deleuze's connection maps,

> a map meant for those who want to *do* something with respect to new uncommon forces, which we don't quite yet grasp, who have a certain taste for the unknown, for what is not already determined by history or society.
>
> *(Rajchman, 2000, p. 6, emphasis in original)*

Thus, not only would the thesis grow like a rhizome, but I would grow with it, as I too was part of the rhizome. I had also allowed myself to break, to get upset, to connect, to reconfigure myself, to let 'things' in and out, to be carried away or not by lines of flight and, above all, to have 'a trust that something may come out though one is not yet completely sure what' (Rajchman, 2000, p. 7). Developing a thesis rhizomatically entailed adopting a state of becoming, a processual and always in transformation/creation work. And this for me was very liberating, challenging and exciting.

Towards an ontology of becoming

This chapter focuses on the concept of becoming taken from Deleuze's ontology of becoming (Carlin & Wallin, 2014; Coleman & Ringrose, 2013). It is because it connects with the spacestimematterings[2] (Barad, 2007; 2010; 2014) of a research based on this specific ontological approach. It presents an understanding of reality as multiplicities, groupings that move and change because they affect and are affected by other multiplicities. Reality consists of assemblages of forces, intensities, and velocities. Entanglements of intra-actions[3] constantly reconfiguring themselves. All this leads, on the one hand, to an understanding of the subject and subjectivity, not as fixed entities, and attributes, but as a nomadic (Braidotti, 2015). According to jagodzinski (2014), 'the ontology of becoming emerges as a chance event that actualizes Being' (p. 22). On the other hand, to research that no longer focuses on subjects and things, but on the relationships and movements created.

Therefore, it means to understand the subject as an I-multiple-in-relationship and in constant change, moving in a reality also multiple and in constant change. Reality is presented as unfinished, indeterminate and open (Coleman & Ringrose, 2013), which considers for the research more than the facts, processes, forces and movements that affect and force different ways of thinking. Becoming promotes a type of research that, more than looking at what has happened, looks and searches for potentialities, for what is about to happen (Lara, 2015; Carlin & Wallin, 2014). Hence, we can ask: How ethnographers could embody an ontology of becoming in our research? How could we walk towards a state of becoming in our inquiry processes? How we may 'become-in-research'?

Becoming in research

Living the educational research rhizomatically invites us to a change of state, a change of attitude and gaze. For everything to flow and frameworks of thought not clashing too much with research in education, this change is necessary. But where do we focus? What changes does this onto-epistemology propose?

Atkinson, for example, invites us to adopt a state of *wander*, of *wonder*, and of *what if*. According to the author, the normative, pre-established and fixed does not allow real learning, does not allow to go beyond what we already know in research. What precipitates learning is the 'feeling of wonder we experience when we are confronted with something, we find strange, when we encounter something that is inexplicable or surprising' (Atkinson, 2011, p. 22). And he follows: 'this passionate state is what precipitates a search for understanding' (Ibid., p. 23). 'The site of real learning is a place of wonder, uncertainty and experiment' (Ibid., p. 163), and it is crucial if we are doing research differently from the pre-established. And this is what the becoming in research as a rhizome proposes. Continuing with this author, 'Whereas conformal propositions perpetuate a stable, social order non-conformal propositions constitute an adventure, a

Ontology of becoming and ethnographic research **95**

wandering and a wondering, without clear sight of an outcome' (Atkinson, 2018, p. 80).

To adopt a state of *wonder* is understood as letting oneself be surprised, taking an interrogating attitude, open to the thinkable and the not yet thinkable. Do not worry about reaching a concrete end but rather let yourself be carried away and go through the circumstances, reconfiguring yourself in them, having the conviction that research always leads you somewhere and creates new knowledge. Similarly, we are also invited to adopt a *wandering* state, referred to as that in which we allow ourselves to wander through the planes of reality, through the spacetimematterings to which Barad refers. Thus, taking the educational theories of Atkinson (2018), we can think of becoming in research as 'an on-going series of relational forces precipitating wanderings, pondering, lines and shapes. Territorializing—deterritorializing—reterritorializing on different planes, a proliferation into not-yet-known spaces and times, rich in potential' (p. 59). This quote invites us to think about ethnography in a very different way. On the one hand, from the relational point of view, from the connections and their relations of forces of power and desire. On the other hand, to pay attention to how these precipitate a diverse erratic and reflexive walk, which opens us to new lines and forms, to new ways of thinking, saying, feeling and living that from the pre-established and prescribed would not be possible.

We are required to open ourselves to the unknown. Because in research, it is challenging for us to recognize that ethnographers do not need to have answers to everything, nor can they have everything under control. Precisely Atkinson (2011, 2018) invites us to pay attention to the gaps, to what we do not know because, according to this author, it is precisely from those unknowns that we can create real learning, necessary to generate knowledge. Stability does not allow movement or create knowledge. The dynamic, instead, what moves (and moves us) does so because not knowing pushes us to want to know, to ask ourselves, to explore and experiment. It forces us to move away from our frameworks of thought.

And here we can ask ourselves, why in our day-to-day research do we not allow ourselves to take these directions and attitudes? If we have detected the tensions, contradictions, problems and limitations of our current onto-epistemology and methodology in research, why not explore other ways of doing? Thinking about research from a state of becoming invites us to take other paths and other ways of thinking about research. And at this point, a third element is added to confront becoming-in-research: To adopt a 'what if attitude'. According to Löytönen (2017, p. 6, italics in original) 'thinking in rhizomes will be done through the speculative question of *what-if*. This is because, according to her

> the *what-if* question is tentative, open, and partial, drawing attention to connections, movement (flux), and the constant becoming of things (see also St. Pierre, 2013). Hence, the *what-if* questions open toward questioning educational certainties and expanding difference and creation in pedagogy and educational development
>
> *(Ibid., pp. 6–7, italics in original)*

96 Judit Onsès-Segarra

Likewise, St. Pierre (1997, p. 370) talks about the nomadic ethnographer by saying that

> A nomadic ethnographer might, for instance, appear in one local space and then another without defining transitions and paths to connect those points into a fiercely ordered grid of striations. A nomadic ethnographer speeding within connections and conduits and multiplicities might gnaw a smooth space to extend her territory (the field grows)… She might be more interested in the surprising intensity of an event than in the familiar serenity of essence.

Becoming in research allows openness, creating questions and new lines of thought and action. It invites ethnographers to let themselves be surprised by the subjects in research, by the spaces, times and matter. To let themselves be carried away by circumstances. It is to know oneself part of the rhizome-research. Not only not to resist unforeseen and last-minute changes, but to take them as an opportunity for learning-in-the-researching; incorporate them into the research process; be open to the unexpected and spread this attitude throughout the research community. As jagodzinski (sic) states, 'there are no "guarantees" when it comes to "becoming"' (2014, p. 17). And this is the real power and potentiality of it.

Becoming-Ph.D thesis

Doing a dissertation based on an ontology of becoming entailed to approach research differently. In this case reflected in: Putting at work theory; the conversation with authors; reporting the fieldwork; the writing process; and the structure of the doctoral dissertation. What follows are some decisions made in the realisation of a Ph.D thesis.

The thesis as a worktable

The development of the dissertation consisted of having year after year a more significant accumulation of short texts without order, some conference papers, few papers in the process to be published and lots and lots of doubts. The entanglement was too big. I was lost in threads, ideas, memoirs, materials, readings, connections, experiences, questions, concepts, abstractions, maps… Few months before delivering the report, I still had in my computer dozens of folders and documents full of fragments and little texts without any sense nor order. There was not a clear table of contents. I was trying to make a puzzle that I knew had many pieces missing, and many pieces left over.

In front of that *mess*, and thinking and looking for papers related to cartographies, during the process of writing and thinking about the Ph.D thesis, I recovered Aby Warburg and his *Atlas Mnemosyne*. Didi-Huberman (2010) connected that artwork with the concept of a worktable. This idea helped me to think of the becoming-dissertation as a worktable too, by accepting that all that entangled

Ontology of becoming and ethnographic research **97**

material was indeed what the research wanted to be(come). The thesis was shaped by doing it, so as I was writing a specific section, I imagined that what would follow would have its comings and goings, its configurations and counter configurations, its mutations, lines that could be pointed out but later on lead nowhere... Inspired by Koro-Ljungberg (2012), who claims that 'research and methodology could also be seen as processes of creation and connections that are always becoming, newly invented, adapted, and fabricated' (p. 808), I wondered if I could write a doctoral thesis 'on the go'. If everything is moving and reconfiguring, if everything is flowing, you cannot write anything other than 'on the fly'. So, I decided to try it.

That mainly meant:

1. Understanding writing as inquiry and, in a similar way to St. Pierre (1997, p. 365), I 'decided to attempt a nomadic journey, to, in fact, travel in the thinking that writing produces in search' of a becoming-PhD thesis. This decision entailed making explicit the processes of thinking-writing the report by dialoguing with the reader and with myself in the process of writing; making questions about how to follow and write it down in the same dissertation. According to Britzman (1995), in the thesis writing, I took

    the odd position of moving behind the scenes of my own ethnographic work to elaborate the theoretical and narrative decisions I made in producing my text. As a 'hidden chapter' in my own ethnographic text, I offer thoughts about the narrative dilemmas unleashed when one attempts to write a poststructuralist ethnography

    (p. 231)

2. Using references as a 'montage' of quotations. With the desire of making explicit the idea of decentring the subject in research—that is, the researcher as a subject-in-relation-to-, I put at work literal quotations from the idea of collage in photography, or montage in cinema and the technique of found-footage.[4] I was interested to 'assemble' the quotes, to wander through the readings and rescue and concatenate segments of them in such a way as to create a story with openings to other readings and thoughts. Creating a story that my multiple and in relation 'I' was building from segments of texts, deterritorialising them from their original place and reterritorialising them in the thesis. Arranging the pieces on the board, on the blank paper, on the worktable. There was not an accumulation of quotations without criteria and with any organization, but an assemblage of literal quotations.

Using another structure-language

For Deleuze & Guattari (1994, p. 2) 'philosophy is the art of forming, inventing, and fabricating concepts'. And throughout their work, they are inventing and creating concepts as well as deterritorializing others from their original field and reterritorializing in philosophy (e.g. rhizome, plateau, ritornello). At the time I was engaged in the process of writing the report, I had several tensions and doubts regarding the structure and form of traditional writing. I was thinking of another kind of text. I needed to think of other concepts that helped me more to organize the research than the usual sections of the theoretical framework, state of the art, methodology and conclusions. Because in my study, everything was entangled and was developing at the same time. Therefore, I could not compartmentalize the knowledge that it was being created in a state of becoming. In this way, I took (deterritorialized) some concepts from different authors and reterritorialized them as articulating ideas of the research. Those were: Plateau, drift, diffraction and cartography.

Plateaus instead of 'chapters'

When I became aware that I must start to shape all the pieces of texts I had until that moment into a report, it was beneficial to start with a map of maps. Those maps were the 'most' similar image of maps that comes to us when we think of a map. Entering those maps, I could recognize which concepts and moments I wanted to explore in the thesis. And I realized that the report could not be structured by chapters but by plateaus.

During the time I was in the writing process, I was so fascinated by Deleuze & Guattari's *Thousand Plateaus* (1980/1987). That work helped me to understand many movements of my research and the dissertation. In fact, it was a book organized not in chapters but in plateaus. Deleuze (1995) understands plateau as a 'sort of bursts" (p. 147); 'plateau isn't a metaphor, ... they're zones of continuous variation, or like watchtowers surveying or scanning their own particular areas, and signaling to each other ... that is, to a polytonality' (p. 142). According to the author, plateau maps out 'a range of circumstances' (p. 26).

The concept of plateau helped me to organize the thesis in 'maps of circumstances' and in a big map made of watchtowers and other maps. In the PhD thesis, the different plateaus that composed it had been growing and increasing/decreasing according to the needs of those that already existed. That meant to have several plateaus and sub-plateaus and sub-sub-plateaus open at the same time and create the new ones when the writing itself required it. According to jagodzinski (2014), in a process of becoming in writing, 'new actualizations can take place as new becomings emerge' (p. 30).

Theoretical drifts

Paying attention to how I was relating to readings and authors, the drift emerged as the best option. It was consistent with wandering between theories and texts; to be open to the unexpected and to what I found, and not closed only by looking for either what I already knew or what I did not find. Thus, theoretical drifts presented as an adventure, as a way of giving an account of the processes I was following to become familiar with the theory. But also, as space to rehearse or investigate how to put the theory in relation to the experience lived during the

Ontology of becoming and ethnographic research **99**

fieldwork. And, to give an account of the processes followed to consolidate decisions taken for the research. Besides, theoretical drifts acted as a plateau, a high plateau to resort to if in the wandering of the other plateaus there is some concept that escapes us, that we do not know where it was obtained or what it is there for. In this way, plateaus had internal references that connected concepts between them to make the deambulation throughout the report easier, inviting the readers not to follow the text linearly but in the way they feel.

Diffractions

The concept of diffraction was taken from Haraway and Barad. These authors propose the notion of diffraction as an alternative to reflection (and reflexivity). In line with their methodological and ethical onto-epistemology, where knowledge is situated and embodied (Haraway, 1988; Barad, 1996) and the subject becomes part of and makes the phenomenon (Barad, 1996, 2003, 2007), reflection cannot be a 'valid' strategy in research. According to them, reflection supposes a distance, a separation between researcher and object or investigated subject. That is why these authors propose diffraction because it does not separate the phenomenon from the researcher, but rather 'moves' the phenomenon, unfolds and refolds it in different ways although the phenomenon remains there, the same changing phenomenon, but the phenomenon in its totality.

I was into this concept as an alternative to analysis as a strategy to activate and deactivate processes and materials created during the research and the writing process. Instead of explaining them, dialoguing with them, reflecting with them or analysing them, I decided to diffract them among themselves; with me as a multiplicity in the becoming that I am; with other readings and authors; with other concepts; and with other learning phenomena that were appearing and connecting themselves in the same diffraction. That allowed me not to distance myself from the research and the materials created, but to take them as part of the phenomenon in which they and I were involved. And move them to think from their folds and intra-actions, how those modify the relations between them and the other parts of the thesis.

A Ph.D thesis-cartography

The concept of cartography was one of the cornerstones of the research. The whole process was carried out by overlapping and putting at work different ways to understand maps. The result was a report as a living map of maps with different layers and dimensions. The first cartographical dimension was the *Maps of situation*. It consisted of diagrams arisen from the need to situate key moments, learning phenomena, mini-events that had made me write and think in the way I did. They showed an overview of the processes I went through and lived throughout the research. To me, those maps set up the 'real' dissertation table of contents. Coming back to *Thousand Plateaus* (Deleuze & Guattari, 1987), I realized that the whole book could be considered as an excellent cartography of contemporary thought organized by plateaus. So, we could find a second cartographical dimension, the map plot by the thesis dissertation's plateaus. Finally, diffraction acted as a dimension of connections. It was the strategy that kept alive the other cartographical dimensions. Diffraction allowed the other maps to fold, unfold, refold, connect, disconnect and jump between them, configuring and reconfiguring themselves depending on the reader and the section they were reading or make them flee in other directions, into unexplored territories. Indeed, all those cartographical dimensions could be understood as a big knot diagram moving in the diffractions for a becoming-Ph.D thesis. According to de Freitas (2014, pp. 113–114),

> The singularities of the knot diagram are precisely where signification is refused, where the diagram punches through the surface of meaning, breaks with flatness, and dethrones its own capacity to depict or refer, opening up instead a space of becoming.

A thesis with no conclusions

Just like St. Pierre (1997, p. 367), 'I resisted writing an ending, since I did not know how to end something that had no beginning'. In this sense becoming is always in the middle and research is understood as a learning process, in which knowledge is generated in the same becoming and developments in research. Thus, it seemed contradictory that a doctoral thesis carried out in constant becoming, with movements, intensities, speeds and open systems had a closed and stable end. Unlike other researches that have the objective of discovering or demonstrating a premise or question, this one had the objective of wandering, exploring and experimenting with the same act of investigating. Namely, to give an account of developments in research and processes through which inquiry was becoming. Therefore, it did not make sense to add a final section of conclusions.

However, since the academy asked me for a section like that, I ended up adding a plateau with non-final thoughts. This plateau functions as a place from which, looking in some directions, one can see the knowledge generated in the thesis dissertation and, looking in others, one can see where the lines launched that have not yet found a place are going. I understood this section as a stop on the way, from where I continued diffracting with the other plateaus of the report, connecting with each other and with the senses of the inquiry; throwing lines of thought towards different communities and populations and thinking about possible continuities for that investigation.

Unfolding sump up thoughts

The processes outlined to carry out a research from the ontology of becoming calls into question many dimensions and attempts to propose alternatives to some problematisations in qualitative research, which has potential but also risks.

Proposing a thesis that it is not developed in an expected 'traditional' way entails to take the risk that not many academic researchers would accept the work as such. Ethnographers who decide to explore these territories must be aware that the course of this kind of research is neither linear nor predictable; quite the contrary. They have to be prepared to start from an attitude open to the unknown, to allow themselves to be surprised by the research process, to let in elements not initially foreseen, but which can enrich and make the research grow.

Besides, thinking research from these parameters entails a different relationship with theories, texts and authors. Instead of just wanting to understand what they say and translate it into their (the researcher's) own words, it invites to intra-act with the texts and to diffract them with our spacetimematterings. Exploring intra-acting in the fieldwork and with texts may help to transit through the process of inquiry. What these experiences and materials allow us to think about, what new territories allow us to glimpse, what new connections they allow us to make within the research. According to Hroch (2014, p. 50), 'rather than simply hold out hope for a different future, we, in our constant becoming-other, our on-going yet-to-come-ness, are recognized by Deleuze & Guattari as agents with the potential capacity to bring such futures about' and, in the case of the Ph.D thesis, bring new ways of thinking a doctoral dissertation and research in education.

As Britzman (1995, p. 237) states,

> If ethnography is to provide a critical space to push thought against itself, ethnographers must begin by identifying their own textual strategies and political commitments and pointing out the differences among the stories, the structures of telling, and the structures of belief.

This positionality asks for a different commitment from readers and academia. In line with this, and following with Britzman (1995),

> readers of ethnography must also be willing to construct more complicated reading practices that move them beyond the myth of literal representations and the deceptive promise that 'the real' is transparent, stable, and just like the representational. Poststructuralist theories of writing and reading may allow readers [and researchers from academia] to challenge and rearrange what it is that structures the reader's own identity imperatives ... reading and writing ethnography might provoke a different way of thinking, an ethic that refuses the grounds of subjectification and normalization and that worries about that which is not yet.
>
> *(p. 237)*

Writing this kind of dissertation entailed an exciting journey, ideal to adventurers and lovers of the unexpected and the creation of new worlds. However, one must be aware that it also can be challenging for other researchers and academics. You might invite them into fields and territories that they may not want to explore;

102 Judit Onsès-Segarra

leading them to complexities that may put in crisis their beliefs or 'safe' lands, pushing them to think 'out of the frame'.

Notes

1 http://diylab.eu
2 Barad's onto-epistemology understands reality as an entanglement of spaces, times and matter. According to her, 'Phenomena are not located in space and time; rather, *phenomena are material entanglements enfolded and threaded through the spacetimemattering of the universe*' (Barad, 2010, p. 261, italics in original).
3 Barad refers to intra-action as that type of relationship in which all the agents involved in a phenomenon, since conforming an entanglement, are concerned with each other affecting each other in such a way that their nature is reconfigured at the same time as the phenomenon itself is reconfiguring. According to her, intra-action is 'the fully contextual be-in' where the matter and meaning meet' (1996, p. 179). In another work, she claims: '*matter comes to matter* through the iterative intra-activity of the world in its becoming ... All bodies, not merely 'human' bodies, come to matter through the world's iterative intra-activity— its performativity' (Barad, 2003, p. 823, italics in original).
4 Found footage in cinema could be thought of as equivalent to collage in photography. It consists of creating a story from frames or offcuts from different movies or video recordings.

References

Atkinson, D. (2011). *Art, Equality and Learning. Pedagogies Against the State.* Sense Publishers.
Atkinson, D. (2018). *Art, Disobedience and Ethics. The Adventure of Pedagogy.* Palgrave. doi:10.1007/978-3-319-62639-0.
Barad, K. (1996). Meeting the Universe Halfway. Realism and Social Constructivism Without Contradiction. In L.H. Nelson & J. Nelson (Eds.), *Feminism, Science, and the Philosophy of Science* (pp. 161–194). Kluwer Academic Publishers.
Barad, K. (2003). Posthumanist Performativity: Toward an Understanding of How Matter Comes to Matter. *Journal of Women in Culture and Society,* 28 (3), 801–831.
Barad, K. (2007). *Meeting the Universe Halfway.* Duke University Press.
Barad, K. (2010). Quantum Entanglements and Hauntological Relations of Inheritance: Dis/continuities, SpaceTime Enfoldings, and Justice-to-Come. *Derrida Today,* 3 (2), 240–268. doi:10.3366/E1754850010000813.
Barad, K. (2014). Diffracting Diffraction: Cutting Together-Apart. *Parallax,* 20 (3), 168–187, doi:10.1080/13534645.2014.927623.
Braidotti, R. (2015). *Lo Posthumano* (1a ed.; Juan C. Gentile-Vitale, trad.). Gedisa. (Original work published in 2013).
Britzman, D.P. (1995). The Question of Belief: Writing Poststructural Ethnography. *International Journal of Qualitative Studies in Education,* 8 (3), 229–238. doi:10.1080/0951839950080302.
Carlin, M., & Wallin, J. (Eds.) (2014). *Deleuze & Guattari, Politics and Education: For a People-Yet-to-Come.* Bloomsbury.
Coleman, R. & Ringrose, J. (Eds.) (2013). *Deleuze and Research Methodologies.* Edinburgh University Press.
de Freitas, E. (2014). Diagramming the Classroom as Topological Assemblage. In M. Carlin, & J. Wallin (eds.), *Deleuze & Guattari, Politics and Education: For a People-Yet-to-Come* (pp. 95–115). Bloomsbury.

Deleuze, G. (1995). *Negotiations 1972–1990* (Martin Joughin, trans.). Columbia University Press. (Original work published in 1990.)

Deleuze, G. & Guattari, F. (1987). *Thousand Plateaus* (Brian Massumi, trans.). University of Minnesota Press. (Original work published in 1980).

Deleuze, G. & Guattari, F (1994). *What is Philosophy?* (Hugh Tomlinson and Graham Burchell, trans.). Columbia University Press. (Original work published in 1991.)

Didi-Huberman, G. (2010). *ATLAS ¿Cómo llevar el mundo a cuestas?* [exhibition brochure]. Museo Reina Sofia.

Haraway, D. (1988). Situated Knowledges: The Science Question in Feminism and the Privilege of Partial Perspective. *Feminist Studies*, 14 (3), 575–599.

Hroch, P. (2014). Deleuze, Guattari, and Environmental Pedagogy and Politics. Ritournelles for a Planet-Yet-To-Come. In M. Carlin, & J. Wallin (Eds.), *Deleuze & Guattari, Politics and Education: For a People-Yet-to-Come* (pp. 49–75). Bloomsbury.

jagodzinski, j. (2014). On Cinema as Micropolitical Pedagogy. Is there an Elephant in the Classroom? In Mathew Carlin, and Jason Wallin (eds.), *Deleuze & Guattari, Politics and Education: For a People-Yet-to-Come* (pp. 15–47). Bloomsbury.

Koro-Ljungberg, M. (2012). Researchers of the World, Create! *Qualitative Inquiry*, 18 (9), 808–818, doi:10.1177/1077800412453014.

Lara, A. (2015). Teorías Afectivas Vintage. Apuntes sobre Deleuze, Bergson y Whitehead. *Cinta moebio*, 52, 17–36. Retrieved April 13, 2020, from www.moebio.uchile.cl/52/lara. html.

Löytönen, T. (2017). Educational Development Within Higher Arts Education: An Experimental Move Beyond Fixed Pedagogies. *International Journal for Academic Development*, 22 (3), 231–244, doi:10.1080/1360144X.2017.1291428.

Onsès, J. (2018). *Documentación Visual en los Fenómenos de Aprendizaje con Estudiantes de Primaria. Una Indagación Rizomática Difractiva Desde las Teorías 'Post'* (Doctoral Thesis). University of Barcelona.

Onsès, J., & Hernández-Hernández, F. (2017). Visual Documentation as Space of Entanglement to Rethink Arts-Based Educational Research. *Synnyt/Origins*, 2, 61–73.

Rajchman, J. (2000). *The Deleuze Connections*. The MIT Press.

St. Pierre, E.A. (1997). Nomadic Inquiry in the Smooth Spaces of the Field: A Preface. *International Journal of Qualitative Studies in Education*, 10 (3), 365–383. doi:10.1080/095183997237179.

9

OPENNESS TO THE UNFORESEEN IN A NOMADIC RESEARCH PROCESS ON TEACHERS' LEARNING EXPERIENCES

Fernando Hernández-Hernández

Introduction[1]

Mruck and Breuer (2003) justify the need to speak from ourselves—and not of ourselves—in the relevance of our positionalities and options in the research process, to despise 'characteristics of objects' as 'existing realities':

> Why is it necessary to talk about ourselves and our presuppositions, choices, experiences, and actions during the research process in a sufficiently precise way so that it allows others to follow what we mean and did? It is necessary because without such reflection the outcomes of the research process are regarded as 'characteristics of objects,' as 'existing realities,' despite their constructed nature that originates in the various choices and decisions researchers undertake during the process of researching.
>
> *(Mruck & Breuer, 2003, p. 2)*

Simons (20) also maintains that showing transparency in our written reflections has three advantages: The first is that it allows us to identify when our subjectivity evokes a research project; the second is that it will enable us to reflect critically on the actions and decisions we make throughout the research process; and, the third is the possibility of pointing out our trends in the research process and identify what measures we have chosen to counteract them.

I take into consideration these two contributions that emphasize the importance of making the position of the researcher visible and transparent to situate my becoming positionality in the research process. I understand positionality as 'political process' (Fares, 2010), as 'relational construction, insofar as the conditions of possibility for an agent depends on his position concerning others' (p. 81).

Research as a process that makes the becoming of the researcher transparent

To give an account of this process that crosses positionalities and becoming, I take as a guiding thread my interest—both from teacher development, accompanying transformation processes in schools, and research—in how teachers learn. This interest started within the framework of the reform promoted in 1990 by the Spanish socialist government with the General Organic Law of the Education System (LOGSE). This law, in addition to transforming the structure of the Spanish education system, tried to transmit to teachers a constructivist approach to learning, based on Piaget (1967, 1970, 1972) and Vygotsky (1978)'s contributions, which, it was supposed, would guide their practices; practices that should be planned considering the Instructional Elaboration Theory indications (Reigeluth et al, 1978; Reigeluth, 1983). A national teacher development program was designed based on the idea of teachers' learning by reception and repetition, and later, with these bases, reflect reform ideas in the classroom. To disentangle this oxymoron—putting together constructivism and instructional planning—we try to explore the question of how teachers carry out (or not) with this contradictory process (Sancho et al., 1998). With this purpose, we conducted three ethnographic studies to try to put some light on how teachers in three schools—with different historical, organisational and curricular trajectories—appropriated, replicated or transformed the proposals of the education reform. During the field work I published an article entitled 'How teachers learn' (Hernández, 1996–1997). From this article, I tried to raise the need for research into teacher learning as an alternative to the research promoted by the Centre for Educational Research and Documentation (CIDE), and the reviews (Marcelo, 1995; Barquín, 1995), focused mainly on teachers' sociological characteristics, teacher thought and teachers' school stress.

A few years later, and after a trajectory of making professional life stories of teachers at the school and university (Hernández et al., 2010; Hernández & Rifà, 2011; Hernández-Hernández & Sancho Gil, 2013) in which the importance acquired by biographical experiences in professional paths was revealed, we decided to investigate how teachers learn inside and outside educational institutions. But, just as it happened to us when we approached the topic of how one learns to be a subject in primary school (Hernández-Hernández, 2010), the challenge before us was how to investigate the experience of learning, which is a slippery notion (Fendler, 2015) and which slides through our fingers when we approach it, if we want to convert it into data. The experience of studying this elusive phenomenon put into question my research positionality of understanding the world as a given... and brought me to approach the research phenomena of my interest as permanently new, as part of a process of becoming into the unknown (Atkinson, 2011).

Becoming in research as encounter with the unknown

Taking into account this previous journey, in this chapter, I explore my process of becoming from being part of a research project[2] under an ethnographic approach (Reeves et al., 2013; Atkinson et al., 2001) and by using ethnographic methods (participatory observation, interview, sites and interaction description...). In this project, we described teachers learning movements in and beyond their/our cartographic encounters to understand how secondary school teachers experience their learning movements and processes; their times and spaces of learning (Hernández-Hernández, 2019).

This research situation demanded a nomadic attitude that implied imagining a research praxis as unstable and requiring a constant openness to the unforeseen. This generated a relationship with the disturbing characteristics in which the investigation was becoming. This openness demanded rethinking the meaning of how a methodological approach is usually understood and its relationship with the onto-epistemological and ethical foundation of research. From a post-qualitative position (Lather, 2013; Lather & St. Pierre, 2013; St. Pierre, 2011; Hernández-Hernández & Revelles Benavente, 2019) it is not a question of designing a situation that allows generating some data to later analyse them and account for their possible meanings following previously established decisions. To assume a 'post' position supposes, according to St. Pierre (2011, p. 615), '[...] a radical break with the humanist, modernist, imperialist, representationalist, objectivist, rationalist, epistemological, ontological, and methodological assumptions of Western Enlightenment-thought and practice'. In this framework, the notion of becoming is critical because it enables us to approach research and account for it as a process in motion, not as a predefined place from which to start and to reach. Assuming this nomadic positionality implies, as Semetsky (2006) points out, that the 'subjects' of research (teachers and researchers) are subjects in the process, because

> as becoming, (are) always placed between two multiplicities, yet one term does not become the other; the becoming is something between the two ... Therefore, becoming does not mean becoming the other, but becoming-other.
>
> *(Semetsky, 2006, p. 6)*

This becoming experience implies a relationship, an in 'between' movement that reflects our encounters with others and with materiality embodying all relationships. Atkinson (2018) says that becoming takes place when we participate in 'a dynamic series of prehensional relations through which beings try to take account of each other, and such relations are underpinned by a composition of feelings and conceptual processes' (p. 129).

Being 'within', 'between' and in 'becoming' leads to assume that the research approach adopted does not seek to find and reveal what is 'out there' since it is recognized that the outside is entangled with the researcher gaze and positionality. It was from this position that we tried to ask ourselves not what we wanted to find, but what we were experiencing in the research process, as well as on the concepts that emerged and illuminated teachers' learning trajectories.

In this becoming journey, the writing process is traversed by sudden movements and displacements of the research, making it part of the research. By writing as researching frees us, following the invitation of Richardson and St. Pierre (2005, p. 962), 'from trying to write a single text in which everything is said at once to everyone [...] writing is validated as a method of knowing'. This approach towards writing is what I am trying to display in this chapter.

This journey placed me in an unstable position as a researcher, as it questioned not only the initial design of the research, but the very meaning of what research should be from a qualitative perspective. I was beginning to get what St. Pierre says happens when the researchers place themselves in a 'post' research positionality.

> each researcher who puts the 'posts' to work will create a different *articulation ... remix, mash-up, assemblage, a becoming* of inquiry that is not a priori, inevitable, necessary, stable, or repeatable but is, rather, created spontaneously in the middle of the task at hand, which is always already and, and, and...
>
> *(St. Pierre, 2011, p. 620, emphasis in original)*

In this framework, the notion of becoming is essential because it makes the focus of research and the process of writing about it become becoming, rather than being a predefined place from which to start and to arrive. Thus, becoming leads to research which does not seek to reveal what is 'out there', since it recognizes that the outside is entangled with the gaze of the researcher. This positionality makes the process of inquiry a relational journey where one is attentive not to what one hopes to find, but to what is happening in a process that is not linear, but rather full of bifurcations, doubts and places of not-knowing (Atkinson, 2018).

It was from this position, from a groping move and not from the certainties from which educational and social science research is usually approached, that we tried to ask ourselves not what we were trying to find, but what research displacements allow us to think. As Deleuze & Guattari (2001) suggest, we paid attention to concepts that we made emerge, in the process of creation of cartographies by teachers of their learning transits inside and outside educational institutions. We came to the cartographies because we thought we could not approach teachers with a question like, 'Can you tell us how you learn in and out of school?' We consider that this is not only a question that is difficult to answer because of its inherent nature, but also one that can be uncomfortable since it seems to be a way of examining our interlocutor. The choice of the cartographies was also given by the relationship of some of us with research based on the arts (Barone & Eisner, 2011; Leavy, 2018; Souminen et al., 2018) and visual methods (Margolis & Pauwels, 2011; Pain, 2012). This previous experience led us to consider cartographies as a possibility for creating visual representations of concepts, questions and meanings, as well as for taking risks in revealing and exploring themes that resist the fantasy of reification and the measurement of learning experiences (Atkinson, 2011). Besides,

108 Fernando Hernández-Hernández

cartographies allow the configuration of a space that can contain multiple perspectives, conceptions, skills, and modes of understanding of a problem, such as
that of teacher learning, including dissonant and conflictive movements (Garoian &
Gaudelius, 2008).

Research journey as process of affecting and being affected

The research proposal we sent for the Ministry of Economy, Enterprise and
Competitivity call gave an account of the desired path, from a realistic qualitative
ontology and epistemology, in which we presented the rationale and methodology
as two parts of what was supposed to be a coherent and structured process. The
initial objectives were:

1. Mapping scenarios in which teachers learn to reveal their value as a source of
   knowledge and experience.
2. Detect teachers' learning experiences in these scenarios and what perspectives
   on learning emerge.
3. Explore ways of learning how teachers move between the stages/areas identified and their practices and professional decisions.
4. Establish a framework for comparison between the ways of learning of teachers in early childhood, primary and secondary school, to systemically
   represent regularities and differences.

However, from the beginning, when the researchers carried out a workshop to
carry out researchers' cartographies responding to a premise of the ESBRINA
research group[3] (Hernández-Hernández, Sancho-Gil & Domingo-Coscollola,
2018) of not asking others to do what we do not do first, we realized that we were
entering a terrain of not knowing. Our cartographies involved an interweaving of
images, words and stories that gave an account of biographical journeys, but also of
desires articulated between the unusual and the unspoken. Cartographic experience
was part of our becoming, because, as Lather (2013) points out, we were able to
re-imagine and carry out research that can produce different kinds of knowledge.
At this point, in approaching cartographies to draw teachers' learning journeys, I
felt like Kunda (2013), when he talks about ethnography 'as a method that pro-
blematized and examined, rather than sanctified, assumptions about human behaviour' (Kunda, 2013, p. 6).

Being involved in cartographies with teachers (and with ourselves) evoke what
Marcus (2007) says about ethnography 'as composed of networked, rhizomic, viral
knowledge processes. Yes, it is following out connections and relations, but of
ideas and maps or topologies that are not given, but found.' (p. 1132).

With this background, after conducting a pilot study with two teachers who
anticipated the openness of what we were going to find, we contacted three teachers and proposed them to participate in the research. But the unforeseen event
broke out through the proposal they made to us: 'why don't you come to our

Openness to the unforeseen in a nomadic research **109**

school instead of doing it individually and do it with all the teachers who want to participate'. From this invitation, we found ourselves readapting what we had thought of as an individual approach to bring it into a group relationship. This movement challenged the fantasy of myself as an omniscient researcher who records in his observations—without interference—what happens around him. Going to the schools and meeting a group of teachers placed me in a relationship with multiple focuses, which demanded to be open to the unforeseen and to not knowing. We decided, after thinking about how to face the new situation, to 'put ourselves on hold' and write to each participant thanking them and advancing what we could do together. We sent them an ethical agreement in which we summarized the project, explaining what we expected and what we offered them. We also sent two examples of cartographies that two teachers had done during a 'pilot' study. With this, we somehow thought that the situation in which we would find ourselves would already be informed, and the teachers would be able to carry out what we proposed to them. But it did not happen quite as we had thought.

We went to all three schools, and in each one, we found a different situation that we could not foresee beforehand. When we arrived at the first one, the group (nine women and two men) was affected by a father's intervention against a teacher; this situation generated a discomfort that made them doubt about whether or not to participate in the proposal we had made to them.

In the second one, those who participated (five women and two men), maintained links between them because they shared a project of language integration and had responded to the invitation because of the interest communicated by one of the participants, who had been our initial contact.

In the third, six women and one man came. One of them was the principal, with whom we had initially connected, and the rest shared with her their interest in improving school practice. These three situations demanded different ways of relationship, not only with the groups but with each teacher during the cartographic process.

We went to the schools on two occasions. During the first one, we participated in a conversation to introduce the study ourselves and invite teachers to talk about their expectations and trajectories. We wrote field notes, visually (by video and photo) documented the encounter and accompanied teachers in the creation of their cartographies. Finally, we opened a conversation in front of each cartography on teachers' decision process and made a balance of the contributions of being part of this experience. On the second, four months later, we shared what the cartographies, teachers' narratives and conversations had made us think. Thus, opening an alternative relationship in which we exchanged how the shared experience had affected them and us. Our stay at schools made evident what Merriman (2012) has mentioned in a broader view:

> The world may be in constant movement, flux and becoming, but this does not mean that those movements are flat, linear and uniform. Movements and

110 Fernando Hernández-Hernández

becomings may be approached as qualitative multiplicities, and they are clearly underpinned by diverse political strategies.

(Merriman, 2012, p. 5)

This journey placed me in an unstable position as a researcher, as it questioned not only the initial design of the research, but the very meaning of research from a qualitative perspective. It happened to me, as Green (2013) points out, that the movements of research were configured as

a continual process of flux or differentiation even though this fact is usually masked by powerful and pervasive illusory discourses of fixity, stability, and identity that have characterized most of western philosophy and theory since at least Enlightenment.

(Green, 2013, p. 751)

This research situation demanded from me a nomadic exploration attitude that involved imagining a practice of 'travelling in the thinking that writing produces, in search of the field' (St. Pierre, 2000: 258). A nomadic, a becoming unstable approach that required a constant openness to the unexpected, which generated a relationship with the disturbing characteristics that the research was becoming. Something similar happened when I found myself before the cartographies and tried to map the learning trajectories of teachers, not as results, but 'questioning guidelines, the points of entry and exit, as a constant deployment' (Braidotti, 2006, p. 160). This operation, which ceased to be normative, meant questioning, as Snaza & Weaver (2014) point out, the phenomenon of *methodocentrism*, according to which the methodology of researchers and their faithfulness to a method are the primary concern, relegating human beings, other living people and inanimate objects to a subordinate position, from which the role of these beings and their realities form the work of the researcher.

At this point, the initial research question 'How do teachers learn in and out the workplace about disciplinary content; pedagogical references; student learning; technologies, particularly digital technologies; cultural and social dimensions; and self-references' became another question. A research interrogation that now did not seek results, but opened a path of thought in the following terms: 'What enables us to think, what allows us to expand from the process of mapping by secondary school teachers their learning journeys within and outside educational institutions'.

This is no longer a question of obtaining results, but of generating concepts and thus thinking about what happens to us and them in the research. A question linked to a research notion where ontology (reality), epistemology (knowledge), methodology (modes of inquiry) and ethics (the relationship with the other) do not each go their way but are assembled in the course of the research. Where questions we want to answer do not at first mark the process and destiny of the inquiry. We were now open to the issues emerging from the process of research. We also considered that the human, the non-human and the material are articulated on the same relationship. Finally, we propose to think of each of these elements in an (inter)connected way, where their existence and execution cannot be conceived independently from the assembly of which they are part.

All of the above links to a notion of learning that emerges in research and, as Atkinson points out, is characterized by a creative process, which allows one to authorize oneself, 'which must have moments and forms of stabilization, since one cannot always be moving forward. There must be points of stability. But this "how one move" is complex in terms of ontogenesis, since learning is not only cognition, but is also affectively integrated' (Atkinson, 2015, p. 4).

Discussion and conclusions

This itinerary, presented here with an emphasis on the research movements that affected the researcher, also allowed a series of considerations about learning as becoming; not understood as something that is out there and that the researcher 'rescues' through a series of data collection and analysis strategies. But explorations of how to conduct research has made it possible to think about how teachers learn:

- Teachers learn in a network of relationships, by linking biographical and corporeal, as well as cognitive aspects of their lives.
- Teachers learn by moving from the 'outside' to daily school life, in relationships with colleagues and students.
- Teachers also report an expansive dimension of their learning in the links they make with their life experiences of learning.
- These experiences cannot be viewed in isolation since teachers 'assign a territory or space in their cartographies to the different areas in which they learn (family, friends, leisure, culture, school...) while making explicit multiple intersections and transits between them' (Bosco, Alonso & Miño Puigcercós, 2019, 87).
- Finally, learning 'is constituted as discursive material phenomena made up of organisms, objects, technologies, times, spaces, situations, experiences, values and entangled concepts' (Sancho-Gil & Correa-Gorospe, 2019, p.134).

What these 'findings' tell about the consideration of learning as a process of becoming means, as Lundborg (2009) mentions, that becoming 'does not have a pre-determined goal. It presents only a "flow of life" that can take on new paths and create new ways of thinking and perceiving' (p. 3). This idea of becoming implies that there is no middle point, or a present, in which—in his/her learning process—the subject is located. Becoming consists of an unrestricted movement that 'produces nothing but itself'. In this sense, we understand becoming as incorporeal; it is never present as such and has no direct relationship with an already present body (Lundborg, 2009, p. 3 paraphrased).

112 Fernando Hernández-Hernández

To continue thinking about the meaning of ethnographic educational research as becoming

Isabelle Stengers (1997, 2010)—a researcher who walks the intersection of scientific studies, the history of science and post-humanism—accompanies and allows me to substantiate the orientation of research that I try to share in this article. Mainly because her contributions help me 'to find our way when the way was hidden because we had strayed from the paths we were told to follow' (Ahmed, 2018, p. 33).

Stengers is suspicious of fields of knowledge that claim to be science by displaying a multitude of tooling objects (lab coats and lab spaces, graphics, statistics, normative writing sequence, technical vocabulary, etc.). In contrast to those who emphasize the continent, she believes that what makes a science 'science' is that it looks for ways to let its 'object' speak or become a subject. The 'what' of the study must be able to participate, to surprise the researcher. When a researcher decides in advance what will be considered and how the 'results' will be presented, the surprise is impossible. All that can happen is 'confirmation' or 'denial'. When this happens, the system is completely closed.

Therefore I share with Stengers the need for an open science, a science that is not afraid to remember the cultural-political-historical construction of science within the humanist networks; a science that goes beyond science as we know it to help us think about the meaning of the denied relationships in which we are always entangled. These relationships involve humans, animals, machines, and things (Snaza, et al. 2014).

As I mentioned at Hernández-Hernández (2019) all the above has implications for ethnographic educational research if the displacements described in this article are to be expanded, as Stephanie Springgay (2015) does. Springgay calls for maintaining a sense of movement, which positions itself against the use of pre-established 'methods', and in favour of procedures that emerge 'in the midst of the research process' (p. 81). She also invites one to adopt a process construction, which regards research not as rigid or limited by a method, but as an 'ongoing construction' (p. 84) which can only lead 'to approximate rigorous abstractions' (idem). This becoming displacement implies challenging traditional notions of research focused on linear causality.

Finally, responding to the invitation of Elizabeth St. Pierre (2013), Springgay asks educational researchers—in a request particularly relevant for ethnographers—to consider the idea of research without pre-set, fixed, concrete and isolated data, since the research that the post-qualitative perspective pursues is that which is relational and processual. An investigation configured, not in a planning that predetermines before carrying out the study, but in the process of writing, since '[W]riting is thinking, writing is analysis, writing is indeed a seductive and tangled method of discovery' (Richardson and St. Pierre, 2005, p. 967, emphasis in original). This research as writing, which is essential in ethnographic research, makes possible to explore what we do not know, and which surprises us. At the same time, it enables us to understand in new ways what arouses our curiosity and opens

Openness to the unforeseen in a nomadic research **113**

other ways of thinking and knowing. This orientation towards research like becoming happens, as Lather (2013) points out, as researchers reimagine and carry out research that can produce different knowledge.

In the case of the research presented in this chapter, on how teachers and researchers learn, it was an account of becoming encounters 'which resists being completely understood in the present' (Ahmed, 2018, p. 27). However, these encounters and displacements generate what Sara Ahmed calls 'sweaty concepts' (Ibid., p. 27)—concepts that 'contribute things to the world' (Ibid.: 28) and not only to the career of researchers.

Notes

1 This chapter is written in 'I' and 'we' voices because it focuses on the changes that affect the author and the group of researchers participating in a research, in which the initial question changed when they came into contact with the research collaborators.
2 APRENDO (I learn): How teachers learn: educational implications and challenges for social change- Ministry of Economy and Competitiveness/EDU2015–70912-C2–1-R
3 https://esbrina.eu/en/home/

References

Ahmed, S. (2018). *Vivir una Vida Feminista.* (María Engueix, trans). Edicions Bellaterra.
Atkinson, D. (2011). *Art, Equality and Learning: Pedagogies Against the State.* Sense.
Atkinson, D. (2015). Pedagogía de lo Desconocido. *Cuadernos de Pedagogía*, 454, 34–39. (interview made by Fernando Hernández & Juana M. Sancho).
Atkinson, D. (2018). *Art, Disobedience and Ethics. The Adventure of Pedagogy.* Palgrave. http://dx.doi.org/10.1007/978-3-319-62639-0.
Atkinson, P., Coffey, A., Delamont, S., Lofland, J., & Lofland, L. (2001). *Handbook of ethnography.* SAGE Publications Inc.
Barone, T.; Eisner, E. (2011). *Arts Based Research.* SAGE.
Barquín, J. (1995). Lo Investigación Sobre e Profesorado. Estado de la Cuestión en España. *Revista de Educación*, 306, 7–65.
Bosco, A., Alonso Cano, C., & Miño, R. (2019). Geografías e Historias de Aprendizaje de Docentes de Secundaria. Intersecciones, Tránsitos y Zonas de no Saber. *Educatio Siglo XXI*, 37 (2), 67–92. http://dx.doi.org/10.6018/j/387021.
Braidotti, R. (2006). *Transpositions. On Nomadic Ethics.* Polity Press.
Deleuze, G., & Guattari, F. (2001). *¿Qué es la filosofía?* (6a ed., Thomas Kauf, trans.). Anagrama. (Originally published in French in 1991.)
Fares, G. (2010). Los Estudios Fronterizos y sus Descontentos: Un Manifiesto Posicional. In N. Hochman (ed). *Pensar el Afuera* (pp. 81–102). Kazak Ediciones.
Fendler, R. (2015). Navigating the Eventful Space of Learning. Mobilities, Nomadism and Other Tactical Maneuvers (unpublished doctoral dissertation). University of Barcelona.
Garoian, C., Gaudelius, Y. (2008). *Spectacle Pedagogy: Art, Politics, and Visual Culture.* SUNY Press.
Green, J.C. (2013). On Rhizomes, Lines of Flight, Mangles, and Other Assemblages. *International Journal of Qualitative Studies in Education*, 26 (6), 749–758. https://doi.org/10.1080/09518398.2013.788763.

114 Fernando Hernández-Hernández

Hernández, F. (1996–1997). *¿Cómo Aprenden los Docentes? Kikirikí. Cooperación Educativa*, 42–43, 120–127.

Hernández, F., Rifà, M. (Coords.) (2011). *Investigación Autobiográfica y Cambio Social.* Octaedro.

Hernández, F., Sancho, J. M., Creus, A., Montané, A. (2010). Becoming University Scholars: Inside Professional Autoethnographies. *Journal of Research Practice*, 6 (1), art. M7. Accessible at: http://jrp.icaap.org/index.php/jrp/ article/view/204/188.

Hernández-Hernández, F. (Coord.) (2010). *Aprender a ser en la escuela primaria.* Octaedro.

Hernández-Hernández, F. (2019). Investigar en Educación Desde una Posición de no Saber: dar Cuenta de los Tránsitos de una Investigación en Torno a Cómo Aprende el Profesorado de Secundaria. *Investigación en la Escuela*, 99, 1–14. http://dx.doi.org/10.12795/IE.2019.i99.01.

Hernández-Hernández, F. & Revelles Benavente, B. (2019). La Perspectiva Post-cualitativa en la Investigación Educativa: Genealogía, Movimientos, Posibilidades y Tensiones, *Educatio Siglo XXI*, 37 (2), 21–48. http://doi.org/10.6018/j/387001.

Hernández-Hernández, F. & Sancho Gil, J.M. (2013). Històries de vida en educació: un balanç. *De Didàctica de la llengua i de la literatura*, 61, 9–16.

Hernández-Hernández, F., Sancho-Gil, J. & Domingo-Coscollola, M. (2018). Cartographies as Spaces of Inquiry to Explore of Teacher's Nomadic Learning Trajectories. *Digital Education Review*, 33, 105–119. https://doi.org/10.1344/der.2018.33.105-119.

Kunda, G. (2013). Reflections of Becoming an Ethnographer. *Journal of Organizational Ethnography*, 2 (1), 4–22. https://doi.org/10.1108/JOE-12-2012-0061.

Leavy, P. (ed.). (2018). *Handbook of Arts-Based Research.* Guilford Press.

Lather, P. (2013) Methodology-21: What do we do in the Afterward? *International Journal of Qualitative Studies in Education*, 26 (6), 634–645. http://dx.doi.org/10.1080/09518398.2013.788753.

Lather, P., & St. Pierre, E.A. (2013). Introduction: Post-qualitative research. *International Journal of Qualitative Studies in Education*, 26 (6), 629–633. http://dx.doi.org/10.1080/09518398.2013.788752.

Leavy, P. (ed.). (2018). *Handbook of Arts-Based Research.* Guilford Press.

Lundborg, T. (2009). The *Becoming* of the "Event": A Deleuzian Approach to Understanding the Production of Social and Political "Events". *Theory & Event*, 12 (1), http://dx.doi.org/10.1353/tae.0.0042. Retrieved from https://muse.jhu.edu/article/263142.

Marcelo, C. (1995). Constantes y Desafíos Actuales de la Profesión Docente. *Revista de Educación*, 306, 205–241.

Marcus, G.E. (2007). Ethnography Two Decades After Writing Culture: From the Experimental to the Baroque. *Anthropological Quarterly*, 80 (4): 1127–1145. http://dx.doi.org/10.1353/10.1353/anq.2007.0059.

Margolis, E.M., Pauwels (eds.) (2011). *The SAGE Handbook of Visual Research Methods.* SAGE Publications Inc.

Merriman, P. (2012). *Mobility, Space, Culture.* Routledge.

Mruck, K., & Breuer, F. (2003). Subjectivity and Reflexivity in Qualitative Research—The FQS Issues. In K. Mruck (ed). *Forum: Qualitative Social Research.* 4 (2) Art. 23. Accessible at http://www.qualitative-research.net/index.php/fqs/article/view/696/1505.

Pain, H. (2012). A Literature Review to Evaluate the Choice and Use of Visual Methods. *International Journal of Qualitative Methods*, 11 (4): 303–319. https://doi.org/10.1177/160940691201100401.

Piaget, J. (1967). *Six Psychological Studies.* Random House.

Piaget, J. (1970). *Genetic Epistemology.* Columbia University Press.

Piaget, J. (1972). *The Principles of Genetic Epistemology.* Viking.

Reeves, S., Peller, J., Goldman, J., & Kitto, S. (2013). Ethnography in Qualitative Educational Research: AMEE Guide No. 80, *Medical Teacher*, 35 (8): 1365–1379. https://doi.org/10.3109/0142159X.2013.804977.

Reigeluth, C.M. (1983). *The Elaboration Theory of Instruction, Instructional Design Theories and Models: An Overview of Their Current Status*. Lawrence Erlbaum.

Reigeluth, C.M., Merrill, M.D., & Bunderson, C.V. (1978). The Structure of Subject Matter Contents and its Instructional Design Implications. *Instructional Science* (p. 7). 107–126.

Richardson, L., St. Pierre, E. (2005). Writing. A Method of Inquiry. In N.K. Denzin & Y.S. Lincoln. (Eds.), *The SAGE Handbook of Qualitative Research* (3a ed., pp. 959–978). SAGE Publications.

Sancho, J.M., Hernández, F., Carbonell, J., Tort, A., Simó, N., & Sánchez Cortez, E. (1998). *Aprendiendo de las Innovaciones en los Centros. La Perspectiva Interpretativa de Investigación Aplicada a tres Estudios de Casos*. Octaedro.

Sancho-Gil, J. M., & Correa-Gorospe, J.M. (2019). Intra-acciones en el Aprender de Docentes de Infantil, Primaria y Secundaria. *Educatio Siglo XXI*, 37 (2), 115–140. http://dx.doi.org/10.6018/j/387041.

Semetsky, I. (2006). *Deleuze, Education and Becoming*. Sense Publishers.

Simons, H. (2009). *Case Study Research in Practice*. SAGE Publications Inc.

Snaza, N., Appelbaum, P., Bayne, S., Carlson, D., Morris, M., Rotas, N., Sandlin, J., Wallin, J., & Weaver, J. (2014). Toward a Posthumanist Education, *Journal of Curriculum Theorizing*, 30 (2), 39–55.

Snaza, N., & Weaver, J. (Ed.). (2014). *Posthumanism and Educational Research*. Routledge.

Souminen, A., Kallio Tavin, M., Hernández Hernández, F. (2018). Arts-based research traditions and orientations in Europe: Perspectives from Finland and Spain. In P. Leavey, (ed.). *Handbook of Arts-BasedResearch* (pp. 101–120). Guilford Press.

Springgay, S. (2015). "Approximate-Rigorous-Abstractions": Propositions of Activation for Posthumanist Research. In N. Snaza & J. Weaver (Ed.). *Posthumanism and Educational Research*. (pp. 76–88). New York: Routledge.

St. Pierre, E. (2000). Poststructural Feminism in Education: An Overview. *Qualitative Studies in Education*, 13 (5), 477–515. https://doi.org/10.1080/09518390050156422.

St. Pierre, E. (2011). Post Qualitative Research. The Critique and Coming After. In N. Denzin & Y.S. Lincoln (Eds.). *The SAGE Handbook of Qualitative Research*. (3rd ed.). (p. 611–625). SAGE Publications Inc.

St. Pierre, E. (2011). Post Qualitative Research: The Critique and the Coming After. In N. K. Denzin & Y.S. Lincoln (eds.) *The Sage Handbook of Qualitative Research* (4th revised edition), (pp. 611–625). SAGE Publications Inc.

Stengers, I. (1997). *Power and Invention: Situating Science*. University of Minnesota Press.

Stengers, I. (2010). *Cosmopolitics* I. University of Minnesota Press.

Vygotsky, L. (1978). *Mind in Society: The Development of Higher Psychological Processes*. Harvard University Press.

PART III

Becoming as a concept that allows to re-signify the subjectivity

10

AN ACCIDENTAL INSTITUTIONAL ETHNOGRAPHER

Reflections on paradoxes and positionality

Garth Stahl

Introduction

As debate grows internationally over the corporatization of schooling, this chapter focuses on the paradoxes and positionality in *being* and *becoming* an ethnographer within a charter school in the United States. Neoliberal in both their governance and pedagogic enactment, charter schools, as a mix of public and private resources, remain contentious not simply because they are evidence of the state divorcing its responsibility to educate its citizens through eliciting private enterprise but also due to their lack of regulation, which makes them vulnerable to corporate interests. My journey to *becoming* an accidental institutional ethnographer (Smith, 1987; 2005) in an age of uncertainty is set against the backdrop of the neoliberal affront to public education, where unprecedented private resources are expended in an effort to increase forms of school choice in urban markets. Despite extensive critique and scrutiny, policies and legislations which are conducive to fostering growth in the charter school sector continue to become more robust and embedded.

By definition, within the world of charter schools, Charter School Management Organizations (CMOs) are consistently high-performing networks of small schools who are financed by venture capitalists (Gronberg, Jansen, & Taylor, 2012). The school culture of a CMO is often deeply tied to education reform ethos in the United States, which consistently promotes the belief that education *can* and *should* borrow heavily from the 'best practices' of corporate culture. Given their unprecedented freedom from bureaucracy and staunch non-union stance, common practices include a high level of attention to teacher effectiveness, accountability and surveillance and their cultures centre around data-driven instruction (Bulkley, 2012), scripted curriculums and pedagogic approaches (Golann, 2015), bodily control (Stahl, 2019a) and teaching to the test (Ravitch, 2013). In defence of such practices, CMOs contend that their model of schooling ensures that all students can achieve regardless of their circumstances.

Research on the daily practices, ethical dilemmas and lived experience of leaders and educators working in a CMO remains limited; we know very little of how neoliberal policies and ideologies are enacted in daily school life. Working a sixty to eighty-hour work week in a CMO over the course of nine months, this chapter focuses on how my own sense of self was 'caught up in' the principles and ideology of the CMO itself and how daily routines and language practices structured my subjectivity (Stahl, 2020). As I worked in a leadership capacity, I both studied and enacted an uncompromising model of neoliberal schooling, a model that was strategically designed to both raise aspirations and attainment for low-income students of color. Therefore, as an accidental researcher—or an accidental ethnographer—I address how the research involved a negotiation with power, ethics, and my own social justice principles leading to the writing of *Ethnography of a Neoliberal School* (Stahl, 2017). These tensions, which are central to both my analysis and reflection, is what Ball (2016) refers to as 'subjectivity as a site of struggle' (p. 1129).

As an employee at the CMO, my primary role was to study the practices of the institution in order to improve the culture and ensure the best for students (Stahl, 2019b). Working as both agent and observer, I was able to examine the customs, habits and rituals/traditions and alter them if need be. As I think back on this process, what aligns my thinking is how identities are produced in relation to the missionary zeal of the CMO and the enactment of a very specific model of schooling where no detail is left to chance. Within an age of uncertainty, Beck (1992) details how what has replaced wealth production is risk production, an integral part of reflexive modernization. He contends the 'logic' of risk production is now dominant where it is central to most forms of social, environmental and political debates. While I was an auditor of quality, I was also audited through random spot-checks to ensure my focus on pedagogical instruction was consistent. Failure to perform could mean immediate dismissal (Stahl, 2019b). In terms of how institutions negotiate risk, we are attuned to how risk permeates global discourses where it 'brings into being supra-national and non-class-specific global hazards with a new type of social and political dynamism' (Beck, 1992, p. 13).

Dorothy Smith (2005) notes how 'people become caught up in, and how our lives become organized by, the institutional foci of the ruling relations' which is 'mediated by institutionally designed realities that organize relations ...' (p. 27) which, in turn, objectify and assign subject positions. Our realities are coordinated by a complex amalgamation of the state and private enterprise. With this in mind, it is through a reflection on the everyday milieu that we can come to understand how *subjectivities become constituted* (Smith, 1987; 2005) in relation to our understandings of the paradoxes we encounter as well as our own positionality. I detail how Institutional Ethnography (IE)—which I came to after I ceased employment at the CMO—allowed me to critically consider the ways in which my experience was structured by what Dorothy Smith (1987) calls the 'ruling relations.' The chapter is a reflection of the ethical tensions involved in my research in one CMO, specifically how corporate practices shape pedagogic experiences for disadvantaged populations (Stahl, 2017; 2019ab; 2020). I begin by setting the context through recounting some of the socio-historic ideologies and policies that have led to the manifestation of charter schools as well as outlining some of their institutional practices. This is followed by a section which describes my 'accidental' journey to IE and how reading this scholarship structured my reflection, which enhanced my analysis, leading to a variety of hermeneutical deliberations (what Hodkinson (1998) calls the 'hermeneutical circle' (p. 563)). Then, in considering the process of *becoming* as one involving a multiplicity of factors, I return to the notion of personal-subjective and inter-subjective in an attempt to capture my reflexivity as an ethnographer where my subjectivity was enacted upon by neoliberal policies.

Brief overview of Charter School Management Organizations (CMOs)

Regardless of my positionality (e.g. citizen, employee, researcher, etc.), I approach charter schools as a neoliberal project—the result of a policy experiment which now remains a fixed part of the education landscape in the United States. Neoliberalism, with its promotion of 'efficiency', 'productivity' and 'targets' alongside a rhetoric of 'risk' and 'choice', has enabled competition and market-driven results without strategic consideration to the gross economic inequalities they create, particularly for marginalized, low-income communities (Stuart Wells, Slayton & Scott, 2002). While charter schools are diverse and subject to state-based regulatory powers, for the most part they exist as largely autonomous entities, operating under the policy remit that their continued existence is determined by student performance on high stakes state testing. In broad terms, the failure to achieve the necessary test scores would result in revoking the charter and thus the immediate closure of the school. As a result, these institutions are fiercely results-driven environments where nothing is allowed to infringe upon student learning.

Depending on the location, policy climate and the level of philanthropic funding they are able to secure, some charter schools may become Charter School Management Organizations, operating as franchised networks with a specific model, ethos and branding. This is what Ravitch (2013) refers to as the 'McDonaldization of education' where she compares CMOs to the development of retail chain stores. In order to ensure high academic standards, the CMO I worked for was founded on a corporate culture of 'sweating the details' whereby the smallest threat to optimal learning conditions (e.g. poor behaviour, lighting, temperature, smell) is quickly eliminated to guard against further decay. Within this hyper focus to deportment and aesthetics, in terms of academic rigor these institutions ascribe assiduously to 'no excuses' practices (Stahl, 2015; Golann, 2015). As CMOs engage in these controversial practices, it can be argued they are simply practising what in neoliberal language is called 'risk management', to ensure their survival in accordance with the policy remit which allows for their existence.

122   Garth Stahl

Critics have highlighted charter schools as a significant part of the neoliberal assault on the education space. In terms with how we—as educational researchers—seek to comprehend significant societal and political changes, Lipman (2004) asserts we 'must ask what behaviors and identities are being cultivated through current education policies grounded in accountability and centralized regulation of schools' (p. 320). The research addresses how myself and colleagues were deemed worthy in relation to neoliberal measures of productivity—and how targets, indicators and evaluations work to privilege certain subjectivities, performances and configure different ways of becoming (Stahl, 2020). Thus, underlying my research journey are my negotiations with the institutional paradoxes and my own positionality. I now highlight the ways in which IE enhanced my understanding and structured my reflective research.

Becoming an institutional ethnographer

The daily work at the CMO was a powerful experience of inculcation. Before I began this work, I was familiar with historic and seminal work on school ethnography (Willis, 1977; Woods, 1979; Ball, 1981) and, whether consciously or unconsciously, I applied this knowledge in my daily employment as a school leader.[11] The research process rarely develops in a linear fashion or according to ideal types (Hodkinson, 1998). This common issue in research has a significant influence on one's reflexivity (Walby, 2007). I did not actively pursue becoming an ethnographer of the CMO in which I worked. However, as I was fascinated by the experience, I collected institutional texts in the hope of writing about it someday. When I spoke to other scholars about the paradoxes and positionality tied to my experience at the CMO after I had concluded my employment, they asked if I was familiar with feminist sociologist Dorothy Smith's work on developing Institutional Ethnography (IE) as a method of research to explore the social relations coordinating people's everyday lives. As I began to read Smith's corpus of work (1987; 1990; 2005), I entered into a process of structured reflection and hermeneutical deliberation concerning the personal-subjective and inter-subjective,[2] as I attempted to both document and reflect upon my own experience and the practices of the CMO—all existing within a specific time and space.

For Smith, the ethnographic encounter is centred upon 'problematizing the everyday', privileging the dialectic confrontation between experience and shifting subjectivities, where the ethnographer is both the 'doer as well as knower' (Smith, 1987, p. 142). The starting point of any IE is grounded in "the actualities of our lives as we live them in the local particularities of the everyday/everynight worlds in which our bodily being anchors us" (Smith, 1997, p. 393). This is what Smith, and her contemporaries, describe as 'standpoint', which emphasized for me the importance of starting the analysis from the actualities of my own everyday life. IE, as an approach, rebukes traditional sociological methods of inquiry by valorizing the lived realities (Grahame, 1998) over the objectification of research subjects, thus privileging research knowledge.[3] Through acknowledging life is in the actions

An accidental institutional ethnographer **123**

of real people in real places, Smith embraces the subjective. Thus, for Smith (2005), IE is:

> ...exploring the social relations organizing institutions as people participate in them and from their perspectives. People are the expert practitioners of their own lives, and the ethnographer's work is to learn from them, to assemble what is learned from different perspectives, and to investigate how their activities are coordinated. It aims to go beyond what people know to find out how what they are doing is connected with others' doings in ways they cannot see. The idea is to map the institutional aspects of the ruling relations so that people can expand their own knowledge of their everyday worlds by being able to see what they are doing is coordinated...
>
> *(p. 225)*

So rather than capitalize on my previous accrued knowledge in sociology of education—specifically my expertise and experience in school for underprivileged populations—the process became one of foregrounding the problematizing of the mundane everyday milieu of the CMO school culture. In IE the analytic account relies on lived experience where the goal is *an ethnographic synthesis*. As the aim is to 'explore' and not 'answer', the aim is to use social theories—to varying extents—in order to understand day-to-day experiences, ruling relations, micropolitics and perceptions. DeVault (2006) writes:

> Smith's initial sketch for institutional ethnographic research (in Smith 1987; elaborated in Griffith and Smith 2004) demonstrated how one might begin with some embodied experience—in her example it was that of single mothers working to manage their children's schooling—and define a problematic or 'puzzle' that arises from that experience (why should such families be seen as 'defective'?).
>
> *(p. 295)*

Through problematizing the everyday and reflecting upon common practices, routines and rituals, I explore how my own understandings were formed, how my sense of meanings was negotiated, and how my role as part of the institution developed. In terms of the hermeneutical deliberations I encountered, I recalled how Bernstein warned that labels can 'remedy and cure' or 'blind us' (Schwandt, 2000, p. 292) and, additionally, how Bourdieu (1988), reiterating Kant, warns that 'theory without empirical research is empty, empirical research without theory is blind' (p. 775). As the ethnography was written retrospectively drawing on institutional texts and memories, I had to be cautious around the use of both previous knowledge and previous exposure to theory—this is where IE was particularly useful.

Given that my own employment at the CMO required enacting a specific neoliberal model of schooling, my background knowledge of sociological theory at times seemed almost cumbersome to my capacity to reflect on and analyze my experience. How IE was largely neutral in terms of applying various theories—perhaps even apathetic toward theory?—became an important part of departure[4] and how my own subjectivity as a researcher was constituted. In reading various IEs focused on education, I was able to better consider how I had my own views—but those views shifted multiple times. It allowed me to not focus on one theoretical approach (e.g. class inequality, neoliberalism, marketisation) thus I felt I had the freedom to address the *lived experience*, the day-to-day milieu which should, as Smith contends, always be the starting point, what she calls embodied 'standpoint'. Therefore, in writing *Ethnography of a Neoliberal School* (Stahl, 2017), what became central to the text was documenting both my inculcation into institutional practices—which sometimes aligned with my personal values and sometimes did not—and the dialectic between my experience, my own subjectivity and social justice values as well as the subjectivities of the people around me.

Reflecting upon my experience at the CMO through examining the institutional texts (e.g. emails, Blackberry messages, posters, and rubrics), IE compelled me to think of how my reality as institutionally designed and how my actions were organized and regulated by 'ruling relations' (Smith, 2005)—namely neoliberal policy enactment—which works to establish normative practices, privilege certain discourses and contribute significantly to the structuring of certain subjectivities. These texts, or 'textual artifacts' (Smith, 1987; 1990), we know are frequently replicated across time and location to coordinate people in certain processes. Smith (2005) suggests 'texts don't achieve the capacity to regulate just by their existence... the text has no force until it is activated' (p. 81, 82). Furthermore, in writing the institutional ethnography, I drew on these texts outside of their immediate context separated from their intended purpose but still relevant to revealing the complex institutional workings. Smith (1987) asserts that 'the practice of ruling involves the ongoing representation of the local actualities of our worlds in the standardized and general forms of knowledge that enter them into the relations of ruling ... Forms of consciousness are created that are properties or organization or discourse rather than of individual subjects' (p. 3). Critical reflection of how 'ruling relations' come to be represented in texts allowed me, as a researcher, to connect the knowledge of daily work in a CMO with the paradoxes of education reform movements in the United States. Connecting these knowledges led to a deeper reflection on what social justice values and educational equity have come to mean in understanding the cultures in institutions in neoliberal times (Stahl, 2020).

At this point, I briefly consider how autoethnography works in tandem with IE with specific attention to how the IE was composed retrospectively. Coffey (1999) contends the 'construction and production of self and identity occurs both during and after fieldwork' where she argues that through a process of 'writing, remembering and representing our fieldwork experiences we are involved in processes of self-presentation and identity construction' (p. 1). As there were years between the experience of working in the CMO and writing *Ethnography of a Neoliberal School*,

An accidental institutional ethnographer **125**

to structure my thinking I reflected upon when I felt empowered and when I felt disempowered—and the ways I worked as a leader to empower and disempower others in line with the mission of the institution. This supplied a way to carve out the contours of an institutional culture. In her writings on IE, Kerr (2006, p. 48) writes that autoethnography 'tends to privilege the individual "voice," point of view, or experience; it expands the personal-subjective to include inter-subjective and self-reflexive analyses of the socio-political context and the power relations that shape one's experience.' In autoethnography, careful attention is given to the research working to break down their own assumptions and biases where the reader reflects upon and considers what Coffey (1999) calls 'the nature of field relations and identity management' (p. 4). In the case of researching institutions, this is an ongoing process of structured reflective practice where we reflect on ourselves, our values, the institutional practices and the ideologies which structure these practices.

While the conflation between autoethnography and IE is rarely articulated, in my research I found IE to be a compass where, drawing on the work of Smith and her contemporaries, I was able to focus my attention on the experience rather than get caught up in the hermeneutics of what point in the research process certain knowledges came to the fore while other knowledge receded. Certainly, in terms of my own 'identity management', I was embedded in the discourses of the CMO and surrounding the CMO, where I grew to identify strongly with their version of social justice during the course of my employment. After the experience, as time passed and I read further into the history of charter schools and venture philanthropy, I started to question my beliefs. As I have written before, the cult-like practices of the CMO (rigid attention to a mission, exclusivity, urgency, etc.) did influence me (e.g. positionality, subjectivity) and contributed to the ways in which I conducted myself in reference to institutional expectations (c.f. Stahl, 2017).

Reflexivity, theory and becoming in research

All research requires a continual attention to reflexivity. In reflecting upon my accidental journey to becoming an institutional ethnographer, I consider my own reflexivity in three main domains: as a continual and ongoing process relating to *being* and *becoming*; as integral to my hermeneutical circle specifically in relation to the conflation of previous knowledge, theory and experience; and in terms of my inculcation into the norms and values of the institution. Each overlap and mutually inform each other. Walby (2007) writes, 'Reflexivity is often posited as a thing instead of a process, as the opposite of objectivist social science' (p. 1010). In terms of personal-subjective and inter-subjective, reflexivity functions as a consideration of both the ontological implications and the social and intellectual unconscious embedded in analytical operations surrounding research. Reflexivity speaks to the ways of *being* and *becoming* through the process of both working in the CMO and the subsequent years of writing the ethnography. So, I accept that in IE, reflexivity is integral to the intellectual project and how it makes 'explicit a research project's

126 Garth Stahl

goals, intentions, and procedural principles [which] works to displace the position of researcher authority and make the researcher accountable' (Walby, 2007, p. 1015). I adhere to how this is a continual *process*, never fully complete.

In terms of reflexivity in relation to the hermeneutical dimension, I knew a lot about charter schools before I began working for the CMO, I learned a lot as an employee and through writing the IE in the subsequent years. For Bourdieu, reflexivity is a methodological concept which stems from 'critical theory based on a phenomenological questioning of knowledge creation: whether, how, and to what extent a research process allows the subject of knowledge to grasp the object of his or her study in essence' (Grenfell, 2008, p. 200). While IE assisted in the 'object' of study being my own experience, given the immersive nature of IE, the wording of 'object' feels misguided. The issue for me is how my phenomenological questioning was never consistent but instead constantly shifted in relation to both my previous knowledge and experience. In regard to the hermeneutical quandaries all researchers encounter, Hodkinson (1998) writes:

> All researchers are locked into a hermeneutical circle with the subject they are investigating, for they can only see that subject from their own standpoint—a standpoint that is historically, socially and culturally located. This means that not only can there be no logical starting point for research, there can be no 'untainted' truth, or firm foundation upon which to build it.
>
> *(p. 563)*

Considering the notion of *becoming* an ethnographer, or institutional ethnographer, in order to augment autoethnographic approaches with IE, I contend there is a new emphasis on connecting the self (previous self, current self, future self) to the social (global, institutional, familial). This is particularly important in relation to the conflation of previous knowledge, theory and experience. Upon writing the ethnography, I deliberated on what I knew and when I knew it before accepting the immersive nature of the research and how there would always be ambiguity (e.g. the knower—beyond the Cartesian self—who becomes (self)conscious even of the reflexive process of knowing). IEs remain in a delicate balancing act with theory where the tension is integral to how a researcher *becomes*. In drawing upon past IEs, my capacity to consider my narrative or standpoint, as well as the standpoints of other participants, was bolstered as I became increasingly fascinated by how we are caught up in and coordinated by institutional processes. When studying institutions, theory must be employed adeptly to accentuate the analysis of data, yet data must also be allowed to speak for itself. This is what Dolby and Dimitriadis (2004) describe as 'the twin dangers in contemporary social scientific work—the danger of presenting empirical material divorced from theoretical reflection, as well as the danger of theoretical reflection divorced from an engagement with the empirical' (p. 5).

Adding a further dimension to reflexivity is the consideration of one's own positionality; my embedding within the institution meant not only negotiating contentious and paradoxical practices but also the structuring of my own subjectivity in line with the institutional values. In terms of personal-subjective and inter-subjective, identities are constructed within discourses where they acquire different degrees of reflexivity, as identities emerge within the play of 'specific modalities of power, and thus are more the product of the marking of difference and exclusion' (Hall, 1996, p. 4). In writing the IE, I had to recognize my experience influenced how I thought about equity, schooling for underprivileged populations and my social justice values. Taking this into account, in writing the ethnography there were times when I was purposely neutral in the language, establishing a tone of 'recounting' rather than analysis. This was done in an effort to document practices rather than value or devalue the coordinated experiences. Coffey (1999, p. 1) argues in ethnographic research the need to recognize fieldwork as 'personal, emotional and identity work'. Certainly, our life histories and future projections all play an important role in how we negotiate the research process, whether in real-time or retrospectively. The IE was therefore a hermeneutical deliberation, where my own sense of identity shifted (citizen, employee, researcher, etc.). This is reminiscent of Hall's (1996) work on identities, which emphasizes the processes of *becoming*, 'not "who we are" or "where we came from", so much as what we might become, how we have been represented, and how that bears on how we might represent ourselves' (p. 4).

One example of my inculcation into the institutional practices relates to the access and use of texts. In the field of IE, texts remain the principle instruments of ruling relations (Smith, 1987; 2005; Rankin, 2017). Central to my analysis was how texts (e.g. emails, blackberry messages, posters) orchestrate the nature of employees' experiences within the institution and privileged certain subjectivities. In my role within the CMO, I was expected to adopt and use the textual language practices—the institutional discourse—which involved me learning a certain vernacular and using texts to initiate action. Directly related to aligning my subjectivity with the institutional values, I came to understand that certain words had a certain currency, where 'Expressive texts, such as emails and newsletters, state a sense of urgency and are delivered in a state of urgency. Within the CMO, the everyday milieu—the physical movement of people, the emails, the networks of knowledge—moves extremely quickly' (Stahl, 2017, p. 56). For me, these texts often become a vehicle to produce idealized versions where they work to promote and punish certain behaviours. Through the retrospective analysis I was able to draw direct and indirect references for mapping institutional practices and the work they were able to perform within the fast-paced school environment.

Concluding thoughts: Ethnographic tensions in an age of uncertainty

My research on the CMO is positioned within a wider research agenda which considers the uneasy relationship between institutions, corporatization, venture philanthropy, the state of public education and my own subjectivity and conflicted social justice values (Stahl, 2017; 2020). During my time at the CMO and in the years after it, I followed both political and parent blogs as well as tracking policy initiatives at the state level which influenced charter school expansion in order to continue to nuance my understanding of my experience. All of this contributed to my journey towards *becoming* an accidental institutional ethnographer in an age of uncertainty. Working in the CMO was a complex negotiation with power and ethics where I faced the requirement to enact neoliberal policies, which feel uncomfortable but raise important questions regarding social justice. My previous experience working in schools as well as my knowledge of theories associated with inequality contributed significantly to my experience and the subsequent analysis and writing. Adding another layer to the complexity, it is important to consider how the CMO—as an institution—fits within a changing outside world. Reay (2010) writes of the tensions involved in maintaining a 'reflexive and critical lens on identities and identifications within any one of the influential contexts for identity making without losing sight of the impact of other, even broader contexts such as the policy field, the nation state and even the global arena' (p. 281).

Notes

1 Wacquant (2011) argues that one must go in 'armed' with the knowledge of the 'problematics inherited from your discipline, with your capacity for reflexivity and analysis, and guided by a constant effort, once you have passed the ordeal of initiation, to objectivize this experience and construct the object, instead of allowing yourself to be naively embraced and constructed by it' (p. 87–88).
2 Hodkinson (1998) notes the exposure to ideas after the data has been collected is quite common in research.
3 While Smith (1999) argues institutional ethnography rejects the Archimedean point of 'knowing' in traditional sociology, Walby (2007) critiques Smith's work by suggesting the social relations of research always entail a degree of objectification, thus are 'not transcending of objectification, and the institutional ethnographer still retains a high degree of authority over representations of the subject' (p. 1026).
4 This is not to say Smith's work on IE or any of her contemporaries lacks theoretical or conceptual density.

References

Ball, S.J. (1981). *Beachside Comprehensive: A Case Study of Secondary Schooling*. Cambridge University Press.
Ball, S.J. (2016). Subjectivity as a Site of Struggle: Refusing Neoliberalism? *British Journal of Sociology of Education*, 37 (8), 1129–1146.
Beck, U. (1992). *Risk Society: Towards a New Modernity*. SAGE.
Bulkley, K. (2012). Charter Schools … Taking a Closer Look. *Education Digest*, 77 (5), 58–62.
Coffey, A. (1999). *The Ethnographic Self: Fieldwork and the Representation of Identity*. SAGE.
DeVault, M. (2006). Introduction: What is Institutional Ethnography? *Social Problems*, 53 (3), 294–298.
Dolby, N. & G. Dimitriadis (2004). Learning to Labor in New Times: An Introduction. In N. Dolby, G. Dimitriadis and P. Willis (Eds.), *Learning to Labor in New Times*. (1–12). RoutledgeFalmer.

Golann, J.W. (2015). The Paradox of Success at a No-excuses School. *Sociology of Education*, 88 (2), 103–119.

Grahame, K.M. (1998). Asian Women, Job Training, and the Social Organization of Immigrant Labor Markets. *Qualitative Sociology* 21, 75–90.

Grenfell, M. (2008). *Pierre Bourdieu: Key Concepts*. Acumen.

Gronberg, T.J., Jansen, D.W., & Taylor, L.L. (2012). The Relative Efficiency of Charter Schools: A Cost Frontier Approach. *Economics of Education Review*, 31, 302–317.

Hall, S. (1996). Introduction: Who Needs 'Identity'? In S. Hall & P. du Gay (Eds), *Questions of Cultural Identity* (pp. 1–10.). Sage.

Hodkinson, P. (1998). The Origins of a Theory of Career Decision-making: A Case Study of Hermeneutical Research. *British Educational Research Journal*, 24 (5), 557–572.

Kerr, L. (2006). *Between Caring & Counting: Teachers Take on Education Reform*. University of Toronto Press.

Lipman, P. (2004). *High Stakes Education: Inequality, Globalization, and Urban School Reform*. Routledge.

Ravitch, D. (2013). *Reign of Error: The Hoax of the Privatization Movement and the Danger to America's Public Schools*. First Vintage.

Reay, D. (2010). Identity Making in Schools and Classrooms. In M. Wetherall & C. Talpade Mohanty (Eds.), *The Sage Handbook of Identities*. (pp. 277–294). SAGE.

Schwandt, T.A. (2000). Three Epistemological Stances for Qualitative Inquiry: Interpretivism, Hermeneutics, and Social Constructionism. In N.K. Denzin & Y.S. Lincoln (Eds.), *Handbook of Qualitative Research* (pp. 189–213). Sage.

Smith, D.E. (1987). *The Everyday World as Problematic*. Northeastern University Press.

Smith, D.E. (1990). *Texts, Facts, and Femininity: Exploring the Relations of Ruling*. Routledge.

Smith, D.E. (1997). Comment on Hekman's "Truth and method: Feminist standpoint theory revisited". *Signs: Journal of Women in Culture and Society*, 22 (2), 392–398.

Smith, D.E. (1999). *Writing the Social Critique, Theory, and Investigations*. University of Toronto Press.

Smith, D.E. (Ed.) (2005). *Institutional Ethnography: A Sociology for People*. Altamira Press.

Stahl, G. (2017). *Ethnography of a Neoliberal School: Building Cultures of Success*. Routledge.

Stahl, G. (2019a). Critiquing the Corporeal Curriculum: Body Pedagogies in 'No Excuses' Charter Schools. *Journal of Youth Studies*. https://doi.org/10.1080/13676261.2019.1671582.

Stahl, G. (2019b). 'We Make Our Own Rules Here': Democratic Communities, Corporate Logics, and 'No Excuses' Practices in a Charter School Management Organization. *Journal of Contemporary Ethnography* 49 (2), 176–200.

Stahl, G. (2020). Corporate Practices and Ethical Tensions, Researching Social Justice Values and Neoliberal Paradoxes in a 'No Excuses' Charter School. *British Journal of Educational Research*. https://doi.org/10.1002/berj.3617.

Stuart Wells, A., Slayton, J., and Scott, J. (2002). Defining Democracy in the Neoliberal Age: Charter School Reform and Educational Consumption. *American Educational Research Journal*, 39 (2), 337–361.

Wacquant, L. (2011). Habitus as Topic and Tool: Reflections on Becoming a Prizefighter. *Qualitative Research in Psychology*, 8, 81–92.

Walby, K. (2007). On the Social Relations of Research: A Critical Assessment of Institutional Ethnography. *Qualitative Inquiry*, 13 (7), 1008–1030.

Willis, P. (1977). *Learning to Labor: How Working Class Kids get Working Class Jobs*. Columbia University Press.

Woods, P. (1979). *The Divided School*. Routledge & Kegan Paul.

11

RESEARCHERS AND RISK

Exploring vulnerability, subjectivity, and identity in ethnographic research through collage making

Cleti Cervoni, Corinne McKamey, and Rhoda Bernard

Introduction

We are scholars who use ethnographic methods to work with vulnerable populations and topics, including young children and gender (Cervoni & Ivinson, 2011; Cervoni 2014), music and dis/ability (Bernard, 2016), and immigrant youth and educational care (McKamey 2011; 2013). We believe that ethnographic research is an endeavour that poses considerable risks to the researcher, as well as to the participants. In the words of Ruth Behar (1996), the ethnographer is a 'vulnerable observer' whose deeply personal relationships with the research topic, the informants, the ethnographic process and the field come into play in ways that she can never anticipate, but that always require extensive reflection, examination and discussion. At the same time, participants in ethnographic research place themselves at risk as they uncover and reveal their experiences and meaning making over the course of the project, and as they trust the researcher to portray them to others. In our work, we have found the arts-based method of collage making to be a particularly effective tool for exposing, reflecting on, understanding and working through the risks that we and our participants take (Barone & Eisner, 2012; Franklin-Phipps & Rath, 2018; Finley, 2008; Renold, 2018; Hickey-Moody et al., 2016).

We begin by riding with Cleti in her car, driving through a neighborhood to get to her university. Cleti's recollection of this drive helps us explain, in a very concrete way, our framework of assemblage/collage. We then share three vignettes of our subjective experiences of using collage as a research method, pedagogy, and reflective practice. We hope these vignettes provide a larger space for the reader to think about the dynamics and ways of being and becoming with participants and students within a variety of educational and research spaces.

Murals at the point

There is a neighborhood that I (Cleti) pass through each morning as I drive to the University. The neighborhood is unlike any other in this small city (pop. 50,000) in the northeast United States. The neighborhood consists of three streets, and the buildings are all concrete and high rise with multiple apartments jumbled on top of one another. It is called 'the Point' by the locals, and it was the neighborhood that recent immigrants flocked to when they arrived in the area. In the early twentieth century, the Point was occupied by French-Canadians who had recently immigrated from the north. More recently, the Point has been populated by immigrants from the Dominican Republic. A few years ago, an organization called Punto Urban Art[1] commissioned seventy-five large scale murals painted by thirty renowned and twenty-five local artists. Almost overnight the Point became 'El Punto'. As I drive through the neighborhood, I notice that the images fall into several categories. There are inspirational images titled 'trust thyself', and 'don't hate/meditate'. Others are more fantasy-based with bots and galactical creatures. Yet others are of houses with flower boxes called 'home'. There are multiple images of women (one or two with men), but many more as a single image/face of a woman.

New Materialism (Fox & Alldred, 2015; 2018) coupled with the ontology of Deleuze and Guattari (1987), encourages me to consider this space as an assemblage with points of relations among the human and the non-human (Semetsky, 2006). The word assemblage comes from the French root *agencer*, which means 'to arrange, lay out, to piece together' (Nail, 2017, p.22). As an analytical tool and a concept, an assemblage gives the researcher a lens with which to examine social relations and connections in new ways. In the neighborhood, the assemblage consists of the LatinX community, the concrete high-rise buildings, the colorful images, the people who visit and live in the neighborhood, and those like me who drive through on a regular basis. This assemblage is dynamic, with a multiplicity of moving parts and spaces in-between that are always in relation to each other. Deleuze & Guattari talked about these points of relations as 'becomings' (Semetsky, 2006). Drawing from the new materialism paradigm that 'dissolves the boundaries between the natural and the cultural, mind and matter' (Bradiotti, 2013:3), we focus on the processes and interactions in assemblages (Deleuze & Guattari, 1980/ 1987) with its notion of becoming rather than being. Deleuze & Guatarri (1987, p. 293) write 'Becoming is not a process of transforming one thing to another; a line of becoming has neither beginning nor end, departure nor arrival, origin or nor destination... A line of becoming has only a middle'.

What becomings do I imagine for myself? I too am entangled in the middle of this space as a frequent visitor. How does my identity as a middle class, white, cisgender professor shift as a result of the relations in this space? The concept of an assemblage with the notion of in-between spaces ever changing resists definitive data conclusions, and puts the researcher in a fluid understanding of the data, participants and self.

Collage as assemblage

Where assemblage is a concept that provides a framework for analyzing social multiplicity, the process of collage-making is a practice of assemblage. Collage is defined as an artistic composition made of various natural and made materials (such as paper, cloth or wood), glued onto a surface (Butler-Kisber, 2008). Collage has been employed effectively in qualitative research, where researchers engage their informants in creating collages and discussing them (Butler-Kisber & Poldma, 2010; Luttrell, 2003; Vaughan, 2005). Collage-making provides an accessible venue for creating visual representations of concepts, questions and meaning making, and for taking risks by exploring vulnerable topics. It also provides a medium through which participants and researcher can project and discuss multiple conscious and unconscious beliefs and assumptions. This 'plurality of vision' opens up a space that can hold multiple perspectives, beliefs and understandings about a topic, including dissonant and conflicting discourses (Garoian & Gaudelius, 2008; Restler, 2017).

While collage-making has been employed with informants in ethnographic studies (Adriaens, 2014; Luttrell 2003; Kostera, 2006; Mannay & Creaghan 2016) we have also used it as a means for exploring complex and vulnerable issues of our researcher subjectivity and identity. Many scholars have written about the importance of researcher subjectivity (Behar, 1996; Josselson 2011). Understanding their identities helps researchers recognize the tensions created by the 'gaps between authority of experience (the participant's understanding of his or her life) and the authority of expertise (the researcher's interpretive analysis of that life)' (Josselson 2011, p. 33). Minding that gap requires researchers to interrogate who they are and what they bring to the data as well as listening intently to their participants. This reflexive process can be difficult, and sometimes the researcher's key identities and filters are known to the researcher, and sometimes, as McKamey (2011) argues, they can be tacit and unconscious.

As ethnographers of education who also work as instructors and administrators in higher education, we use collage as a research methodology that informs our scholarship and our practice. Our multiple roles are part of the larger assemblages in which we engage.

In the following sections we describe how we have used collage and the multiple ways it has informed how we think about concepts, pedagogies, connections with our participants and program designs. Taken together, the three vignettes we share below function as a content assemblage. We therefore welcome the reader to engage with a mindset of becoming, to stay in-between the relations and to reflect on the dynamics of your relationship to the examples. As you read them, ask yourself: What themes, dissonances and ideas live within and between these vignettes and me? What risks are involved for the researcher and participants as they explore their vulnerabilities? How does the medium of collage help people negotiate these risks?

Becoming—what is nature? (Cervoni)

I teach a course in a public university, *Study Nature not Books*. The course is designed for freshmen to help orient the students to campus. Professors are encouraged to teach the course based on their passion for a topic. I chose learning about the natural world because it is my passion, and I thought given the current political focus on climate change and environmental sustainability, students might be interested. A diversity of students signed up for the course, (white, latinX, middle and working class) with many students being first generation college students. I designed the course to give students as many experiences as I could think of—to immerse them in nature. We spent time outdoors identifying and observing trees; we hiked to a local conservation area along a salt marsh and I taught them about the plants and animals that make up that habitat. We read articles on the historical nature-study movement, and I introduced them to authors that argued the importance of nature-study with children. At some point towards the end of the semester, I invited the students to make a collage. I asked them what magazines they would like me to bring in and suggested that they, too, bring images in. I made available glue sticks, scissors and different colors and shapes of paper as well as a piece of heavy cardboard for them to mount their images on. The prompt was 'to make a collage of your relationship with nature'.

Through watching and listening to my students assemble their nature collages, I noticed that they chose images that were very individual to who they are. For example, Monte spoke of how 'nature to me is the out of doors and hiking' and he described for me a particular time hiking in Maine where he got new boots and picked fresh blueberries. These were tangible things that he brought to the concept of nature. His collage had a quote that said 'nature is waiting for you'. Emily said she chose images personal to her interest in becoming a nurse and her desire to teach others about natural medicine like CBD oil. Brianna said that there was 'a piece of nature in all of us' and used an image of a runner to explain 'getting away from the hustle and bustle of everyday life'. She showed me images of gardens and flowers saying, 'there is nature as more feminine with gardens and flowers'. Many students spoke about advocating for nature by not cutting down more Xmas trees and using artificial ones. Others talked about being part of a start-up group called *Sunrise Moment* to work on climate change issues. My impression was that students did not focus their descriptions on naming and identifying as I often had done with them. Instead, students described their connection with nature in personal, emotional, and subjective terms. I had designed the course to bring students in touch with nature, but had expected the students to use more academic naming and categorizing in their descriptions of nature in their collages. As a student of science in the university, I was taught to recognize and name the plants and animals in my local environment. Telling was one of the ways that I would describe my relationship to nature/science based on my academic background, yet I have always wrestled with this masculine, objective orientation since my personal relationship with nature/science has been one of feelings and emotions. I was entangled in the debate.[2]

134   C Cervoni, C McKamey, & R Bernard

In mapping their images, my students taught me that there was not just one way to relate to nature, but there were multiple relations and that naming was only one way. As my students talked about their unique ways of connecting to nature, I began to understand the continuum and fluidity of knowing and relating to something well. I began to see beyond the fixed binary of nature/culture and see these connections as part of a more fluid way of knowing.

Deleuze and Guattari (1987) use the concept of rhizome. In the rhizome metaphor, knowledge does not emanate from one root but rather spreads horizontally in all directions (Guerin, 2013). This model allows for surprises, multiple forms of knowledge and new ideas to emerge. As they engaged in choosing which images to use and how to position them on the paper, my students discovered new things about themselves and their relationship with nature. Making collages together within the larger assemblage of the course allowed me as the instructor the opportunity to engage with and to hold space for a multiplicity of learner subjectivities (Hickey-Moody et al., 2016). I found that as a result of this risk-taking on all of our parts, I am now even more inclusive in my pedagogy. I encourage my students to take the lead as they immerse themselves into the course content we create together. In this entanglement of mind, matter, human and non-human, we are all becoming.

Becoming—what is a youth worker? (McKamey)

I have found that using collage as a pedagogy and research method opens up a space that provides me and my students to re-consider our beliefs, relationships, and identities. For instance, in my introduction to youth development class, I prompt undergraduate students to build a collage—using natural and recycled materials and magazines—that represents 'who they are' as youth workers. As a researcher, I find that providing students with the space and time (an hour) to create these collages elicits complex representations that students can speak about at length to each other and to me (Luttrell, 2003; McDermott, 2002). As an instructor, I notice the pedagogy of collage making opens up a deep reflective space, positioning students as creators of knowledge (Franklin-Phipps & Rath, 2018; Garoian & Gaudelius, 2008).[3] I am also an observer of myself and of what I as a white cis woman project onto the collages and students. For instance, when talking with one of my students, Jason, about his youth work collage, we both seemed to become entangled in representations of gender and masculinity in relation to care work.

Jason, a broad-shouldered, athletic white student wearing a sports jersey, pasted a lime green felt heart centred in the middle of his collage and the words 'thrive', 'No days off,' 'service',' and 'global' edging four magazine images. As I looked at the other images all depicting men, I saw valences of masculinity: A conquering explorer on an ice floe, a group of athletically fit men on bicycles wearing brightly colored jackets talking and perhaps blocking a road, a gardener wearing a grey baseball hat, kneeling as he pulled a green fern from a pot, a small goalie, with knees bent and outstretched arms. The images centred around the heart and also formed a sort of pyramid, with the man on top of the iceberg at the pinnacle and the other images forming the base under the heart. As I looked at Jason's collage, I stumbled over my own stereotyping of the images as expressions of masculinity.

Jason's narration of the images on his collage carried a very different valence, and emphasised care, community and relationships. 'Tell me about the images you have chosen,' I asked. Jason pointed to the image at the top of his collage. 'A kid is like an iceberg,' he said. 'You only see a small amount on the surface, but there is much more to the person the deeper you get.' He went on to explain the other images. 'I chose this man gardening because working with kids is a lot like gardening. Gardeners need to make sure plants have water, and sunlight, and the right containers. In youth work it's the same, making sure that kids have a good environment and resources so that they can thrive.' He pointed to the cyclists: 'And these bikers, they are a community. It's important to help build a sense of community.' 'This heart,' he said, 'well, working with kids is a lot about relationships and caring.'

'What about this image?' I asked, pointing to the image of the goalie.

'That's me,' he said in a quieter voice.

'That's you?' I asked. 'How does that represent you?'

'I just liked that image,' he said. As he pointed to the figure, I noticed that the goalie was the smallest image on the collage, surrounded by the other images representing community building, creating healthy environments and healthy young people.

This exchange and 'assemblage' of which I as a teacher researcher was a part, opens up multiple associations about gender, masculinity and care work within my classroom and the U.S. context. As Marsiglio (2008) notes, western social expectations most often identify caring for children and young people as women's work. In this western dichotomous gender frame, to identify as a caring man risks conveying a masculine identity. Jason's collage, his explanation of his collage to me, his professor in a course on youth work, and my own interpretations, embrace multiple gendered notions of self and youth work. In considering the collage imagery, perhaps Jason explicitly chose images with a masculine valence to express a tough exterior—a masculine expression of himself that maybe his peers and me and society expected (Kimmel, 2008; Kivel, 1998). Maybe these images were representative of the images of men in popular magazines that Jason had as source material (Luttrell, 2003). Maybe I as a white cis-gender woman was projecting my own stereotypes and assumptions of masculinity—Jason's and his images—upon his visual collage. At the same time, Jason's narrative explanation focused on relations that are more often associated with femininity: Relationships, community and developing caring contexts. As Jason and I considered his answer to the question, 'Who am I as a Youth Worker?' his visual collage, narrative responses and my own interpretations embodied the complexities and vulnerabilities related to negotiating self, youth work and gender. These assemblages resisted a single conclusion and kept me and Jason in an 'in-between' space of possibilities. Garoian & Gaudelius (2008) note the potential of these in-between spaces, 'where knowledge is mutable

136 C Cervoni, C McKamey, & R Bernard

and undecidable, opportunities exist for creative and political intervention and production—a kind of educational research that exposes, examines, and critiques the academic knowledge of institutionalized schooling' (p. 92).

★★★★

Becoming—what is inclusion? (Bernard)

I have used collage as a method to explore my subjectivity as an ethnographic researcher and administrator. Through creating and analyzing collages, I have uncovered some ways in which I am engaging in an intellectually and emotionally risky process of becoming. Creating and examining assemblages about some of the complex issues in my work provides me with a forum to step back and gain a new perspective on my identity and on my relationships with my participants. Specifically, as a non-disabled person who studies and works with musicians with physical and intellectual disabilities, I have constructed collages in response to the question: 'What does disability mean to you?' Through this work, I have explored my understanding of dis/ability, access and inclusion. As an arts-based method of inquiry, creating collages makes it possible for me to express myself without using words or more 'linear' forms of expression (Barone & Eisner, 2012; Cahmann-Taylor & Siegesmund, 2018; Leavy, 2018), revealing some of the unspoken assumptions that lie beneath my thinking. Furthermore, the assemblages that I produce enable me to do more than just examine ideas and express myself —though those processes in and of themselves are certainly valuable. They provide me with a forum in which I can immerse myself in the complex dynamics between me and my informants and gain an understanding of how their relationships play out in my thinking and in my work.

For example, creating and analysing a collage that I made about 'inclusion' enabled me to come to understand a greater range of the ways that the social model of disability (Shakespeare, 2017) plays out through attitudes that serve to disable. According to the social model of disability, disability lies in the barriers created by society. These may be concrete barriers that are easily visible, like those in architectural structures, or they may be barriers in attitudes, policies, assumptions and practices that might be less easily visible (or visible in a different way). In these collage activities, I identified and contrasted representations of inclusion with representations of exclusion, using images and words from magazines. I used photographs of diverse groups of people and accessible spaces, and I found words that related to inclusion, such as 'welcome', 'open',' 'invitation',' and 'family'.' These images and words were juxtaposed in the collage with photographs that depicted standardization and sameness, and words that related to exclusion, such as 'outside, 'different', and 'normal'. I felt connected to the words and images about inclusion and alienated from those about exclusion. In my work, I strive to create safe and welcoming spaces for arts education for all people. I am particularly sensitive to the fact that people with disabilities are too often excluded from arts education opportunities and arts experiences (Bernard, 2020). It is very important to me that others see me as someone who opens up opportunities. At the same time, I struggle with my own privilege as a white, non-disabled, highly educated, upper middle-class woman. I have not known first-hand the exclusion that my participants face every day. I am limited in what I can fully understand about their experience, and their perception of me limits how they can trust me and relate to me.

My collage efforts have also prompted questions about some of the ways that I, as a well-meaning, informed, progressive musician-researcher-scholar-administrator may be unknowingly contributing to these barriers. They have illuminated areas where I would benefit from engaging with my informants more deeply as partners. One such area has to do with whom is served by my organization. I direct an Institute that provides arts education programs for people with disabilities. The programs are all what is known as sub-separate programming —programs only for individuals with disabilities. The aim of the sub-separate programming is to provide a safe space for people with disabilities to learn in and experience the arts. Our mission and work are grounded in the belief that individuals with disabilities need a space, just for them, to learn and gain experiences in the arts. We offer a range of highly effective and engaging classes, ensembles, and lessons. Participants often express their gratitude and happiness. My staff and I observe and measure very impressive artistic skill development in our students, who grow as artists through our programs. Clearly, many aspects of our work are successful. Yet, at the same time, I cannot help but worry that, as we segregate our programs across (dis)ability, we run the risk of perpetuating larger forces in our society that segregate and oppress people with disabilities. I sit with this tension every day in my work, in-between in relation to these two perspectives. As a result of my collage activities, I have reached out to people with disabilities and have begun conversations about the issue of inclusion versus sub-separate programming and how my organization might negotiate these tensions.

For me, the experience of creating collages and speaking about these and other issues with my colleagues has illuminated the ways that my process of becoming is rife with intellectual and emotional risks. Intellectually, it has stimulated and complexified my thinking about myself, my work and my participants. Emotionally, it has provided me with a forum in which to continue to work through my feelings, some of which are uncomfortable.

Discussion

Collage as an ethnographic research strategy and pedagogy can invoke in-between spaces where educators, scholars and participants can negotiate ambiguity, towards new ways of thinking and doing (Franklin-Phipps & Rath, 2018). In our vignettes, we illustrated how the process of collage can provide opportunities to think critically about policies that may reinforce and/or resist systemic oppression; to negotiate and expand identities within educational spaces; and to learn knowledge and ideas while at the same time making space for new knowledge.

Our interactions with collage have helped us become more comfortable with risk in these in-between spaces, including the separations among images and objects and the differing experiences and subjectivities among participants and researchers. We can consider multiple overlapping and changing layers of possibilities and truths. As we work within these in-between spaces, we engage in becoming—the process of growth and new understandings. The process of becoming is inherently risky because it is deeply personal and involves relationships among researcher and participant(s), the research context, and the researcher's understanding of her identity. It is also risky because it is laden with uncertainty and is constantly changing. We believe this process of becoming can help us think more deeply about issues of representation and inclusion, and work with our students and colleagues in opening up new possibilities in our classrooms and institutions.

Notes

1 The Punto Urban Art Museum is a mission-driven social justice art program created by North Shore CDC, a community development non-profit founded in the neighborhood in 1978.
2 Feminist scholars of science have argued that science is gendered and that science instruction needs to take into account multiple ways of knowing including emotion, intuition, imagination, and creativity (Berman, 1992; Keller, 1983; Kelly, 1985; Harding, 1992; Haraway, 1988; Rose, 1983; Rosser, 1989; Schiebinger, 1987).
3 Following the suggestions of participants in a collage workshop at the European Educational Research Conference in 2019, and Subini Annamma (2018), I now make artwork alongside my participants as a way of disrupting the researchers' gaze and to share my own subjectivity and connection with the topic and participants.

References

Adriaens, F. (2014). 'Diaspora Girls Doing Identities': Creating Ideal Television Programmes and Narratives of the Self. *European Journal of Cultural Studies*, 17 (2), 101–117. https://doi-org.ric.idm.oclc.org/10.1177/1367549413508096

Annamma, S.A. (2018). Mapping Consequential Geographies in the Carceral State: Education Journey Mapping as a Qualitative Method with Girls of Color with Dis/abilities. *Qualitative Inquiry*, 24 (1), 20–34.

Barone, T., & Eisner, E. (2012). *Arts Based Research*. Sage.

Behar, R. (1996). *The Vulnerable Observer: Anthropology That Breaks Your Heart*. Beacon Press.

Berman, R. (1992). From Aristotle's Dualism to Materialist Dialectics: Feminist Transformations of Science and Society. In A.M. Jagger & S.R. Bordo (Eds.), *Gender/body/knowledge: Feminist Reconstructions of Being and Knowing*. (pp. 224–255). Rutgers University Press.

Bernard, R. (2016). Disciplinary Discord: The Implications of Teacher Training for K-12 Music Education. In J.H. Davis (Ed.), *Discourse and Disjuncture Between the Arts and Higher Education*. (pp. 53–74). Palgrave Macmillan.

Bernard, R. (2020). Shattering Barriers: Exposing and Understanding the Narratives of Musicians with Disabilities. In A. Dequadros & K.T. Vu, (Eds.), *My Body was Left on the Street: Music Education and Displacement*. Brill Publishers.

Braidotti, R. (2013). *Metamorphoses: Towards a Materialist Theory of Becoming*. John Wiley & Sons.

Butler-Kisber, L. (2008). Collage as Inquiry. In J.G. Knowles & A.L. Cole (Eds.), *Handbook of the Arts in Qualitative Research* (pp. 265–276). Sage.

Butler-Kisber, L., & Poldma, T. (2010). The Power of Visual Approaches in Qualitative Inquiry: The Use of Collage Making and Concept Mapping in Experiential Research. *Journal of Research Practice*, 6 (2), M18-M18.

Cahmann-Taylor, M. & Siegesmund, R. (2018). *Arts Based Research in Education: Foundations for Practice*. Routledge.

Cervoni, C. (2014). Identity, Materials and Pedagogy: Girls in Primary Science Classrooms in Wales. In L. Swiniarski (Ed.), *Moving Forward in a Global Age: World Class Initiatives in Early Education*, (pp. 67–80). Springer.

Cervoni, C. & G. Ivinson. (2011). Girls in Primary School Science Classrooms: Theorizing Beyond Dominant Discourses of Gender, *Gender and Education*, 23 (4), 461–475.

Coleman, R. & Ringrose, J. (2013). Introduction: Deleuze and Research Methodologies. In R. Coleman & Jessica Ringrose (Eds.), *Deleuze and Research Methodologies*. (pp. 1–22). Edinburgh University Press.

Deleuze, G., & Guattari, F. (1980/1987). *A Thousand Plateaus: Capitalism and Schizophrenia*, trans. B. Massumi. Athlone.

Finley, S. (2008). Arts-based Research. In J.G. Knowles & A.L. Cole (Eds.) *Handbook of the Arts in Qualitative Research*. (pp. 71–82). Sage Publications.

Fox, N.J. & Alldred, P. (2015). New Materialist Social Inquiry: Designs, Methods and the Research-Assemblage, *International Journal of Social Research Methodology*, 18 (4), 399–414.

Fox, N.J. & Alldred, P. (2018). New Materialism. In P.A. Atkinson, S. Delamont, M.A. Hardy & M. Williams (Eds.), *The SAGE Encyclopedia of Research Methods* (pp. 1–16). Sage.

Franklin-Phipps, A. & Rath, C. (2018). Collage Pedagogy: Towards a Posthuman Racial Literacy. In C. Kuby, K. Spector, & J. Thiel (Eds.), *Posthumanism and Literacy Education*. (pp. 142–155). Routledge.

Garoian, C. & Gaudelius, Y. (2008). *Spectacle Pedagogy: Art, Politics, and Visual Culture*. SUNY Press.

Gerstenblatt, P. (2013). Collage Portraits as a Method of Analysis in Qualitative Research. *International Journal of Qualitative Methods*, 12 (1), 294–309.

Guerin, C. (2013). Rhizomatic Research Cultures, Writing Groups and Academic Researcher Identities. *International Journal of Doctoral Studies*, 8, 137–150.

Haraway, D.J. (1988). Situated Knowledges: The Science Question in Feminism and the Privilege of Partial Perspective. *Feminist Studies*, 14 (3), 575–599.

Harding, S. (1992). Rethinking Standpoint Epistemology: What is 'Strong Objectivity?'. In L. Alcoff & E. Potter (Eds.), *Feminist Epistemologies* (pp. 49–82). Routledge.

Hickey-Moody, A., Palmer, H., & Sayers, E. (2016). Diffractive Pedagogies: Dancing Across New Materialist Imaginaries. *Gender and Education*, 28 (2), 213–229.

Josselson, R. (2011). "Bet You Think This Song is About You": Whose Narrative is it in Narrative Research? *Narrative Works* 1 (1), 33–51.

Keller, E.F. (1983). *A Feeling for the Organism: The Life and Work of Barbara McClintock*. Freeman and Co.

Kelly, A. (1985). The Construction of Masculine Science. *British Journal of Sociology of Education*, 6 (2), 133–153.

Kimmel, M. (2008). *Guyland: The Perilous World Where Boys Become Men*. Harper.

Kivel, P. (1998). *Men's Work: How to Stop the Violence that Tears our Lives Apart*. Hazelden.

Kostera, M. (2006). The Narrative Collage as Research Method. *Storytelling, Self, Society*, 2 (2), 5–27.

Leavy, P. (2018). *Handbook of Arts-based Research*. Guilford Press.

Luttrell, W. (2003). *Pregnant Bodies, Fertile Minds: Gender, Race and the Schooling of Pregnant Teens*. Routledge.

Mannay, D., & Creaghan, J. (2016). Similarity and Familiarity: Reflections on Indigenous Ethnography with Mothers, Daughters and School Teachers on the Margins of Contemporary Wales. *Studies in Qualitative Methodology*, 14, 85–103. https://doi-org.ric.idm.oclc.org/10.1108/S1042-319220160000014017.

Marsiglio, W. (2008). *Men on a Mission: Valuing Youth Work in our Communities*. Johns Hopkins University Press.

McDermott, M. (2002). Collaging Pre-service Teacher Identity. *Teacher Education Quarterly*, 29 (4), 53–68.

McKamey, C. (2011). Uncovering and Managing Unconscious Ways of "Looking": A Case Study of Researching Educational Care. *Psychodynamic Practice* 17 (4), 403–417.

McKamey, C. (2013). Ensuring Success in School is About More than Getting A's: Layered Stories. *In Education*, 19 (1), 19–33.

Nail, T. (2017). What is an Assemblage? *SubStance* 46 (1), 21–37.

Renold, E. (2018). 'Feel what I feel': Making da (r) ta with Teen Girls for Creative Activisms on how Sexual Violence Matters. *Journal of Gender Studies*, 27 (1), 37–55.

Restler V. (2017). *Re-visualizing Care: The Digital Assemblage. In Re-visualizing Care: Teachers' Invisible Labor in Neoliberal Times*. (Unpublished doctoral thesis). City University of New York. Accessed on 2/25/2020 at https://scalar.usc.edu/works/re-visualizing-care/index?path=index.

Rose, H. (1983). Hand, Brain and Heart: A Feminist Epistemology for the Natural Sciences. *Signs* 9 (1), 73–90.

Rosser, S.V. (1989). Feminist Scholarship in the Sciences: Where are we now and when can we ever Expect a Theoretical Breakthrough? In N. Tuana (Ed.), *Feminism and Science*. (pp. 3–14). Indiana University Press.

Schiebinger, L. (1987). The History and Philosophy of Women in Science. *Signs* 12, 305–332.

Semetsky, I. (2006). *Deleuze, Education and Becoming*. Sense Publications.

Shakespeare, T. (2017). The Social Model of Disability. In L.J. Davis (Ed.). *The Disability Studies Reader* (5th ed.) (195–203). Routledge.

Vaughan, K. (2005). Pieced Together: Collage as an Artist's Method for Interdisciplinary Research. *International Journal of Qualitative Methods*, 4 (1), 27–52.

12

ETHNOGRAPHIC EDUCATIONAL RESEARCH AS ASSEMBLAGES OF TEACHERS' AND RESEARCHERS' MOVEMENTS AND THEIR LEARNING ENVIRONMENTS

Juliane Corrêa

Introduction

The theoretical-methodological foundation of my research about the difficulties of incorporating new information and communication technologies in educational contexts has been building up in line with educational ethnography, a constructionist perspective, and a qualitative research approach. Therefore, it was possible to understand that the use of a specific educational space reflects the use of the other settings of the school and that its comprehension depends on the information related to the context. That is to say; the reality is built in many ways of interaction with the space, the body, social networks and relationships.

The field of my research was the context of professional development of primary school teachers involved in the Undergraduate Course carried out in partnership with the Department of Education of Minas Gerais State and the Federal University of Minas Gerais (Brasil). In this course participated six hundred teachers from two hundred and sixty primary schools, carried out on-line with face-to-face sessions in the schools where the teachers worked and at the University. From this group, forty schools were selected, according to their geographical distribution, to carry out my observations and interviews.

The initial objective of this research was to map out the uses of educational spaces and computer labs. With that purpose, this work took into consideration the spaces of these forty public schools. However, when I studied the context of the teacher's work, I noticed that something affected my perception of the experience and that an unknown materiality often overlooked in teacher professional development was present.

Recently, in my readings (Ellsworth, 2005; Freitas, 2012; Cumming, 2014; Clarke and Parsons, 2013; Atkinson, 2018; Semetsky, 2006, 2010; Masny, 2014; Massumi, 2002) about post-qualitative research, cartography and rhizomatic perspectives allowed me to integrate something that I realized in my research but did not know how to express by then. I started to realize that we can understand how teachers affect and are affected by these learning spaces just as I, as a researcher, became entangled with these shared environments. In other words, I recognized the rhizome researchers/teachers and ethnographic educational research as assemblages, and I have expanded my understanding of the educational experience through my experience as a researcher.

This study focuses on three school scenes, fragments of assemblages, and it gives a small illustration, maybe a sketch of the educational ethnography research: Sound space; moving space; shared space and, at the end, it introduces some approaches that allow us to understand the learning environment through an ethnographic and rhizomatic perspective. This chapter does not aim to explain what happens in schools but seeks to approach, to map out the 'becoming of' educational spaces.

As a university teacher and an educational researcher, I would like to understand what is happening in the educational spaces and computer labs that make up the daily life of schools. I aim to provide significant elements for proposing new teacher professional development itineraries, contributing, thus, to the advancement of teaching practices and educational policies.

Educational ethnographic research—travelled paths

This work has been done by studying the cultural phenomena that occur in everyday school life and the teaching practice. The focus of the research was to analyse how teachers use computer labs, but the approach to research generated a set of indications that changed the initial question. In the beginning, I was doing ethnography research about computer labs and virtual environments, but surprisingly I discovered learning settings in different spaces of the school, including the material environment. Consequently, this changed my perspective.

In the ethnographic perspective, according to Green et al. (2012), it is crucial to give visibility to the decisions that make changes and reconstruct the logic-in-use. Throughout the process, it was possible to include the objective of mapping the social networks that make up daily life at school and to recognize the implications of the individuals inserted into them. We also witnessed the presence of everyone in every space. By doing so, new questions began to emerge: How do the teachers get involved in the learning space? What happens in the computer labs?

Sancho (2013, p. 83), emphasizes the need 'to take into account the complex phenomena created by the multifaceted aspects of culture' to understand 'the cultural changes related to the values, ways of accessing and assessing information and knowledge, ways of relating to others'. And Hernandez-Hernández & Fendler (2013) also point out that when they inquired how students give meaning to the experiences of silence in university classes, they evidenced the possibilities of displacement due to the potential of the research to generate stories, images, perceptions and affects. So, these complex phenomena and this displacement were central points in my research and allowed me to express my perspective as an educational researcher.

Moreover, my reference of ethnography was 'a non-linear system, guided by iterative, recursive and abductive logic' (Green et al., 2012, p. 309). This perspective shows that an ethnographic study is not based on 'the length of time involved but the logic-in-use guiding the researcher's decisions, actions and work across all phases of the study' so that the most important 'are moments where ethnographers are confronted with a surprise or something that does not go as expected' (Ibid., p. 312).

On my initial visits to each school, the spaces were introduced to me by their functionality such as recreational, service, circulation, communication, collective, specialized, external settings, as well as by their conditions of use such as run-down schools, abandoned ones or well-taken care. I found painted, unpainted schools, graffiti-vandalized, graffiti-cleared schools, schools with gardens, without gardens, with a concrete paved patio, with a dirt patio or without a patio. I gradually realized how those spaces were composed of small networks of interaction that dialogued with other systems as well as with possibilities of each new element, object or person present in educational places. Besides that, the data collection allowed me to identify the material constitution of the building, the use and appropriation of physical spaces as its architecture that made it possible to identify the foundation time of the school building.

Cumming (2014) reminds that any data, which includes gestures, objects, tonalities of voices, ways of walking, glances, preferred, and non-preferred spaces are within assemblies and connecting elements of different groups. From this, you can only trace the connection lines, the possible movements and the 'becoming'. Thus, the use of visual cartographies (Hernandez-Hernández et al, 2018) enables an epistemological, methodological approach that allows for micro-ethnographic descriptions and a mapped out 'process of becoming, characterized by forces, flows and fluxes that disrupt the unity of the subject' (p. 106). Furthermore, the use of visual cartographies can be an epistemological medium, an apparatus of capture (Cumming, 2014) that registers and visually documents the experience where something escapes, comes through, resonates, affects, produces a transformation in the body, in the brain and the feelings.

Therefore, that learning means moving along with a specific environment (Semetsky, 2010) in a meeting with an unknown problem through its unfolding experience. Ontologically, in the Deleuzian conception 'to be' in itself is a fold, so in our experiences 'we go from fold to fold' (Deleuze, 1993 as cited in Semetsky, 2006, p.15). Due to the knowledge of the educational ethnographic research, I discovered that subjects and contexts became present in assemblages, that something was present and insisted on appearing. And, in this way, one exercises a 'mental correction', experiments with 'ways of disrupting familiar dualisms that can disconnect and stabilize assemblages' (Cumming, 2014, p. 38). In other words, one exercises the logic of 'AND' that allows for thinking the unthinkable. This experience is not limited to what is immediately perceived because it is oriented to the future, to the becoming, which takes place in the lines of flight.

In this regard, I could recognize unfolds and assemblages in those observed scenes that were experienced through the immersion in the daily life of schools due

144 Juliane Corrêa

to the ethnographic research carried out, that is, scenes that allowed me to approach the 'learning environments' or 'pedagogical becoming'.

Becoming rhizome researchers/teachers—unfolds and assemblages

When I carried out this ethnographic educational research, I perceived a complexity of day-to-day interconnections that included students, teachers, researchers in different contexts and, as a result, something happened and grew beyond the separated identities. For this reason, new perspectives on educational research were necessary. Clarke & Parsons (2013, pp. 36–37) consider that 'Research changes the researcher in often inexplicable ways', that is, 'research as rhizomatic or becoming rhizome researchers'. This statement was vital in this work and, therefore, I considered the 'new perspectives that emerge from thinking as a rhizome researchers' (Ibid., p. 39) highlighted by these authors:

1- Start where they are.
2- Listen to the voice/things connected to them.
3- Embed themselves in the lives of their research/students.
4- Develop sensitivities to elements/people that are not part of the status quo.
5- Search for sometimes ignored research aspects.
6- Desire a life of becoming rather than copying what is seen.

These aspects helped me understand that something affected me as a researcher in my interaction with contexts and teachers of the visited schools and I verified that being available for research is not only an availability of time, but it also implies the quality of presence in the space.

According to post-structuralism and the new empiricism, Semetsky (2010, pp. 477–79) approaches the experience as 'that milieu which provides the capacity to affect and be affected; it is a-subjective and impersonal'. It is necessary to highlight that, for the author, learning means moving together within a given environment in an encounter with an unknown problem through unfolding experiences. She approaches difference not as a personal or individual attribute or aspect, but as a condition for the manifestation of each phenomenon. Therefore, affects, the possibility of encounter, of event, of difference, are embedded in the experience, and it is this ability to affect and be affected that makes learning happen.

Initially, I had the assumption that we reveal ourselves together in the act of knowing and that the emphasis of our premises affects what we testify so that we can gather information that confirms what we think, avoiding what disconcerts us. Besides, something that I contacted escaped in my comprehension of what emerged. I noticed that the experience is not limited to what is immediately perceived. According to Semetsky (2010) the experience is oriented towards the future, the becoming that takes place in the flight lines that allow us to access the possibility of the creative, the unthinkable, the unpredictable. She approaches the experience as an active experimentation in the relationship with the other. Following her line of

Ethnographic education research **145**

thought, I started to consider something that I did not know and looked to my research in an attempt to understand the school from other perspectives.

To clarify that active experimentation, I selected some scenes from my observation records made in primary schools and the University computer lab. The first two scenes introduced lines of flight that affected my perception of the school space, and the third scene allowed me to become 'We', changing the research and the researcher.

Scene 1: Sound space

I was waiting for the teacher at her classroom door and listening to her, speaking loudly to the students. I waited until recess so I could interview her. The noise was tremendous from the children. It took us a while to find a quieter place; we went to a room at the back of the library, but it was in vain. The noise made the conversation difficult, and she told me that that noise remained in her head night and day. She did not notice how high her tone of voice was, because this noise was present in her readings, when preparing the lessons and even when her class was silent.

Ellsworth (2005, pp. 28–29) argues that the experience of an event, the movements, the bodily sensations constitute the 'materiality of pedagogy' and that it is possible to materialize this pedagogical force in and through 'places of learning' where teachers become active participants in the 'pedagogical becoming'. This statement is evident in reports and experiences, allowing one to move through 'sensations, pre-linguistic and pre-subjective' that precede concepts, images, or recognitions as things made and promised to 'bring something new and unexpected into the loop'.

In this research, I realized that the materiality of learning consists of an invitation to go beyond, to unfold minds and bodies, allowing self-learning to emerge. That in the sound space in which the teachers immersed themselves daily, it was possible to perceive the noises of the school and the children in movement; noises that permeate, which remains beyond working hours. In fact, through the pedagogical becoming, I was discovering how things happened, not what they meant, but how in that specific context, they were 'beings'. The point was not to talk about school; it was to feel the space of the school in this self-perceived contact and be aware of it. By inhabiting this sound space or being inhabited by it, the teachers developed a specific perception about themselves, the other teachers, the students, and their context. It is confusing, like a cloud in our minds, in our bodies or of a barrier that prevents us from listening, understanding and thinking.

Furthermore, the capacities of bodies in the assemblage are the productive capacity of the assemblage itself (Cumming, 2014). Assemblages, in a Deleuzian sense, are processes of arrangements that continuously shift through movements that stabilize, destabilize and restabilize spaces. As Cumming (2014, p. 144) explains, I had time to 'collect myself', I saw these deterritorializing movements as reminders to decentralize and to connect myself as an element in the assemblage, rather than holding the research assemblage at a distance.

Scene 2: Moving space

We met in the boardroom, and our conversation began formally. As we walked through the school spaces, we passed the kitchen, the storage room, the patio, the library, the computer lab. The conversation changed in tone, corporeality, and even content. The moving body gained gestures, approximations, and distances according to the spaces we travelled. When we went into the toilets, it was as if we were accessing something very precious because the teacher's tone of voice changed, her body approached, as in the promise of telling a secret. She showed me the toilets with great satisfaction and pride, in a tone of intimacy, for this was the best of all local public schools' bathrooms.

Green et al. (2012, p. 313) state that 'events are constructed by members in and through discourse and actions among participants, and that an event may involve multiple levels of timescale and activity.' This view can relate to the rhizomatic perspective due to their conception of events as dynamic and developing, as potentially existing across time. Besides, Cumming (2014, p.138) tells us that 'this focus of rhizoanalytic approaches on movements makes them well suited to enquiry what seeks to generate new possibilities, change, and transformation.' That is, rhizoanalytic approaches 'focus on what is produced in the interactions of parts of assemblages, rather than centring on meanings produced by or for participants' and so that every moment of interaction looks like a lot of things.

I could observe how the discourse varies according to the spaces covered, gaining greater intimacy, explaining other meanings and identifying a correlation between the occupation, the movement in the physical area of the school and the characteristics of the language and the content addressed (Corrêa, 2018). Teachers' connections and interactions were restricted to the immediate vicinity of the space they occupied: The teachers' room and their classroom, not extending much beyond that limit. At first, I noticed that primary school teachers avoided using different information and communication technologies and expanding their possibilities of interaction. After this research, I realized that they had other needs, of which I was unaware. Usually in teachers' professional development, the courses do not acknowledge the intimate life that unfolds, that emerges apart from the curricular planning and that breaks out in the daily life of schools.

In a broader sense, Atkinson (2018) considers human beings as existing in relation to all other entities; a conceived mind and body as entities which are not separate—and he disagrees on the view which considers the identities of teachers and learners as something already inscribed. He says that 'We don't know what a body is capable of doing or thinking; we don't know what teaching or learning is capable of' and that 'we don't have a full understanding of our bodies or those bodies that affect us, human or non-human' (p. 45). For 'Our ideas and affects are constantly succeeding each other in the process of experiencing, according to where we are, who or what we meet, what we do, what we see, and so on' (Ibid, p. 43). Thus, I could never have imagined that the toilet would be the most important space of a school.

Scene 3: Shared space

It is Saturday. We are in the computer lab at the Faculty of Education. We have one of the groups of students that are primary school teachers. All have been registered in our system and have their usernames and password; that is, they can use the Internet. At this point in the course, the task is to send an email. A lady is very nervous, not knowing what to do. I crouch down beside her and ask what is happening; if she has difficulty turning on the computer or accessing the browser or typing the text. 'What's the matter, what's the difficulty?' She tells me whispering: 'I have no-one to email'. At this moment, the space unfolds, something escapes, and we are in an intimate space.

When the digital inclusion of six hundred primary school teachers was done by the University, through weekly classes in the computer lab of the Faculty of Education, the reality of teachers was unknown. There was no contact, but only an idea of digital inclusion and teachers. At that moment in the computer lab that teacher gained a face, hands, she expressed a fragility from a body movement that we did together, a respectful approach that allowed something to emerge. This situation allowed our space to emerge; our intimate space and I became 'We'. This experience was of fundamental importance because from that point on, I began to explore a place that I could not name, which destabilized me as a researcher. The experiences do not fit in the questions; they are vanishing points that deterritorialize the question, that go beyond and deconstruct the initial problem. As Semetsky (2006, p. 16) quoting Deleuze tells us: 'I do not encounter myself on the outside. I find the other in me.' I could conclude, from that lab experience, that we are part of the assemblage, including our materiality and the matter of all things.

Besides that, Ellsworth (2005, p. 16) states that: 'I will locate the experience of the learning self as a self not in compliance but in transition and in motion toward previously unknown ways of thinking and being in the world.' She understands that 'when we think of experience as a question of sensation, we remind ourselves that we do not have experiences. We are experiences' (Ibid, p. 26). That is, we live through these places of learning not as observers, but rather in a space where there is 'neither self nor other but the reality of relation', and 'the world and I exist in difference, in encounter' (Ibid., p. 30). What she means is that the inside and the outside are interdependent since the outside requires an engagement from the inside; it needs to 'go beyond'. Moreover, she considers that these places of learning allow for one to live the experience as an emergent event and to access the pre-linguistic and non-linguistic, printing a quality to the learning experience, an understanding of what is learned. In this way, we can reach the materiality of places of learning, as events of the body, being something that affects us in the body, but beyond subjectivity.

In this episode, I was affected as if we were not separate one from the other, and for a moment, we fused. Knowledge happened directly without mediation, without being necessary to explain. It became clear that we had to change the route, which achieved something else. What we had was no longer enough. It was

148 Juliane Corrêa

another quality, another texture. And yet with a capacity to generate other actions, other interactions and even another perception of ourselves.

Little by little, I was building the understanding that educational ethnographic research allows approaches to assemblages and unfolds. Then, I could observe by rhizoanalysis the scenes, the tellings that emerge from an assemblage, 'that affect and are affected in an assemblage' (Masny, 2014, p. 358); in other words, this space where something from the other manifested in me.

Ethnographic educational research as assemblages

Usually, in my classes, I approach the notion of learning as change, in the sense of provoking, having displacement because of learning. Now I begin to perceive another dimension of this process: That learning and displacement happen together. It is not before or after. It is neither a cause nor a consequence. And it is not easy to break this mental pattern. I notice that we often incorporate new concepts within the same thought structure and reformat them to fit in, and most of the time, we do not even realize what we do. We think we have learned something new, but we are using the same logical mechanisms to interact with our perceptions.

In this ethnographic educational research, I describe some scenes throughout the text in which, through my corporeality, I put myself in relation to the context, to the other, to myself and 'WE' reach one space inside 'AND' outside at the same time. With that in mind, I consider that we can, little by little, allow for the necessary resourcefulness to perceive this space between, where the 'being' is in sensation, the reality of relation occurs and the 'becoming of' the educational spaces changes us. In other words, a learning environment of interactions that upholds the 'experience of the learning self' as 'in the making' and participates in the 'unfounded and unmediated in-between of becoming' (Ellsworth, 2005, pp. 33–34).

All this makes me think of Massumi's (1995) approach that considers the event as processual unfolding of forces of expression, the 'happening doing' in the middle of something already underway. Therefore, it is not possible to witness something because, unexpectedly, the subject is already part of what happened. It goes along with the emphasis of Semetsky (2006, p.74), who throughout her texts tells us 'it does not live in an environment; it lives by means of an environment' recollecting what Dewey had already told us.

Recently, while revisiting the documentation of my experience in research, I realized that at certain moments, some meanings unfolded, changed, disfiguring the initial script and allowing for a new configuration to emerge as well as a new experience of myself as a presence in the space. So, in my postdoctoral studies at the University of Barcelona with Juana M. Sancho Gil and Fernando Hernandez, I had the possibility of reviewing and reorganizing my process, my data, my perception of this research.

Ethnographic education research **149**

I discovered the cartographic perspective as a possibility to present rhizomatic connections, a contact with the unfolding, the 'becoming'. I did not use the cartography method in my research. Still, when I reviewed the initial organization of data in the form of the scenes, I noticed that when grouping them in a linear structure by using bidimensional representation, this process made it possible to visualize the empty spaces and the silent spaces. And when arranging them in a non-linear structure by using three-dimensional representation, it created the possibility to visualize the shadows, the depth and gravity.

In my analyses of the scenes, the sound space one is above the other scenes, and it creates a shadow in the body, in the perception which affects one in an unknown way. It is often difficult to find the necessary clarity for the understanding and the expression of thoughts and emotions. Consequently, it can compromise dialogue and interaction with oneself and others. Similarly, the distance from the toilet affects the position of the library and the computer lab. That distance is in turn affected by the shadow of the library and the computer lab overlapped. The void between the intimate space and the space in movement points to lines of escape that lead to other places, which sometimes coincide with the spaces of run-down schools, abandoned or well cared for areas. New questions arise from voids and shadows: How does my movement affect the empty and shadowed spaces? How do those spaces affect me? How does the intimate space with the other affect and become affected by all of this?

When organizing the experiences in scenes, I explicit something that Freitas (2012) identifies as a rhizome whose characteristic is being able to be cut, but which starts up again elsewhere on one of its old or new lines; that is to say, the maps or diagrams 'can function as pragmatic exercises of finding out how something works' (p. 594), and they make it possible to identify a 'knot', that according to Freitas is an event, a potentiality. She says that these maps or diagrams 'capture the ontogenetic nature of classroom interaction' (Ibid., p. 599). In my research, I discovered they could also capture the ontogenetic nature of school interaction. As I explained earlier in the presented scenes, when we allow the face, the hands, the fragility of the body in movement to emerge, our space appears as well, and the intimate space breaks out. When I become We, we do not use the protections to avoid contact, and something happens, something unfolds which changes our separate identities. Because 'when a body is in motion, it does not coincide with itself. It coincides with its own transition: its own variation' (Massumi, 2002, p. 4). This author emphasizes that the qualitative transformation that occurs, which we call 'emerging', constitutes a dynamic unity.

In this chapter, I deal with how I experienced in my research the process of palpation that allowed, according to Masny (2014, p. 358), the 'reading data to become intensive and immanent'. She highlights that this process 'can be challenging, ambiguous and difficult.' Indeed, I experienced that and observed how it was possible through this approach to perceive something more, and this was expressed in the scenes presented. This something more connected with the raw tellings 'that resonate with flows of affects engaging multiplicities, complexities and out-of-boundaries messiness' (Ibid., p. 358).

Admittedly, the raw telling affected me as a researcher and a teacher, so I seized this opportunity to analyse my research from another perspective and to rewrite the process I experienced. When Masny (Ibid., p. 359) asks 'might rhizoanalysis entail the interaction of forces with what a body can do and what is it capable of with affect/becoming that happens in reading connecting relations intensively and immanently in an assemblage?' I feel I must keep asking: Is it possible that the encounters with the outside also provoke the re-engagements of the inside and that it puts something of the inner reality to process? Is it possible to discover relations and potentialities beyond oneself?

According to Denzin (2005, p. 1084), when talking about the future of qualitative research,

> we seek a set of disciplined interpretive practices that will produce radical democratizing transformations in the public and private spheres of the global postcapitalist world. Qualitative research is the means to these ends. It is the bridge that joins multiple interpretive communities. I can conclude, through my experience as a teacher/researcher, that ethnographic educational research enhances this process as it allows for connecting the immanent, the context of schools so that ethnographic educational research becomes an assemblage of teachers and researchers' movements and their learning environments.

References

Atkinson, D. (2018). *Art, Disobedience, and Ethics. The Adventure of Pedagogy*. Macmillan. doi:10.1007/978-3-319-62639-0.

Clarke, B. & Parsons, J. (2013). Becoming Rhizome Researchers. *Reconceptualizing Educational Research Methodology*. 4 (1), 35–43.

Corrêa, J. (2018). *Insufficient or Inadequate – Teacher Training for the Use of ICTs in Educational Contexts*. OmniScriptum Publishing.

Cumming, T. (2014). Challenges of 'Thinking Differently' with Rhizoanalytic Approaches: A Reflexive Account. *International Journal of Research & Method in Education*, 38 (2), 137–148.

Denzin, N.K. (2005). The Future of Qualitative Research. In N.K. Denzin, & Y.S. Lincoln (Eds.), *The Sage Handbook of Qualitative Research, Third Edition* (pp. 1083–1087). SAGE.

Ellsworth, E. (2005). *Places of Learning: Media, Architecture, Pedagogy*. Routledge.

Freitas, E. (2012). The Classroom as Rhizome: New Strategies for Diagramming Knotted Interactions. *Qualitative Inquiry*, 18 (7), 588–601. doi:10.1177/1077800412450155.

Green, J.L., Skukauskaite, A., & Baker, W.D. (2012). Ethnography as Epistemology: An Introduction to Educational Ethnography. In J. Arthur, M. Waring, R. Coe, & L.V. Hedges (Eds.), *Research Methods and Methodologies in Education* (pp. 309–321). SAGE.

Hernández-Hernández, F., & Fendler, R. (2013). An Ethnographic Approach to Researching Students' Experiences of Silence in University Classes. In F. Hernández-Hernández, R. Fendler, & Sancho-Gil, J.M. (Eds.) *Rethinking Educational Ethnography: Researching on-*

line communities and interactions (pp. 54–64). Universidad de Barcelona. http://hdl. Handle. net/2445/44009

Hernández-Hernández, F., Sancho-Gil, J.M., & Domingo-Coscollola, M. (2018). Cartographies as Spaces of Inquiry to Explore of Teacher's Nomadic Learning Trajectories. *Digital Education Review*, 33, 105–119. doi:10.6018/rie.36.2.30442.

Masny, D. (2014). Disrupting Ethnography through Rhizoanalysis. *Qualitative Research in Education*, 3 (3), 345–363. doi:10.4771/qre.2014.51.

Massumi, B. (1995). The Autonomy of Affect. *Cultural Critique, 31* (2), 83–109.

Massumi, B. (2002). *Parables for the Virtual – Movement, Affect, Sensation.* Duke University Press.

Sancho-Gil, J.M. (2013). Rethinking Educational Ethnography: Researching on-line communities and interactions. – Final remarks. In F. Hernández-Hernández, R. Fendler, & J. M. Sancho-Gil (Eds.) *Rethinking Educational Ethnography: Researching On-line Communities and Interactions* (pp. 54–64). Universidad de Barcelona. http://hdl. Handle.net/2445/44009.

Semetsky, I. (2006). *Deleuze, Education and Becoming. Educational Futures: Rethinking Theory and Practice.* Sense Publishers.

Semetsky, I. (2010). The Folds of Experience or Constructing the Pedagogy of Values. *Educational Philosophy and Theory*, 42 (4), 476–488.

INDEX

Note: 'n' indicates chapter notes.

15M Movement 81–82, 87, 90n2

abductive processes 19, 21, 22, 56, 58, 65, 143
access 17, 43, 76, 86, 127, 136, 142
accountability 119, 122
Actor-Network Theory 32, 35, 82–84
Adler, P.A. 35
affects 3, 83–89, 108–111, 144, 150
Agar, M. 24–25, 26, 34, 56, 76
Ahmed, S. 113
Arrival Education 64
artifacts 18–20, 22, 34, 36, 124
assemblages 3, 81–87, 130, 131, 142–150;
    collage as 132, 134, 135
Atkinson, D. 87, 94, 95, 106, 111, 146
Atkinson, P. 34
auto-ethnographic perspectives 7, 40–48,
    124–126

Baker, W.D. 58
Bakhtin, M.M. 66
Ball, S.J. 44, 46, 120
Barad, K. 4, 49n5, 99, 102n2–3
Barker, R. 42
Bateson, M.C. 52, 61
Beach, D. 33, 36
Beck, U. 120
Becker, H.S. 31, 34
'becoming' concept 3–7, 17
Behar, R. 130

being, ways of 20, 24, 26, 52, 55, 59,
    60, 61
Bellour, R. 84
Berger, P.L. 26
Bernstein, B. 45, 123
Blok, A. 35
boundaries 19, 54, 59
Bourdieu, P. 123, 126
boyd, d. 3
Breidenstein, G. 32
Breuer, F. 104
Britzman, D.P. 97, 101
Butler, J. 4–5

Callon, M. 83
cartography 88–89, 93, 98–100, 107–108,
    141–142, 143, 149
Cazden, C. 36
charter schools 119–128
Chicago School 35
Clarke, B. 144
climate 87, 89; *see also* spaces, educational
Coffey, A. 124, 127
collaboration 24, 26
collage 130, 132–138, 138n3
connections 19, 131, 132, 134, 138n3, 143,
    144, 146, 149
contexts 40, 42–46, 48
culture 2, 19–21, 110
Cumming, T. 143, 145, 146

Index 153

de Freitas, E. 88–89, 100
Delamont, S. 34
Deleuze, G. 4–5, 81, 87, 92, 93, 97–101, 107, 131, 134, 143, 145
Denzin, N.K. 150
DeVault, M. 123
Didi-Huberman, G. 96
diffraction 98, 99, 100, 101
digital ethnographies 2–3, 34, 48, 92, 147
Dimitriadis, G. 126
disability 136–137
discomfort 56–57, 107, 109, 128
displacement 107, 112, 113, 142, 148
Dixon, C.N. 54
Dolby, N. 126
Domingo, M. 48
Donin, J. 75
drift 98–99
Duneier, M. 35
Duranti, A. 36

Ellen, R.A. 66
Ellsworth, E. 145, 147
emic/etic perspectives *see* insider/outsider perspectives
epistemological perspective 1, 2, 3, 6, 17, 33, 53, 54, 55, 58–61, 86, 110–111, 143
Estalella, A. 85
ethical perspective 1, 2, 3–4, 6, 47, 48, 99, 106, 109, 110–111, 120–121, 128
ethnocentrism, setting aside 17, 19, 25, 26, 56, 58

Faber, R. 4–5
Fendler, R. 142
Fiction Workshop (FW) 81–89
fieldnotes 3, 18, 20, 47, 109
fieldwork 29, 34, 35, 85–87, 92, 93, 101
Fine, G.A. 33
folds/unfolds 143–145, 148
Forsey, M. 35
frame clash 24–25, 64, 67
Frederiksen, C.H. 75
Freitas, E. 149

Garcia, A.C. 36
Garfinkel, H. 30
Garoian, C. 135
Gaudelius, Y. 135
gaze 40, 42, 46, 48, 94, 106–107, 138n3
Geertz, C. 2
gender 134–135
General Organic Law of the Education System (LOGSE, Spain, 1990) 105
Giddens, A. 67

Goffman, E. 31, 34
Green, J.C. 110
Green, J.L. 19, 20–21, 24, 54, 58, 142, 146
Guattari, F. 4, 5, 81, 92, 93, 97–101, 107, 131, 134
Gubrium, J.F. 32
Gumperz, J. 36

Hall, S. 127
Hammersley, M. 29, 34
Haraway, D. 99
Heath, C. 33
Hernández-Hernández, F. 48, 92, 112, 142
Hickey-Moody, A. 87
Hill-Bonnet, L. 65–66
Hillman, T. 36
Hitzler, R. 36
Hodkinson, P. 126, 128n2
Holmes, D.R. 85
Honer, A. 36
Hroch, P. 101
Hymes, D. 21, 36

identity 120, 125, 127, 128, 131–138, 144
imagination 2, 85, 106, 108, 110, 113, 131
in-between spaces 131, 132, 135, 137, 138
inclusion 134, 136–137
insider/outsider (emic/etic) perspectives 21, 23, 25, 26
institutional ethnography 119–128, 128n3
institutions in education 29, 31–32, 34–36
interactional ethnography 64–68, 72, 75–77
interactions 20, 21–24, 26
intra-actions 2, 49n5, 94, 99, 101, 102n3
iterative processes 19–23, 26, 65

Jackson, A.Y. 2
jagodzinski, j. 94, 96, 98

Kanuha, V. 86
Kerr, L. 125
Knoblauch, H. 35
knowing, ways of 20, 21, 22, 26, 52, 53, 61, 134, 138n2
knowledge production 4, 22–26, 31, 33, 108, 113
Koro-Ljungberg, M. 2, 97
Kunda, G. 108

languacultures 26, 56, 58, 59
language use 24–25, 32, 36, 53, 120, 127, 146
Lather, P. 2, 4, 108, 113
Latour, B. 32, 83

154 Index

learning: processes 22–23, 26, 52–61, 92–95; teachers' 105–113; workplace-based 64, 68
Lipman, P. 122
listening 52, 53–56, 60
lived experience 20, 26, 64, 65, 67, 120, 123, 124
Löytönen, T. 95
Luckmann, T. 26
Lundborg, T. 5, 111

Macbeth, D. 35
maps/mapping see cartography
Marcus, G.E. 85, 108
marginalized populations 120, 121, 123, 127
Marsiglio, W. 135
masculinity 134–135
Masny, D. 149, 150
Massumi, B. 148
Mazzei, L.A. 2
McKamey, C. 132
Mead, M. 42
Mehan, H. 35
mentors 64, 72–75
Merriman, P. 109–110
Merton, R.K. 34
methodological perspective 1–4, 6, 7, 10, 19, 45, 47, 48, 55–60, 83–84, 87, 89, 95, 106, 108, 110–111, 126, 132, 141, 143
Mitchell, J. 65
Morgan, G. 32
Mruck, K. 104

nature-study 133–134
negotiation 17, 20, 122, 123, 126–128, 137
neoliberalism 119, 120–122, 124, 128
new empiricism 2, 3, 144
new materialism 2, 3, 46, 131
Nietzsche, F. 5
nomadic ethnography 40, 94, 96, 97, 106, 110
nonlinearity 22, 56, 58, 65

Obama, M. 61
observation, participant 19, 20, 26, 29–33, 86–87, 130, 134
Occupy Poble Sec Cinema Forum (OPSC) 81–89, 90n1, 90n4
Ogbu, J.U. 35
Onsès, J. 92
onto-epistemology 1, 4, 6, 8–9, 19, 47, 48, 55, 83–84, 89, 94, 95, 99, 102n2, 106
ontological perspective 2, 3, 17, 40–48, 55–56, 84, 92–97, 100, 106, 108, 110, 125, 131, 143

openness 2, 96, 104–113
organization(s) of education 29, 31–36

Parsons, J. 144
peers, engagement with 68, 72–75
perspective 17, 20, 21, 25, 26
Phillips, D.C. 43
philosophy of inquiry 19–20
Piaget, J. 105
Pink, S. 35
plateau 98, 100
positionality 3, 104–107, 119–128
posthumanism 2, 87, 88
post-qualitative perspective 1, 2, 3–4, 10, 106, 112, 141–142
power relations 125, 128
professional development, teachers' 141–150
professional roles 25–26
Punto Urban Art murals 131, 138n1

Ravitch, D. 121
Reay, D. 128
recognition 25, 68–71, 75–76
reflexivity 18, 26, 65–67, 71, 76, 99, 104, 122, 125–127, 128n1
representation 134, 135, 136, 138
'researching through' 34–36
rhizome 92–94, 96, 134, 141–146, 149, 150
Richardson, L. 107
rich points 17, 25, 56, 58, 59, 68
risk 2, 100–101, 120, 121, 130–138
Rupšienė, L. 57–58

Sánchez Criado, T. 85
Sancho-Gil, J.M. 48, 142
science 2, 29, 31–33, 35, 36, 112, 133, 138n2
seeing, ways of 52, 55–57, 60–61
Semetsky, I. 6, 106, 144, 147, 148
serendipity 30–31, 33
Sheridan, D. 21
Silverman, D. 30
Simons, H. 104
Skukauskaite, A. 58
Smith, D.E. 36, 120, 122–124, 125, 128n3
Snaza, N. 10, 110
social contexts 17, 24, 26
social realities 26, 31
spaces, educational 142–149
Spradley, J.P. 68, 72, 76
Springgay, S. 112
Stengers, I. 112
Stern, D. 84
Stewart, K. 88–89
stories 52–55, 61

St. Pierre, E. 1, 96, 97, 100, 106, 107, 112
Strauss, A. 33
subjectivity 94, 104, 106, 112, 120–124,
   127, 132, 134, 136, 138n3
Sudnow, D. 32
surprise 4, 112, 134

teachers' learning 105–113
teachers' professional development 141–150
teaching, learning about 52, 54–61
thinking, ways of 20, 24, 26, 64
transformation 23, 40
transparency 104–105
Troman, G. 33
Trowler, P.R. 35

unknown, the 2, 3, 34, 95, 101, 106–110,
   144–145, 149

van Maanen, J. 34
Vannini, P. 35
virtuality 85–87, 89

vulnerability 56, 130, 132, 135
Vygotsky, L. 105

Wacquant, L. 128
Walby, K. 125, 128n3
wandering 94–95, 100
Warburg, A. 96
Weaver, J. 10, 110
Whitehead, A.N. 4–5
Willis, P. 44
Wolcott, H. 45
wonder 94–95
Woolgar, S. 32
Wright, S. 34
writing processes 81, 83, 85, 88–89, 98–100,
   104, 107, 112, 124–125

Yeager, E. 22, 24
Young, M. 42

Zaharlick, A. 54
Zerubavel, E. 32